Beyond Deception

Volume 2

Tobias Beckwith

Beyond Deception

Volume 2

From the Wizard's Corner

Tobias Beckwith

Triple Muse

Publications

Richmond, CA

Beyond Deception
Volume 2

From the Wizard's Corner

Printed by CreateSpace, and Amazon.com company.

ISBN 978-0-9779843-5-0

First edition
6 5 4 3 2 1

Published by Triple Muse Publications, 5336 Brookwood
Court, El Sobrante, CA 94083
http://www/triplemuse.com

Acknowledgments

Beyond Deception - Volume 2 follows the happy success of Vol. 1 as a result of a project begun after that book was released. For the past several years, the faculty of the McBride Magic & Mystery School have been broadcasting a regular weekly streaming videocast call *Monday Night Mysteries*. I entitled my weekly segments "The Wizard's Corner." Every week we chose a subject and each of us presented a short video essay on that subject. After a couple of years I had more than a hundred of these, and based on the wonderful response from viewers, was encouraged to think they might warrant a slight rewrite and release as this book.

The book itself is less of a collaborative effort than *Volume 1* was, largely because the pieces had already been created and delivered, and because I had enough distance in time from them by the time I decided to create the book that I have felt confident to do most of the rewrites and edits myself. In addition, the book didn't require illustrations.

I do want to thank Kiva Singh for assisting me to create the new cover design, based on the Volume 1 design by Troy Paules. I would also thank Micah Stuart and Kiva Singh, who took the photo of me that is used to start things off. Also Mike Henkel, who agreed to proof-read the book, and thus save you, my readers from the annoyance of my many typos and inconsistencies.

Finally, I want to thank Jeff McBride and my fellow faculty members from the *McBride Magic & Mystery School*. Jeff McBride, George Parker, Bryce Kuhlman, Larry Hass and Jordan Wright continue to inspire me with each and every show we do. As we move forward, each one of us learns a bit more and gets just a bit better each week, each working to keep up with the level the others set, both in terms of the material we offer and the production value of what we produce. Thank you all for your continuing challenges and inspiration!

Table of Contents

Contents

Foreward

by Jeff McBride

In the pages ahead, you will read about the many faces and personas of the magician. Yes, the magician often shape-shifts into many different roles... so does Tobias. As you walk along this adventure with Tobias, you will see him transform and change roles from page to page... and I would not be surprised if YOU transform into a very different performer by the time you reach the final chapter.

In the words of William Shakespeare:

"All the world's a stage, and all the men and women merely players. They have their exits and their entrances, and one man in his time plays many parts, his acts being seven ages."

I have seen Tobias play many parts, both onstage and off. I have witnessed him shape-shift into many stages and ages! Here are just a few.

THE ACTOR

Tobias has spent many years on the stage. He began his theatrical career learning his craft as an actor. He passes his many years of theatrical training and stage experience on to you. His years of acting technique have been distilled down to magic formulas, formulas that he shares with you. Many of his brainstorming techniques and acting exercises can transform your work. Often you will see that these acting and creativity techniques will make you not only a better performer, but a better person!

Be prepared to transform!

THE DIRECTOR

I have seen Tobias work wonders, not only with my stage show, but also with many of the students that attend our *Master Classes* here in Las Vegas. Tobias has a keen eye and observes the theatrical process in his own unique way. He has an incredible attention to detail and often catches subtle mistakes that fly past all the other facilitators who were giving feedback at our sessions. In the following chapters, you will learn how Tobias thinks, and how his years of directing can help you make good choices about your next performance.

THE MANAGER

I've been working with Tobias for 25 years in all venues; television, festivals, casino, theatrical and our classes here in Vegas. Working with Tobias has been one of the most important factors in my success as a performer. As a producer, he has helped many performing artists to manifest their highest visions by assisting them with expert advice and career guidance. Many of his clients and students have gone on to find global fame, and financial success.

THE EDUCATOR

Magic students around the world have had opportunities to meet Tobias in his workshop settings. Each year at our *Magic & Meaning* conference, Tobias challenges us to see beyond our deceptions and misconceptions, into the truths and scientific proofs that support his vision of what a magical performance can achieve.

THE WRITER

Many of you have met Tobias through writings in books, magazines and also his contributions to our Museletter. His first book, *Beyond Deception - Vol. 1,* met with critical and popular acclaim. If you've read Tobias' work in the past, I know you are eager to move ahead and learn more ways to empower your magic. If this is your first time approaching his writings, you're in for a big treat. He will inspire you and fill you with a lifetime of practical knowledge and gems of wisdom. One of the things you may not know about Tobias is how well read he is. It seems he is up on all areas of theater, brain science, and the magical arts. The amount of practical knowledge he has and his ability to distill and share it is staggering! Know that when you read the chapters ahead, you are getting the distilled essence of many of his teachings.

THE WIZARD

In the past few years, I've seen Tobias transform through many stages, the current one being that of the wizard. This transformation into a wizard was very intentional for him. He had worked years towards attaining this goal by pursuing his passions in all the other areas of his interests. Now is the time that he opens to the next stage of his personal unfolding.

Tobias is a messenger of reinvention. He is an exemplar of what he writes. He continually inspires, uplifts, motivates and encourages us all to reach our maximum potential. More than mere words, Tobias gives us his tried and true formulas for a more successful performance and for a better life.

Jeff McBride
April 14th, 2014
Las Vegas, NV

Introduction

As I sit down to write this, it has been almost three years since the release of *Beyond Deception, Vol. 1.* The response to that volume was greater than I had ever imagined it would be, with the first printing of 2,000 now completely sold out. Thanks to all of you who purchased it!

What's more, the critical response, both from the reviewers in magazines and on the web and from readers who have reached out to me by e-mail, Facebook and various other means, has been gratifying. Again, thank you. It is that response which leads me to the current volume. Although it has been several years since I actually released a book, that doesn't mean I haven't been writing all that time!

Soon after Volume 1 was released, we embarked on a fairly ambitious project at Jeff McBride's Magic & Mystery School. We started "Mystery School Mondays," a streaming broadcast which has gone out live each Monday evening on our own channel on the internet (www.mcbridemagic. tv). Each week, I have contributed a piece entitled *The Wizard's Corner.* Most of what follows this introduction first appeared as the text of those Wizard's Corner video pieces. They have been re-edited and I've expanded most of them, so the book is by no means a verbatim transcription of the videos, but that's where it all began.

As part of the experience of having to write and produce a 5 minute video segment each week, I made an interesting discovery. We had a list of subjects we worked from each week, just so each episode could have a basic theme running through it. Sometimes the subjects assigned were things I knew a lot about and writing five minutes was easy. Other times, though, the subjects seemed quite outside my purview. They were things which, at first reflection, I seemed to know nothing about, or could be interpreted in several different ways. Nevertheless, each week, after a bit of thought, I was able to come up with an interesting piece—or at least one that interested me. I found myself exploring different ways of thinking about magic, different ways of generating material— the assignments helped me stretch my own comfort zone.

Thus, I discovered the power of having an assignment to spark my own creativity. It works. And this book is the result. I hope it will inspire you, as the writing of it has inspired me.

On Being a Magician

Magic is a performing art, and specifically a branch of theater. In a way, the theater encompasses all of the other arts - graphic art, dance, music, literature, sculpture, and more. As such it is very rich. Magic is one of many slightly strange offshoots of theater, with many unique aspects. The magician, however, is more than just "an actor playing the part of a magician." Magicians have a different relation to, and effect upon, their audiences than do most actors. Magic is a very special form of performance in which the audience participates directly in the story, and is therefore affected in different ways than a typical audience at other kinds of performances.

Because all theater tells a story, and there is seldom much of a story without multiple characters -- the one-man or one-woman show is a rarity — except in magic. Whereas other forms of theater usually require a second character so that the interactions of a story can take place, this is not the case in magic. In the world of magic, the audience is usually the "other character" with whom the magician character interacts. This creates an entirely different dynamic that we find in other varieties of live theater, and that is one of the things I'll be discussing at some length in the pieces that follow. The longer I find myself working and thinking about the art of magic, the more interesting the thoughts become — at least to me.

Besides the unique nature of magicians' relationship to their audiences, we have the fact that most magicians actually create their own material, and direct themselves and their businesses. As a result, the must necessarily have a broader range of skills than most theater artists, who work in collaborative groups. This fact also opens up a whole range of interesting thoughts, and turns those of us who are passionate about magic as an art into somewhat unusual people. It takes a special kind of person to want to be a magician in the first place, and I suspect most of the people we cross paths with find us to be strange and exotic creatures.

This section contains considerations, then, about just what it means to lead a life in magic. You'll find some ideas of how you can become a better magical artist, whether you perform, build props, direct magicians, chronicle the history of the art, or participate in some other way.

Developing Purpose

In many of my presentations, I speak of the importance of knowing your purpose. What is the purpose of your business – of your show – or of a particular performance piece you have created? Defining your purpose for a project before you begin creating it can help you make decisions and answer the questions that arise in any endeavor. It also gives you a way of measuring the success of that endeavor. All too often we complete a job or performance, and when asked how we did, we find we don't really know. Our audience or boss seemed happy, so we suppose we did well...but unless we know what to measure, we don't really know. A clearly defined purpose can give you just that.

Unfortunately, it is much easier to say "define your purpose" that it actually is to define a good purpose for something. Let's imagine you want to create a new performance piece around a magic trick you have just learned. Let's imagine the magic has to do with finding a spectator's card. That shouldn't tax anyone's imagination too much, though it might tax your creativity to find a new and interesting presentation for this timeworn effect. So... what is your purpose for doing this trick?

I imagine you might say "to fool them," or "to make them wonder how I did it." Some of the more advanced magical artists out there might come up with something a bit more sophisticated, like, "to help them realize they take their own limited point of view a bit too seriously." Take a moment now and come up with one for yourself. Don't spend a lot of time coming up with one, as we're about to change whatever it is you come up with, anyway.

It doesn't really matter what your first idea of a purpose might be. Wherever you begin, what's important is where you take it − because we can always do better. Remember your own answer to the question above: what is your purpose for doing this trick? Now ask yourself "Why?" Why is that purpose important to me? Why do I think it will be important to the person I perform for? Or you might ask "How," instead. When you have come up with an answer for that, ask the same question again, this time about your answer to the first time around. And so on. Several iterations into this, if you work at it, things are likely to begin to get interesting. Your thought process might go something like this:

Q: Why do I want to do this card location trick?

A: To impress people with my skill.

Q: Why?

A: I want them to stick around and see more.

Q: Why?

A: Because I like to perform magic tricks.

Q: Why?

A: It gets me attention.

Q: How?

A: It surprises people. It makes them wonder how I do things. It makes them question their own ideas. That gets their attention.

Q: Why is that?

A: I don't know...I guess because that's what magic

does....it makes us question reality by showing us things that don't seem to fit.

Q: Why would you want to do that?

A: I think it's important for people to open their minds a little.

Q: Why?

A: It makes them happier, more capable people.

Ah...the conversation has finally become a bit more interesting. We've gone from, "I do this trick to impress people" to "I do this trick to help people open their minds so they can become happier and more capable human beings."

See how a little bit of digging can help you turn up ideas about the purpose of your magic – or any endeavor you might undertake – that are deeper and more interesting than the ones that first come to mind?

Try this for yourself to discover bigger and better purposes for various tricks you might do, and with other things in your life. Discovering strong purposes for what we choose to do is one of the ways we can get in touch with our passions, and build a more meaningful and rewarding life and career. Something I strongly wish for every one of you.

It's not important as you go through the above process that you come up with the ultimate purpose of your life or career. Those things will change with experience. The purposes that excite you when you are 18 years old, will be quite different from the ones that appeal to you when you're 30, 45 or 60. In fact, the ones that appeal to you now could change within a few months. But having a clearly defined purpose, right here and now, will help you create more powerful magic, and to be a more effective magician.

Wisdom and Wizards

As performing magicians, many of us are portraying wizards of one sort or another, so it might be good to know a bit more about them. A wizard is not necessarily a magician, and magicians are not necessarily wizards. And yet...they seem to run on parallel paths.

One of the ways I have sometimes defined what it is to be a wizard is to say that they are people who do magic outside of the realm of entertainment. They are people who use magic in real life. But that doesn't reach the heart of the matter...in fact it probably raises as many questions as it answers. A sorcerer or necromancer might also be said to do magic outside of shows.

I've spent the past several years learning more and more about what goes into making someone a wizard...and one of the top things is that real wizards have wisdom. Just listen to the words...you're sure to see the connection:

Wis-dom is Wiz-dom

A Wizard is a Wise-ard

Wisdom is one of the ways someone gets to be a wizard. But that brings us to the somewhat thorny issue of "okay, then...what is wisdom?" Wisdom is not just the ability to hold on to a lot of information. One must gain lots of real knowledge...and I don't mean the kind that comes in books. It is quite possible to have lots of book learning and not a bit of real wisdom. You may have heard the term 'learned fool,' and have probably met a few. We call them 'learned fools.'

Albert Einstein – a wizard if ever there was one – wrote that, "Real knowledge comes from experience. Everything else is just information."

His point, I think, is that if your knowledge hasn't been experienced...used...it isn't useful or real to you. Books contain information – it's up to us to turn that information into real knowledge.

As an example: When you're a teenager, one of the pieces of knowledge you want most is the ability to drive a car. You can go to drivers education classes, read books, read your automobile's user manual, watch films about driving...you can soak up a tremendous amount of information about driving, because it is something you want to do so much. But then, when you finally have a chance to sit behind the wheel of a car -you rapidly discover that you don't have ANY real knowledge of how to drive. Only when you finally get to sit behind the wheel, turn on the engine, and put the car in gear do you begin to truly learn how to drive a car.

It is, I think the same for magic. There a great many collectors of magical information, a great many who dabble at doing magic tricks for their friends. It's fine to be a collector of tricks, a dabbler who shows off simple tricks to one's friends, or a historian of magic who reads all about great magic and magicians of the past. I think most of us involved in the world of magic fall amongst those different categories, and all are necessary and important to keeping our art alive and moving forward.

Far fewer ever reach a point where they have become true wizards or magical artists. That kind of mastery can only be gained by thousands and thousands of hours actually performing magic for others, noticing the results, and reflecting on what happens. We know the true masters the moment we see them begin to perform. When you see Lance Burton or Jeff McBride onstage, you know immediately you are in the presence of a magical master, fully in his power. When you encounter close-up magic at the hands of Eugene Burger or Juan Tamariz, you find yourself totally enchanted, totally within the magical world they create, and completely confident in their artistry and mastery. Why do you suppose that is?

I'm fairly certain that it is because each has developed a unique kind of wisdom about their magic. That wisdom comes from thousands and thousands of hours actually performing magic for live audiences. It comes from performing the same pieces thousands of times, and then reflecting and trying to improve the piece again the next time it is performed. It comes from having developed hundreds and hundreds of performance pieces over the course of their careers, and from trying to improve each of those every time it is done. It comes from being unafraid to try new techniques and ideas and perhaps failing. Not all experiments turn out as expected, but those who fail to try them also fail to learn from the trying. The true masters are happy to fail and learn from their failures, as they know that will lead to greater art, greater success and greater knowledge about themselves and their art than they can ever learn by always playing it safe.

Books, Video and Mentors
Books vs. Video

Different ways of learning are very much a subject of our time, what with the costs of college skyrocketing, our public schools coming ever more under attack for turning out students unable to meet the barest minimum requirements, and the rapid rise of different forms of learning on line. Online programs ranging from the Kahn Academy videos to Codecademy.com for learning basic programming and on to Udacity and Coursera are revolutionizing the ways available to learn almost anything.

In the world of magic, we have followed a similar path. When I was young, there were really only two ways of learning magic: By reading books and by visiting your local magic shop, where, if you were lucky, the owner might be interested in mentoring aspiring magii, helping them learn to perform using the books and tricks they had purchased in the shop. About the time I came back to magic and started working with Jeff McBride, it became economically feasible for large enough organizations like Stevens Magic and L&L Publishing to begin to produce magic instruction on video. Jeff's *The Art of Card Manipulation* series, along with quite a few offerings by Michael Ammar, were amongst the pioneering works in that field.

Jeff's videos really made one of the great advantages of teaching on video clear, at least for me. As a boy of 12 or so, I had attempted to learn some of the sleight of hand with cards which was later taught by Jeff and others on video. Not having a mentor to encourage me, and not being a particularly well coordinated child...I soon came to the conclusion that NO normal human being would be able to execute many of the sleights described and illustrated in the books. Only a manual contortionist could possibly do some of those things! But soon after Jeff's videos were released, we began seeing younger and younger magicians — by the dozens — rapidly mastering many of his very difficult sleights. By actually *seeing* the sleights performed, these young people immediately moved past that "that's impossible" stage that had stopped me, and got down to the business of actually learning the sleights I had thought too difficult to master. Chalk one up for the magic of learning through video!

The other side of that coin, however, was that many, many of the young people learning from the videos also learned to perform the magic in exactly the way Jeff had when he taught it. They became copycats, not real artists. While I've always loved Jeff's card manipulation act, I'd really like to have seen more magicians come up with their own presentations and interpretations... and not just slavishly copy what they saw on video.

Learning   magic   from   books   didn't   share   this

disadvantage. Though the young magician might learn and repeat the patter exactly as written, they had no way of knowing how the original performer had inflected their language when it was delivered, or what the original speed and attitude might have been. As a result, each magician who learned a magic piece from a book, instead of through imitation, came away with a slightly different interpretation. Chalk one up for learning by books!

So...which method is best? In my estimation, both and neither. In studies of education systems, trying to decide whether classes with live teachers or online learning where students can move at their own pace seems to be coming up with the answer that *online learning assisted by a live teacher* is the most effective. I think it's the same with magic. Get your initial information any way you can...through books and by video, depending on where it's available and how you learn best. But, if you really want to move beyond the average, if you really want to master your magic and achieve excellence, find yourself a live mentor or teacher. Get feedback and corrections from someone with experience.

Don't expect a teacher to spoon-feed you every move, every new bit of knowledge. These are best gotten through books and videos. But once you've learned the basics, find yourself a mentor, a teacher... someone who is far beyond where you find yourself in terms of experience...and let them guide you. That's the key to taking your magic to the next level, that level that will help you become a true magical artist, and not just another copycat.

Collect Extraordinary Experiences

Here's a question for you: What have you done lately that really scares you? Or, let me ask in another way: What have you NOT done lately that you would have liked to, but avoided because it scared you?

One of my favorite writers is Tim Ferriss, who wrote both The Four Hour Workweek and The Four Hour Body. One of Tim's mottos is: "Do something that scares you every day." He's a true wizard in many ways, and I highly recommend his books if you're interested in really taking control of your own life and changing the world the way wizards do.

I hear again and again that "magic is an art," and it certainly can be. However, most of the magicians I see who are beyond just the beginner stage, are more craftsmen than artists. They are taking work done by others and learning to perform it competently and well – but they lack the vision and passion to really make it their own, and make it carry their own messages to their audiences. For me, one of the differences between the craftsman and the artist is that the craftsman, though he or she may have put in many hours "perfecting" their performance techniques, has never been willing to go out on a limb and have the guts to actually SAY something with their magic. It can be scary to really express your own thoughts and feelings. What will people think? What if you're wrong? But if you're always careful, and stay inside that comfort zone of doing what has worked for others – you'll never grow and never have anything really worth saying.

Back in the early years of the Italian renaissance, there was an illegitimate son of a country lawyer near Florence who, through his own diligence and intelligence, rose to some prominence, creating great spectacles and events first for the Duke of Milan and then for Pope Alexander VI. On the side, he designed weaponry from Cesar Borgia, and turned his hand a bit to sculpture and painting. He was too poor, however, to attend a university, but managed to get himself accepted into the salon of the painter Verrochio, where he encountered many much richer and better educated young men. He wrote of his experiences with them in one of the notebooks he kept with him at all times. Here is what he wrote:

> *I am fully aware that the fact of my not being a*
> *man of letters may cause certain arrogant persons to*
> *think that they may with reason censure me, alleging*
> *that I am a man ignorant of book-learning. Foolish folk!*
> *Do they not know that I might retort by saying, as did*
> *Marius to the Roman Patricians: 'They who themselves*
> *go about adorned in the labour of others will not permit*
> *me my own'? They will say that because of my lack of*
> *book-learning, I cannot properly express what I desire*
> *to treat of. Do they not know that my subjects require*
> *for their exposition experience rather than the words of*
> *others? And since experience has been the mistress of*
> *whoever has written well, I take her as my mistress, and*
> *to her in all points make my appeal.*
>
> *Many will believe that they can with reason censure*
> *me, alleging that my proofs are contrary to the authority*
> *of certain men who are held in great reverence by their*
> *inexperienced judgments, not taking into account that*
> *my conclusions were arrived at as a result of simple and*
> *plain experience, which is the true mistress.*

H'm...interesting fellow, and a truly great wizard and artist. You may know his work as a painter, especially his *Mona Lisa* and his *Last Supper*. He is, of course -- Leonardo da Vinci.

So, I leave you with the challenge, if you would become wizards or artists, and not merely craftsmen, to get out and create some experiences for yourself that scare you — at least a little bit. Only when you've gone a bit too far, pushed the envelope a bit beyond where it is safe, when you've dared to actually fail a few times – will you begin to really live the life of the wizard and true artist. The world is in sore need of more of those, and could use fewer imitators and hack performers.

You have the power to choose: which will you be?

Diversity

This essay was an assignment. "Write about magic & diversity."

I actually like assignments like this. It is a wonderful challenge to be given a subject to write about each week, and the freedom to interpret that subject in any way we see fit. It's a gift...and one I would highly recommend you give yourselves. Are you up for the challenge? Here's your assignment:

Take a piece of paper, and make yourself a list of general areas you could work on to improve your magic. Here are a few samples to get you started: Scripting, Humor, apparatus tricks, interacting with audiences, applause cues, particular tricks (list them), etc. Now, set aside an hour each week (or more often, if you wish), and take on the assignment of writing one page on one of the subjects, completing the page within the hour you've set aside. For myself, if I simply write the theme word or phrase on my calendar or put it into the to do list for a particular day, that works. Whatever I'm thinking and feeling about that particular subject – that becomes my "Wizard's Corner" essay for that week.

And this week it is Diversity. We could take that to mean, "how do you use magic to help others deal with diversity?" Or it could be, "how much should I diversify the magic I do?" The questions that could be answered under that subject are probably at least as diverse as the number of you out there reading this book!

I'd like to address the diversity within our art on a large scale. I have observed that very few truly successful "stars of magic" have become so by imitating anyone else. Doug Henning, David Copperfield, Criss Angel, David Blaine, Penn & Teller – these are all unique personalities presenting shows as different from one another as you could imagine...but they are all magic shows. On a wider scale, magic serves performers who entertain at private parties, kids' parties, trade shows, luncheon meetings, in the circus, and so on. There are many, many varieties of magic in performance. And not everyone in the art chooses to perform. There are also inventors, script and joke writers, collectors, builders...and together, we form an extremely diverse community. Magic hobbyists come from all walks of life, and all parts of the globe.

I think it is that diversity embraced by magic that, for me, is one of its most attractive attributes. As magicians we get to meet others who are vastly different from ourselves... and yet with whom we share a deep passion. That makes deep connections possible. As magical performers, we are forced to have diverse interests. Because we write our own shows, often create our own props, often have to book ourselves, in addition to actually performing for audiences, magical artists have to develop diverse skills in order to be able to practice their craft. And all this makes magicians more interesting than many other people.

I have just finished a first draft of my book, The Wizard's Way – not about performing magicians, but about real wizards...those amazing people who transform the world in big ways. My original model was the wizard Merlyn from the Arthurian myth – but then I went on to discover how "real wizards" work in history, and in our lives today.

I discovered that one of the primary things that distinguishes the wizard from others is a thirst for a diversity of experience. From Leonardo da Vinci, who used his skills as an artist to invent great public works, war machines and practical gadgets far ahead of his time, to Mohandas Gandhi, trained as a lawyer, whose experiences in South Africa and other cultures led him to a wisdom about how to leverage the non-violent resistance of the poorest of the poor in his native India to overthrow one of the world's most powerful empires, the British Raj — or modern day wizards like Richard Branson – known for creating excellence in a wide variety of industries, and at the same time a passionate balloonist, kite boarder — true wizards embrace a diversity of experience, while non-wizards tend to seek to limit the scope of their experiences. The reward for embracing a diversity of experience is always wisdom and power – and so I hope you'll join me in celebrating the diversity we find in magic and magicians.

I also hope you will make an effort to reach out, not just to magicians who share your particular passions – say for close-up card tricks – but to those within our community but outside your particular niche – and that you will try different areas. If you are a sleight of hand wiz, work with a friend who likes apparatus, and see how you can inspire one another. If your kind of magic is big illusions, take a day to work on close-up, or at least to see some great close-up performers and talk about their work and yours. You'll be amazed at how much the act of getting out of your personal comfort zone, even a little bit, can do to help you grow as an artist and a person.

Our Magical Community

Community among magicians can really be a wonderful thing. I remember when I first moved from Las Vegas to the Bay area, knowing only a few people who lived here. I put out the word on Facebook that I was interested in meeting local magicians, and immediately had a huge response. Several guys invited me out to lunch. A couple more volunteered to organize a series of workshops for me that would take place at Apple headquarters (thanks to Kim Silverman and Rich Meyer for that!). I was invited to several different magic clubs, and to the Magic Garage, a very special place in Sunnyvale where Will Chandler has been hosting magicians every Friday evening for years, and where the community who gather is both enthusiastic about magic and about improving the magic they do.

In short, because of the community of fellow magicians, I felt welcomed like an old friend right from the very beginning of my residence up here. Having that made the move so much easier and happier than it might have been otherwise.

I also remember one of my early trips out of the country with Jeff McBride, when we had been hired to do his show at the Hong Kong Arts festival. A group of 30 or so local magicians met us at the Hong Kong airport with armloads of flowers, then followed our car back to our hotel, and insisted on taking us out on the town for dinner to welcome us to their city. That was 20 years ago, and we still count Albert Tam and some of the other magicians there as close friends.

Why, I wonder, should the magical community be such a strong and welcoming one? Is it because we share a set of secrets not readily available to the general public? Because we recognize that our passion for magic and deception is one not completely understood or accepted by the public at large – and so we're a community of outsiders? I really don't know why it is...but I'm deeply grateful for it. Magicians are truly among my favorite kind of people. It takes a certain amount of courage to take the plunge into magic...to do that first trick which you are sure won't fool anyone, and then be rewarded by their quite amazing responses – or not – and then continuing on anyway, just because you're in love with magic.

In that spirit, I feel especially blessed to have been an integral part of Jeff McBride's Magic & Mystery School right from the beginning. From the first day of that first Mystery School, I have met truly amazing people, deeply dedicated to our craft and to the art of creating magical experiences. I've been blessed to be accepted at once for my own unique contributions by those who most of us think of giants of our art — people like Eugene Burger, Max Maven, Bob Neale and so many others...and been rewarded so deeply for any morsel I have shared by those same people with their own sharing...well, it turns out that a life in magic can be a very special life, indeed.

In this past year or so, we at the McBride School have been exploring more and more ways to reach more and more magicians, collectors, fans of magic and more. Our Mystery School Mondays show has completed well over two years of weekly broadcasts, and we've become better and better at doing it, doing our best to make sure it is an offering worthy of our audiences. And we've been rewarded for doing it. Some of those who watch regularly have sponsored the Jeff McBride Experience in your home areas. Others have paid to come to Las Vegas and study at our classes. Still others have bought books or products our faculty members have put out. All of these are ways our audience has gone out of their way to make us feel supported.

That's how communities work...I offer you something just because you're 'one of us,' and you might give something back...not so much because I gave you something in the first place, but because I'm 'one of you.' This is different from commerce, where I agree to give you something in exchange for money. It's far more than that...a reciprocity built from caring, from a desire to work together toward goals larger than any of our individual interests.

Our art IS a very special one, and we can all work together to continue to improve it. I hope all of us will continue building ways to introduce new audiences to magic in ways that will create ever larger audiences for all our magical creations. One of the ways we make communities stronger is through our service to those communities, and so I feel grateful for the opportunities that continue to come my way to serve this community we're all a part of!

Magic Dealers

Dealers. Those wonderful people willing to sell our secrets to anyone who walks in the door or clicks on their web-pages...and who we love nonetheless, because they also provide *us*...the real magicians, the keepers of secrets, with new ideas, with our magic supplies and, often, with a place where we can experience community.

I have a clear memory from back when I lived in New York City. I had been in a local Barnes and Noble and picked up a book on magic by a well-known magician from their remainders table, so it had only cost me a couple of dollars. It was a book teaching magic to beginners - a.k.a. Laymen. Jeff and I happened to be having lunch with the author, and I thought it would be fun to have him sign the book for me. We had a pleasant lunch, and he was happy to be asked to sign his book, for which I thanked him. He happened to be a high officer with the S.A.M. at the time, and we were discussing having Jeff perform at one of their events. Part of the reason we were getting together was so that I could fill in the papers and put down my dues to become an S.A.M. member myself, and therefore attend the convention as a member.

Towards that end, our friend had brought the application papers with him for me to fill out. As I was scanning through them, I was struck by the statement that, "You agree never to reveal the secrets of any magic tricks to anyone outside our fraternity of magicians." This is the common "magicians' oath" to which we all give lip service. I agreed to take the papers and fill them out later...but I never did. Why? Well...having just bought a book authored by this same gentleman (and he *is* a gentleman and and a wonderful magician), which was doing just that – revealing magical secrets to non-magicians – I felt kind of slammed in the face by the hypocrisy of the whole set-up. "I'll ask you to sign this oath, which I signed myself, even though we both know I've published this book for the mass market that teaches our secrets to others, thus breaking the oath I'm asking you to sign." And if I signed, I'd be making myself just as big a hypocrite, because my business sometimes required me to reveal the way magic worked to non-magicians, simply so they could help us make that magic work for audiences.

So...how important are those secrets, do you think?

I have to say, the longer I am around magic and magicians, the less important I think what I would term "fanatical secrecy" is. Are the dealers who set up in shopping malls, or market heavily on the internet to non-magicians, somehow traitors to the code?

If you are a true believer, how can the answer to that be anything but yes?

And yet... aren't they bringing in new magicians and fans of magic, helping to keep our art alive? Wasn't each and every magician you've ever heard of once a small boy or girl and not a magician, who became one only through reading a book or visiting a dealer — someone who revealed our sacred secrets to them?

Since I operate a web site selling magic to magicians – or to anyone who comes to the site looking for magic – this is a question I have considered more than once. I find myself more and more coming down on the side of "if you're really interested, you should have access." It's really not about those secret workings of different effects, is it? I think what makes magic special is more about how we can create a magical experience *using* those secrets. And I don't think our deepest secrets *can* be revealed by those dealers, any more than a music store can reveal the secrets to becoming a great musician. They're only selling the tools.

I remember sitting in the audience at Caesars Magical Empire one night after one of the episodes of *The Masked*

Magician had aired...in which the star of the show had taught the basic secret of the Linking Rings. Jonathan Pendragon was performing, and had planned to do his version of the rings that week. He chose to keep it in. I don't remember his exact words introducing the effect, but it went something like this: "You may have seen a fellow on television purporting to teach you the 'secret' of the Linking Rings. Well...I'm going to show you my version of the rings. I've been performing The Rings for more than 20 years -- and I'll guarantee you, if he were here tonight, that fellow could not tell you the secrets behind how I do it. This is The Magic of the Rings!" He received a standing ovation after his bravura performance, which included the very difficult "in the air" link that so few have mastered.

I'm certain that some in the audience had seen the TV show the night before, and so felt they were "in the know." I'm equally certain that they experienced mystification and magic in Jonathan's performance. Like any good illusion...even when you "know how it works", you can STILL have the experience of the illusion, and be delighted by that experience. When a great showman like Jonathan Pendragon or Jeff McBride presents that same illusion with all the flair and spectacle they are capable of creating, audiences find themselves dazzled and delighted. They couldn't care less about whether or not they know the secret behind the illusion.

So...let us celebrate all those dealers out there for helping to whet our appetites and those of our audiences for magic. Even those coming in at the lowest level – the 'I need to know how that is done' level — have a chance, through exposure to magic at all levels, to move up and appreciate magic that goes far beyond those secrets supposedly 'revealed.'

I would urge all of you out there to aspire to perform the kinds of magic that will move audiences to the kind of ecstatic response, the joy of experiencing illusion, that goes so far beyond the merest acts of deception. Because when you do that, it really doesn't matter who reveals what to whom.

I would also strongly urge you to visit your local magic shops, and buy from them while you are there. Please don't just go and look, and then buy for a lower price on line. If you do that, you're stealing the extra added value that the shop has added - at the expense of providing skilled demonstrators, paying rent on their space, and providing a place for magicians to gather. If you browse in the shop and then buy on line, you're playing a part in killing that local shop - in killing off your own lifeline to the community of magic. Brick and mortar shops are struggling and going out of business at an alarming rate. Please do your part to help the ones near you survive!

Enchantment

One of the words we associate with wizards – and magic – is enchantment. What does enchantment mean to you? If one of your jobs as a magician is to enchant others...just how would you go about that?

I've been reading yet another fantastic book by Guy Kawasaki. You may know him as the "Macintosh Evangelist," or the author of one of my favorite books on starting a new business *The Art of the Start*. The new book is simply called *Enchantment*, subtitled: *the art of changing hearts, minds and actions*. Sounds like a great description of the job of a wizard.

Here's how Kawasaki defines enchantment. He begins the book with the story of a peace corps worker who was in the Phillippines. Visited one evening by 17 members of the New People's Army, a communist militia from the area who came to visit and intimidate her about her work – instead of being angry and defensive, she told them:

"I'm so glad you're here. Please come in and have some coffee with me." By responding in a completely unexpected way to this armed, intimidating group, she (and I quote here): "transformed the situation from brute force and intimidation to conversation and communication. She delighted him (the leader of the group) with her unexpected hospitality and changed his heart, his mind, and his actions. In short...she enchanted him."

In *Enchantment*, Kawasaki goes on to talk about many ways and means of achieving enchantment. While the book has a definite focus on business, the lessons it teaches are universal. Teachers can enchant students, parents can enchant their children (and vice versa), and performers, hopefully, enchant their audiences. I think we all yearn to be enchanted on some level.

Becoming a powerful enchanter can change your life. Great leaders enchant their followers. They don't badger, threaten or bribe them. They enchant them. But how?

Well... that's your assignment this chapter. Pick someone you would like to enchant. First think of what specific change you might like to see in them? How will you surprise, delight and enchant them so that they will find their way to that change? You will find several methods covered in other sections of this book - things like the giving of gifts, connecting with your audiences, telling stories, and much more. Some from Kawasaki's book, which I would highly recommend that you read for yourselves – others will be from my upcoming book, The Wizard's Way, and some from other sources altogether.

I think the best work you can find on the subject of enchantment, though, will be your own. Each of us is unique, with our own unique ways of relating to those around us...our own strengths and weaknesses. Some are great flirts, others are showmen, still others are brilliant with poetic language or imagery. What are your most enchanting qualities? Figure this out, and you'll be taking a giant step into the power of your own version of what it means to be a truly magical performer.

Ethics in Magic

Ethics in Magic. There are so many ethical issues that we deal with as magicians, it's hard to know where to begin the discussion.

There have been recent articles on Public Radio International and the BBC about magicians stealing from one another and copying one another's performances, something that is unfortunately prevalent... but hardly something that's new.

This is a subject about which many of my friends are passionate. I have a confession: With each passing incident, each passing month and year, I find myself less and less interested in who has supposedly stolen what from whom. There are thieves among us, and we all know who they are. The fact is, though, that we all build on the shoulders of those before us – and each one of us is aware, somewhere inside, of when we cross the line between when that's okay and when it's not. And I think there is a much deeper issue to deal with in the ethics of magic.

Shakespeare wrote (albeit for Polonius, Ophelia's blowhard of a father):

> *This above all: to thine own self be true,*
> *And it must follow, as the night the day,*
> *Thou canst not then be false to any man.*

And that, for me, at least, is at the center of what it means to be a moral person and artist, or not. As magicians, we are required to tell lies, or at least to mislead, our audiences all the time. It can become a habit that bleeds over into the rest of our lives. So much so, that many magicians become habitual liars. What comes out of their mouth is not what they think, but what they think will get them where they want to be.

"Sure, I have a great way to make your CEO appear! We do that all the time!" — when you've never done that, but only know someone who knows someone who can tell you where to rent someone else's prop...with which you've never even rehearsed.

"I've made a deep study of motivational techniques. I'm known as an expert in the field." When you know full well that's not true, and you'll just have to run out and do some research, or buy someone else's script and learn it if you get the job you're lobbying for. But, hey, everyone is doing it!

"I sent that check out two weeks ago. You just can't rely on the post office anymore, can you?"

"Great show! Your performance was remarkable."

You get the idea. And the worst part is that the more often you lie to others, the more you start to believe your own lies. I once worked for a man... a very effective Broadway producer... who often stretched the truth when he was negotiating agreements. On a number of occasions, when someone didn't come through on a point we had negotiated into a contract based on one of his lies, he would become incensed by their failure...and had to be reminded that the thing he was now being "cheated out of" had been based on a lie to begin with.

That's the really awful thing about habitual lying: we begin to lie to ourselves, and not to even notice. We tell ourselves things we know aren't true, but that we want to hear in order to feel better about ourselves. "I killed last night!" "I don't know what more I could have done...I gave that 110% and it still didn't work out." The shame of this kind of lie is at least twofold:

First, you are always caught – eventually. And then the lies destroy your credibility with others.

Besides that, the lies we tell ourselves distance us from any real contact with reality. They distance us from our own authentic experience, and from real contact with others.

I remember a time not too long ago having a discussion with my friend and client, Marco Tempest. I was prepared to stretch the truth a bit in order to get a bigger payment from a client who I knew could afford it. Marco was having none of it: "It's not worth the extra money. If we start lying to clients about our pricing policy, then we have to remember what we told each of them, and we'll eventually slip up and lose all our credibility," was what he told me. He made me realize that anything less than the truth was not only dishonest, but it actually made our lives worse, not better.

So: I hope I leave you inspired to spend a bit of time to think about the fact of having to lie and mislead people in the course of your work, and how that may have bled out into your "real life." It really pays to spend some quiet time with yourself, recovering yourself. "Who am I?" "What do I really want?" "When have I been less than truthful with myself, and with others?" "How can I correct that?" These can be difficult questions for every one of us. But confronting them can change your life in quite wonderful ways.

Evaluating Magic Performances

"How do I evaluate my magic?"

The subject is interesting in that it presumes you have an idea of why you are doing magic in the first place... because if you don't know why you're doing it, you really have no basis for your evaluation. If your sole purpose in doing magic is to have fun...well, if you are having fun doing it, then you're successful. The amount of fun you have determines your level of success. If you want to win magic competitions, you'll measure your success in a different way. If you want your magic to make money for you, well then you'll measure your success in yet a different way.

I'm often hired by magicians or groups of magicians to help them improve their magic. I always try to make it clear to them that I can help them in different ways, depending on what their goals for their magic are. "Do you want to build a career in magic? If so, what kind of magic? You can be a kid-show entertainer, a trade-show magician, a strolling magician for hospitality events, a Las Vegas illusion show magician, a magician who tours to colleges, or some other kind of magician entirely...and the kind of magical performance you need to create in each situation is different from all the others. The kind of intimate magic and performance style that is perfect for entertaining table-side in a high-end restaurant is quite different from that required to draw a big crowd to a trade show booth.

In business, before embarking on a new project or creating a new product, one of the things we do is decide, in advance, how we will measure our success. For example, I'm part of a video-cast each week called Mystery School Monday, which generates no profit directly for the Magic & Mystery School, which produces it. But we will consider it a success if it helps us create an ongoing community of interested followers, and if it introduces a fair number of new magicians to our way of teaching and thinking, which is quite different from many other teachers and magicians out there. It is also successful if it inspires our faculty and staff to participate and work together in new and interesting ways. We are also using it as a means for each of us to learn to present ourselves and our material more effectively on video. So we've been feeling at least moderately successful with Mystery School Monday project. We receive lots of great feedback, the community is growing, and we're learning a lot. If our measure of success were the monetary return, though, the project would be a miserable failure. Only after producing the show for over two years, have we begun to discuss ways we can monetize our investment of time and money over the past year.

If you think of it, this was the same basic business plan that Google used. For their first couple of years, they had no appreciable income. There were no ads on Google back then. No one paid to use the service. They defined their own success as being able to provide the best possible search experience for as many people as possible. At the end of those first couple of years, what they did have was a huge audience using the service every day. At that point it became valuable to advertisers, and in a way that had never before been available to those advertisers, as it suddenly became possible to target those advertised to with an accuracy never before avaialble. So the fact that they showed no profit, or even any appreciable revenue, from their work for such a long time, wasn't a failure in their eyes. By offering the service free, as they still do... they were building something of great value. And they knew how they wanted to measure their success – which was by virtually cornering the market on search, the real "killer app" for the internet.

So: We can't really tell you how to evaluate your magic without knowing your purpose for doing it. As a director, I can help you make it more entertaining and effective for any one of a dozen different kinds of audiences. As a career coach, I can help you build your career and make it more profitable...and if those are the things by which you measure your success, then I'll be helping you be more successful. But if I don't know your criterion, I can't really help you. And you can't really evaluate it, either, until you've spent the time and effort to figure out what your purposes are.

So take some time and write down what excites you

about doing magic. What is your purpose for being a magician? What are your goals...for your career, for particular performance pieces, or for your life? Once you've done that, you should find it relatively easy to create another list, which will be the ways you can begin to measure your success.

One of the great things about taking time to actually measure our success is that by measuring, we gain some degree of control over the level of success we achieve. So, by all means, figure out the parameters you'll use to measure your success - and then set aside time every so often to do just that!

The Gift of Magic
Helping Others with Magic
or: Using Magic to Help Others

At the last *Magic & Meaning* conference I attended, we had a wonderful talk by Tom Verner of *Magicians Without Borders.* You can watch it in the *PEP Talks* section of the *Virtual Magic School*...I'm pretty sure you'll find it just as inspiring as I did. And it is a grand example of one way of using magic as a gift.

There's a very special aspect of our art which really makes it different from all the others. Magic, when done really well, can shatter our preconceptions of the world... and what is possible in it. One might even say this is the core principle of performance magic — the idea that "Hey, you think you know how the world works? How about this?" When the impossible happens in a way that is so convincing it forces us to reevaluate our basic understanding of how reality functions - that can be a powerful moment.

We all think we know what reality is, and that we experience reality on a regular basis. In fact, we're always at least one step removed from reality, buffered by our senses and our mental interpretation of what comes in through those senses. The reality we experience is largely created in our own minds. The ability to shake our convictions that the experiences we have are our "reality," can help change the 'reality' that we live in. And for those living in refugee camps, mired in hopeless poverty, or who are under constant threat, the knowledge that there are other possible realities can be a real lifeline. It can inspire hope, encourage them to take actions they never believed they could have taken...and much more. And that is only one way we can use our magic to help others.

Another key element of magic is that it can so easily surprise us. This makes it a brilliant tool for the story-teller / motivator. A story with a happy ending is great, and can inspire us...but a story with a big surprise that reinforces that happy ending...well that's a story we'll remember and repeat, and which might well change lives.

A third way magic can be used to truly help people is to help them 'let down their guard' for a moment and experience a true connection with other human beings. When I was younger, I used to like to do hypnosis as a party trick. It was always entertaining, even though I didn't do any of the sort of silly comic things that many stage hypnotists do — but the thing I enjoyed most was the close, intimate connection between myself as hypnotist and the subject.

We all yearn for truly close contact with others, but everything in our society seems to conspire against such contact, except between lovers, or between mother and child. As a close-up magical performer, we often connect with those we perform for — by touching them, looking into their eyes, by giving them truly unique experiences, and sharing those experiences with them. This can be a huge gift for many people. So many today feel they are not heard, seen or given the credit they deserve. So many feel isolated, and many feel abused on one level or another. As performers, and especially as magicians, we can help make connections, allow those who otherwise feel isolated, to feel connected — if only for a few moments — and this can be a huge gift.

One of the great things about all these different ways of giving with magic is that you will find you always get just as much as you give. I've watched Jeff McBride and Eugene Burger teaching close-up workers how to get their magic up off the table and next to their faces – partly because it helps make the connection between performer and viewer – but also for the purely selfish reason that when you perform your magic that way, you get to see the look on your audience's faces when the magic happens... and that's the real magic!

I hope you'll take up the challenge to make a gift of your magic at least once during the coming week – the world needs it, and you might just find out that you do, too!

How to be Entertaining

You might think it would go without saying that any performer must, first and foremost, be entertaining. And yet, I'm sure everyone reading this has seen a magician perform who, though technically proficient, perhaps even brilliant – was anything but entertaining. Sometimes they are just dull and boring. Other times the performance is so "off" that it makes the audience uncomfortable. I'm not sure which is worse.

Perhaps this comes about because so many of us come to magic to learn it's secrets. We're so fascinated by how tricks are accomplished, how people can be deceived, that it occurs to us only vaguely that the performance of magic should be entertaining! And, for many, frankly, that's just fine. If you don't aspire to be a performer, there's really no requirement that you should be able to entertain. There are many of us who are big fans of magic, and love to play with it, learning the various tricks and moves just for our own edification, but have no wish to perform.

If you do aspire to perform, though, you had better be able to entertain with your magic!

"But how do I make my magic entertaining?" I can hear you asking. Here are some of the top things I think you must consider:

Connection

First: Good entertainers connect with their audiences. They have learned to be so comfortable making that connection through eye contact, body language, or even touch, that they can engage audiences in the same way two friends engage one another in conversations.

As with any connection – this has to be a two-way street. Great performers are acutely aware of the responses they are generating in their audiences, and they respond in kind. I think we've all seen performers who had decided in advance how an audience would respond to something and planned out their own response to what they imagined would happen. When the audience responds differently than expected, the performer is unaware of it and goes on with his or her now obviously inappropriate response.

On the other hand, the performer who is really tuned in to his or her audience can often create some really great moments just by reacting honestly to what the audience has to give them.

Story

Second: People are entertained by great stories. Even if you don't think of yourself as a storyteller, you must be aware that the performance you give creates stories in the minds of your audiences. Think of the story being created as the one that an audience member will tell their friends about your performance. You definitely don't want that story to be, "This dweeb managed to bore the crap out of us for a full ten minutes. We kept thinking something interesting had to happen sooner or later, but it never did." That's not the story you want to create, is it?

So: What makes a story entertaining? There are more ways than I can begin to enumerate here, but some of the main ones are these:

A great story has interesting characters that the audience can identify with. These characters have intriguing quirks that make them unique. They have desires – goals...and plans for how they can achieve those goals. They have histories that affect who they are and how they act. They have interesting ways of walking, talking, and moving.

Stories get most interesting when they are built around a conflict. Several characters might have conflicting goals, or plans for reaching those goals that will conflict with or thwart the plans of the other characters. The action of these stories is the working out of the conflicts. Who will win, who will lose? And what does it all mean?

Presentation

Then there are all the little presentational choices we, as performers, have to make. How loudly or softly will we speak? How fast, or slow? Will our performance accelerate or slow down at different points? Will there by music accompanying us? What will our costume, props and so on look like?

Just as with conflict and resolution in the story, a performance, like a piece of music, can build and resolve tension. We can use sound, pacing, imagery and lighting to help build comic or dramatic effect, and thus the entertainment value of our performances.

That's just a taste of what you can do to make your magic entertaining. This is one of the areas where a good director or mentor can be invaluable to you, as a performer. Even an inexperienced director can provide you with a point of view outside your own, spotting moments in performance where you seem to be working against yourself, things you're doing that detract from the entertainment value you are seeking. A more experienced director can help you by suggesting changes or additions in staging, your timing, bits of stage business and more, all of which can greatly enhance your magic.

Magic Outside of Shows

One of my first thoughts about performance magic vs. wizardry was that real wizards use magic outside of shows. Let's look at some ways this might work.

I have a clear memory of being at an airport check-in counter on a day when we were experiencing bad weather, and most of the flights out of that particular airport had been delayed or cancelled. I was traveling with Jeff McBride, flying overseas somewhere for an engagement, and as we approached the counter we observed customer after frustrated customer shouting at the check-in clerk. Each one was understandably upset – about late arrivals, missed connections and all the other inconveniences that come up in in that kind of situation. Of course, none of the things that were bothering them was that particular clerk's fault, or even avoidable...but she was taking the brunt of everyone's displeasure, all the while remaining polite and calm and businesslike. But it was easy to see the stress in her face and posture. She was most definitely having a very bad day.

When we got to the window, we knew our extra bags and the size of the group with whom we were traveling weren't going to make things any easier for her. Jeff stepped up with a big smile, and said, "Wow...you look like you could use a little magic in your life about now!" He reached into the air and produced a little rainbow streamer. The clerk's look went from, "Oh, God, now what?" to "Wow...that's amazing." "It's a magic wishing rainbow." Jeff said. "Can you think of a wish you'd like to have come true? Great. Just touch the rainbow and make the wish." She did so, and he then vanished the rainbow streamer. Looking up..."There it goes..." I hope your wish comes true. You're doing such a great job here...I thought you could use a smile." You could see the woman's attitude change. She stood straighter, smiled, and everything about her seemed lighter. I'm sure that little bit of magic not only brightened her day and helped her get through a bad situation, but also made things just a bit better for everyone who followed us to her station for the next hour.

This is only the simplest, most obvious example that crosses my mind of how we might use our magic to create change in the world.

I have another friend who is one of the world's great salesmen, moving millions of dollars worth of product every year. He uses magic as an ice-breaker, a way to cement relationships with his clients. "People like doing business with people they like," he told me. "I show them simple but baffling, fun magic, up close, often right in the palms of their own hands, and I become a special kind of friend. I'm the one who brings them things no one else they know can. Of course, I still have to deliver on my sales pitch, on the quality of what my company provides. But I find the magic works to get and hold their attention in ways some of my competitors can only dream about."

So...your assignment for this section is to find uses for your magic outside of magic shows. Will you use the magic you already know to open someone's mind to a new idea? Brighten the day of someone having a tough time? Make a sale? Perhaps break down a prejudice? Make a point during a discussion? What will you do? I hope you'll let me know!

The Real Power of Magic

I can't really speak for others, but for myself, I got into the world of magic – and then theater – for the powers I hoped they would grant me. The pursuit of power is something we're taught to look down on. Phrases like "power hungry" and "power mad" reflect our feelings about those who openly seek power. There are some good reasons for that: We all think of the Hitlers, the Saddam Husseins and the Gaddafi's of the world when we think of those who have sought and wielded power for power's own sake.

For most of us, I think this 'power hungry' stage is something we go through before we become adults. I forgive myself for having gone through that stage, and chalk it up to youth and adolescence - a time when we're sure we 'know everything,' because we've just learned to think and experience the world around us fully, and are happy to have discovered that the world is a mostly rational, understandable place...except that it appears to be a place where we don't have all of the powers and freedom we think we deserve. We feel we 'know better' than others because we can use logic, and if only they would give us the power to do what needs to be done, we could surely do that.

Fortunately, most of us then continue to grow and experience and become adults. The adolescent power madness fades as we begin to accept more and more responsibility, and to find that life doesn't always follow the most logical or rational path. Things are just a bit more complex than we had realized, and only those who fail to grow and accept that continue on that quest for power. The pendulum swings the other way, you see...and now it is only the crazies seeking the power we once thought should only be ours. If we see someone else actively seeking or expressing power for power's own sake, we see them as being evil, childish, crazy or...whatever. In any event 'not one of us.'

Unfortunately this mindset has led us to a society where most of us actively shun power. Although we are born with certain innate powers, all too often, we deny those powers. We allow society, parents, friends and institutions to beat us down until we willingly give up our personal powers.

But part of becoming a true wizard is the act of reclaiming that lost power. And so wizards do seek power. Some seek power to change the world, or so they can use their power to empower others.

Let's imagine having the powers of the character played by a stage magician. Imagine for a moment that you could actually make objects vanish, and then reappear in other places. A simple enough power, and one we can easily simulate using the techniques we've all acquired as we learned magic. Only suppose for a moment that you discovered you had this power early on in life, and soon tired of using it to show off. Most of us grow out of, "Look, Mommy, see what I can do!" Then we go on and put those things we at first used just to show off, to real use. So, imagine at some point those around you no longer even know you have this power. What could you do with it, then? What would you do with it?

Oddly, most of us jump immediately to the idea of using magical powers for nefarious means. "I could make the money disappear out of a bank vault and reappear in my living room." Things like that. Perhaps it's because just having the power seems somehow illicit, and therefore using it for illicit means seems to naturally jump to mind. Or perhaps it just occurs to us because it would appear to be a way to 'get back' at the very powerful, and balance the books in a more just way.

But let's think how you might use your secret powers

'for good,' however you might define that. Could you, for example, when at dinner with a friend, make the check vanish from it's folder, only to reappear a moment later, with your credit car attached? Perhaps you had a friend who you have learned is secretly using dangerous drugs. Could you make the pills vanish from her pocketbook and be replaced by identical looking sugar pills? What else can you think of? Try and come up with at least 5 things you might do with such a power. Ten would be even better.

I once asked a lot of people what they would do if they had the powers of Merlin. MOST of them responded with "I would certainly not be performing a magic show for entertainment."

So: Let's look at that list I asked you to make up above.

How many of these things that you would do if you had the power to make things vanish and then reappear, could you do using the techniques of performance magic? I'll bet you'll find at least one or two. Here's your challenge. Pick the one that would make you feel best doing it.

Mine, which I actually did recently, was a really simple bill switch. There's a tip jar at the coffee shop I like to frequent. One day as I was waiting for the girl behind the counter to get my order, I reached out and took one of the dollar bills out of the jar, looked at it...and put it back. But it was now a $10. No one noticed at the time...but it made me feel great to know the response it got when they counted their tips at the end of the day. No one saw anyone put in a $10...but there it was. Magic...and good magic.

So, your challenge for the week is to go and use your "powers" – the ones you already have – to do some covert good. Change someone's life in some small way, using your magic...without them ever knowing.

At the end of the day when you do this, sit down and write yourself a couple of paragraphs about what you did and how it made you feel. You see, you already do have the power to change the world, and to do it in the way Merlin himself might have done. Enjoy the power!

Mastery

What does that mean to master something?

I think most of our definitions come from the medieval guild system, in which there were apprentices on the lowest level – would be craftsmen who learned their trade not by going to some vocational school, but by apprenticing themselves to master craftsmen. The apprentice worked without pay – because they were not yet skilled, their labor was not yet highly valued, and their pay, such as it was, came in the form of room, board, and, mostly...the eduction they were getting by working in the workshop of their master. After three or four years of work as an apprentice, if the apprentice had become sufficiently proficient at the craft, they could join the guild as a journeyman, still working for a master craftsman. They would receive journeyman's wages – just enough to live on, and, if they were thrifty, enough so they could save a bit over the few ensuing years when they continued to hone their skills under the master. Ultimately they would achieve two things: the skill to become a master themselves, and enough money to invest in order to set up their own business – and find some apprentices and maybe a journeyman to work for them.

By the time the craftsman reached a level where he could call himself a "master," he had been presented with pretty much every situation that one practicing his craft might run across. He had worked with every known kind of material used to create whatever that craft created. He had learned the economics of how to set up his business, set prices for his products, how to deal with customers, and, most important, how to craft truly excellent products. Wealthy clients bought the boots made by the master boot maker...poorer folk had to settle for the boots made by the journeymen and apprentices.

Notice, in the above example, that the mastery was a measure of the time put in and the skills built more than it was about so called "natural talent," or a formal education.

I recently read a book called The Talent Code, by author Daniel Coyle. Coyle is fascinated by what it takes to create real mastery – and more than that, what it takes to create the very best in a given field, whether that field is sport, the arts, or industry.

While there may have been dozens of "master painters" during the renaissance, there were only a few truly great painters – the Michealangelos and Da Vincis. And so it might be that there is a way to go even beyond mastery to achieve greatness.

What Coyle found, through his research and reading, was that mastery comes through a very specific process – something built into our biology. To oversimplify, the process comes from the building up of the myelin around specific nerves. Myelin is to our nerves like the insulation is to an electrical cord...it insulates the nerve, keeping the signals that nerve carries inside, and protecting them from signals from the outside. The more insulation, the cleaner and better the signal will be, and the more expert you will be at performing the action that is controlled by that nerve or group of nerves.

As it turns out, the way we build myelin is through repetition. If you want to build maximum myelin around the nerves you use, for example, to swing a bat...you swing the bat again and again...and each swing helps add an infinitessimal bit of myelin to all the nerves involved in the act of swinging a bat. As the myelin builds up, you are training the skill into your nervous system. And after about 10,000 times, you've built up enough that the action has become as good as it can be: You have mastered the act of swinging a bat. Sound familiar? We call this process practice. Practice is, quite simply, repeating an action again and again until you have built enough myelin around the nerves involved that you have mastered it.

However, and this is hugely important: it is possible to build mastery without building excellence. If you practice, for instance, a back palm again and again – you'll eventually become very good at doing the back palm...exactly the way you have practiced it. But if you've practiced it in a way that allows the edges of the cards to 'flash' each time you execute the back palm...what you will have mastered is a bad way to perform the back palm.

And that is why we need teachers, directors, and video cameras to provide a critical eye when we practice or rehearse. That is why students come to our master classes in Las Vegas – to study with true masters like Jeff and Eugene. By getting the input from these masters, artists who have gone way beyond the basics of our profession and are willing to share their knowledge, these students can assure themselves they won't be wasting their time practicing to become mediocre performers.

This pretty much matches what Coyle found in his book: You can achieve mastery just by putting in the time, but to achieve excellence at another level, you need to be confronted with, to experience something special that will put your practice on the right path – the path to true excellence and artistry.

Mentorship

Mentorship is one of the great keys to success in any field.

I think my own greatest mentors were the producers I worked for on Broadway. Particularly Richard Barr, who was one of the producers for *Sweeney Todd* – my first Broadway show. Richard and his partner, Charles Woodward had, at that point, produced all of Edward

Albee's plays on and off Broadway. He was president of the League of New York Theaters and Producers (now the League of American Theaters and Producers). I worked in his office as a production assistant, which meant I got to do things like drive Angela Lansbury back and forth to the theater, talk to investors on the phone when they wanted to attend a performance or opening night party, answer phones in the office, and handle house seats for all of the principals on the production. We had quite a list of those: Ms. Lansbury, Hal Prince, Steven Sondheim...a virtual who's who in the musical theatre. In spite of his very busy work days, Richard always took time out to explain why different decisions were being made, and why he wanted me to do things in a certain way, even though it didn't always seem to me that was the most efficient way to do them. What's more, he had an open office. He and Chuck Woodward sat at opposite ends of a long table at one end of the office, and their personal assistant and I sat at desks at the other end of the same room. Everyone got to hear everything that was said. And everything that was said included not only what was going on with our own productions, but often the business of Broadway in general, because of Richard's position as president of the League.

As a result, I learned more about the operation of the theater business in my first 6 months in that office than I had in my 6 years of undergraduate and graduate school in college combined. And it was an education I was being paid to get!

My second great mentor was Norman Kean, producer of the nudie musical Oh! Calcutta! and owner/operater of The Edison Theater – one of Broadway's smallest. I would never have aspired to work for Norman. He was known to be a real hustler, operating a show that was a bit questionable in a theater that barely qualified as being a Broadway house. The show was not a good show...but he somehow kept it open.

However, once I was hired, I learned more and faster from Norman about the real workings of many aspects of the theater than I had in all my life before. He was very much from the "throw them in the deep end if you want to teach them to swim" school of education, and immediately piled as much responsible work on me as he thought I could handle. "You're going to make mistakes," he would tell me. "Make sure they are big ones, because there's no excuse except laziness for the small ones. And the only sin is not reporting in the minute you realize you've made a big one. We can deal with them when we know they've been made...it's the mistake that goes undiscovered that winds up wrecking a business."

Norman loved to negotiate. He was one of the lead negotiators for the League of Producers with all the Broadway unions, and he taught me to read long contracts and tear them apart. Each day he would come back to the office from negotiations and toss a pile of papers on my desk. "Tell me how to get around this. Is it possible to misinterpret it?" He didn't always want to get around it. What he really wanted was bulletproof language that couldn't be misconstrued in a way that would hurt the producers. As a result of doing all that work – for which I had no credentials – I learned to read and write complex contracts. While the other managers of Broadway shows were learning to comply with the current union agreements (usually 150 page booklets), I was learning how to write and negotiate those agreements...something that has served me very well over the years.

I know that without the mentorship of these two remarkable men...I'm sure I would have had a far more difficult time succeeding in my business of mentoring the careers of Jeff McBride & Marco Tempest. And mentoring really IS my kind of management. Other managers are primarily business managers and glorified agents, handling the nuts and bolts of getting bookings, developing marketing, etc. But my personal brand of management style has much more to do with helping my clients discover and figure out what is really important to them, and then create businesses that support that core mission.

So...if you don't have one or more mentors for your magic career – and you are interested in building a career in magic – I strongly urge you to start looking. Don't be too eager, though. Mentorship is a bit like marriage – when you're young and just feel like you 'ought to be married by now,' you're exceedingly prone to choosing the wrong mate. It's the same with mentors. Go ahead and accept the help of whoever offers...but wait to deepen that relationship into a true mentoring one until you're quite sure you have the right mentor.

Key's to Character - Mirroring

I've talked in other sections about the power of role-playing...the various masks we wear which can give and take away our personal powers. Performers are virtually always playing a role, even when we feel we're just being ourselves. Part of the need to entertain is linked to the ability to be somehow larger than life - so even as ourselves, we play a heightened version of that self. As I write this, I'm sitting in an airport, waiting for a flight, and watching the stream of passing people. People watching is a favorite pastime of mine...largely because you can learn so much about how character manifests.

It's amazing how much you can know about another person just by mirroring the expression they habitually carry on their face, the tilt of their head, or their overall body posture. Here is a slightly overweight 60-something "grandma." There, a slightly stoop-shouldered, head-forward middle-aged businessman dragging his roller board suitcase...his mind obviously having moved forward in time to what he expects to be doing in an hour or two, with little awareness of his surroundings. There's the young airline pilot...talking on his phone leaning "casually" against a post as he waits for his plane to be ready for boarding. Obviously trying to look cool and confident... but the pose is just a bit too studied...I think he is secretly not as sure of himself as he would have us (and himself) believe. Across the way is a tall, black-bearded Hassidic Jew. He keeps shifting from one foot to the other as he chats with the woman next to him in line. He doesn't make eye contact with her, but looks out the window as they chat. Impatient, but not overly so. He searches in a jacket pocket, shuffles through a pack of business cards, then leans toward the woman (that overweight grandma I saw earlier) to hand her his card, at last making eye contact. I imagine him to be a diamond merchant, or that he has something else he may be offering her – she is suddenly more interesting to him, and he to her, now that a real contact has been made.

Here is a middle aged woman in comfortable shoes and sneakers, walking slowly as she stretches. She seems comfortable, unhurried and unworried. Has she just gotten off a plane? Tired of sitting, but in no hurry. Maybe she is an employee at the airport on a break, or early for work.

My wife is an extraordinary healer – people come for emotional healing, but also for more physical manifestations that seem somehow tied to their emotional well being. One day we were at a local shopping center and she had me sit with her on a bench just out of the flow of traffic and watch people. "Tell me about that man," she would say. After I had described what I saw, she pressed me, "What else? What makes you think that?" After a few minutes of this, she would surprise me with: "He and his wife just had an argument. Maybe about his health, because I'm fairly sure he has heart disease. Maybe had a heart attack not too long ago. He wants to avoid talking about it, and she's angry with him because he did something that wasn't good for his health. He is annoyed with her for calling him on it, but trying not to show it. I think they might be shopping for their grandchildren." She got all that from watching this couple walk by - in a matter of seconds.

How could she know all this? "His skin color shows a lack of oxygen...you get that when your blood flow is bad, as in people with heart disease. He also moves a little sluggishly, like someone not long out of hospital bed. You can tell by her color...a little flushed...that she is, or just has been, emotionally upset. See how she holds herself? Try putting your body in that position and see what you feel."

"Oh...look...that guy has parasites. A belly like that usually means someone has intestinal parasites. And see how one foot drags slightly?..."

Try it...go watch people, and imagine yourself "in" their bodies. Holding yourself the way they are, moving in the way and at the same rhythm. Even just the angle someone holds their head on can change their whole outlook on the world. What must it feel like to be that person, or that one? What experiences are they having today?

Hey — there goes that "stretching woman" in the t-shirt. I think it's a logo T for one of the merchants here, though she really looks more like she's in sweats. She's more overweight than I thought, and now she looks a little tired and out of breath. Even though she has just been walking, I'm suddenly sure it was for exercise, and she's worn herself out, but with that "good feeling" you have when you've exercised enough to get your blood flowing faster. I think she finds it difficult to do this...maybe she has had some problems and her doctor told her she had to do this, at least a couple of times a day, in order to avoid more serious problems.

If you practice this kind of observation regularly, you'll most likely find yourself developing a deeper understanding of, and empathy for, those around you. I strongly urge you to try it. Try it especially with people you instinctively dislike. What is it that makes them tick? Why do they do the things they do that upset you so much? Once you get "inside" them, you will find that you have a much better idea about these things. You'll probably also either find yourself in sympathy with them, or in a position to help them - or yourself - change for the better.

This is something actors are taught to do. It is one of the keys they learn for how to "become" different characters. It is magic, in a very real sense, because it allows us to discover things about ourselves and others we could never know otherwise. They are things for which there are often not words, so even if people wanted to tell you how they felt, they couldn't. But you can know, beyond a shadow of a doubt, just by mirroring them.

I hope you'll try it. I think our world will be a better place if we all learn to empathize a bit more with those who are different from ourselves. It's easy to understand and by sympathetic with those who are very much like ourselves, but that just leaves us feeling smug and comfortable with our lot. Learning to understand and empathize with those who are very different will help stretch who you are, what you are capable of, and the way you tolerate and support those different from yourself.

So please go out and try this. Watch people, mirror them, and write down what you see and feel. See what you can learn — and have fun!

The Magic of Non-Attachment

As I write this, we've just passed the shortest day of the year, and are about to celebrate the "New Year" according to the calendar. For centuries, cultures all over the world have celebrated this 'turning of the year' in many different ways. In our ever more globally aware society, we find ourselves all aware of Christmas, Kwanza, Hanukah, Yule and other celebrations at this time of year.

So, what does this mean for those seeking the Wizard's Way? I think of it as a time for letting go of the old, and moving forward enthusiastically with the new. There is a Buddhist doctrine known as "Non-Attachment." It's a kind of a tricky concept to embrace, because in practice, it means that, without giving up any of your passion or thirst for life – you let go of your attachment to particular outcomes.

If you think of it, all disappointment is the result of our attachment to a particular outcome. Put in another way, if you have no expectations, you'll have no disappointments — and when you DO feel disappointment, it's an indicator that you had an expectation and were attached to a particular result.

As artists, we often develop emotional attachments to the works of art that we create. If you're a performer and you create a performance piece that is particularly well received, it might become a "signature piece" for you – and you might become emotionally attached to it. Your fans might become emotionally attached, as well. Imagine your favorite band playing a concert and not playing their biggest hit songs, the ones for which their audiences have formed a strong attachment. Forming emotional attachments is a natural part of our lives.

However, it can be immensely freeing if we can let go of those attachments. Performers who are able to let go of their attachments in connection with a particular performance piece often find themselves suddenly freed up to create a whole series of even better new pieces. An author or composer who is able to let go of his or her self image (to which they've become attached) as a "pop" artist, or a "jazz" artist, or "classical composer," might suddenly find themselves creating some amazing new works in a field other than the one in which they've become known.

My challenge for you, then, is to take one of your creations to which you've become particularly attached. A favorite. And re-create it from scratch. If your trick is a particularly clever presentation for the cups and balls, for example, the challenge might be to come up with a completely different presentation for cups and balls. Or to take that special premise which has allowed you to create a special piece for cups and balls, and apply the same principle to a different trick. As you do so, you'll find the older piece and your attachments clawing at you all the way. Again and again, you'll find yourself telling yourself, "but it's better the other way." Don't let that stop you. Face the challenge. Remember, it's not so much about whether or not you can create a better piece (you can), but about the process of forcing yourself to break those attachments. That kind of attachment will only inhibit your growth — and as true wizards and artists, we all want to continue to grow and develop.

And that's my New Year's wish for you – that you may find the courage and energy to continue your own growth and development, no matter what age or status you might now have.

Props & Costumes

When we go to see a play or movie, we seldom stop to think that many of the set pieces and props pieces we are watching are not at all what they seem. Walls are actually flats made by stretching canvas on a wooden frame. What appear to be fabulous bejeweled golden crowns are actually made of rubber and rhinestones. That amazing small town in the western movie is really only a row of facades, propped up with two by fours. But it all looks fantastic from the audience.

A strange truism in the theater is that the "false" set and props pieces often actually appear to be more 'real' than the real ones. They are enhanced...given bigger than life elements so they will be more immediately recognizable for having a particular character than a real life object would be likely to have.

I remember spending a full day while in graduate school "painting on" the woodgrain for a large set piece. The piece was made from wood, and it had a nice grain... but the natural grain was too fine to be seen from the audience. And so we recreated it, a bit larger and with more contrast, using paint. About halfway through the job, I went out into the audience to see how what I was doing. Surprise – the portion we had painted looked like natural wood grain, and the part NOT painted looked like it had a nice smooth coat of wood colored paint on it!

I think it's the same with magic props. We want our audiences to completely accept our props as being what they purport to be...but we also want those props to generate an emotional response, and sometimes our audiences need visual cues a bit stronger than the "real" every day objects our props pretend to be actually have.

At the same time, the "enhancement" must never look less than real from a few feet away. We're in the business of illusion...and the illusions we create must be of a certain quality. Props that look tacky or amateurish will leave our audiences feeling they've seen a tacky and amateurish magician.

Perhaps I can give you an example. My friend Scott Hitchcock is married to a lovely woman who used to work at Ringling Bros. Circus. When they started performing together, she insisted on helping him upgrade all his costumes. Now, Scott was always a meticulous dresser, and had very nice costumes even before this. But they didn't sparkle the way they did when Marissa was done with them. She found tiny, real crystal rhinestones, and sewed them onto all his costumes at small, evenly spaced intervals. Up close, in a dimly lit room, the rhinestones were so small you would never notice them. Even on stage, you wouldn't look at Scott and say, "Oh, he's covered with rhinestones." But you would know that he sparkled. Something about him was now bigger than life, a bit more elegant and sparkly...and though you might not know exactly what it was, you would know he was the hero of the drama that was his magic act. The costumes had moved from being nice, slightly unusual clothing to being COSTUMES...and ones that sent a special message to Scott's audiences.

So...please have a look at all the props, costumes and set pieces you are using. Realize that they don't need to be "the real thing," and that sometimes NOT being real, but LOOKING real is more desirable. Then, think of how you can change them to add emotional impact, how you can make them "bigger than life" for your audiences...and you'll find very soon that you've taken a giant step towards improving your performances.

Who's Responsible?

I've been thinking about responsibility lately.

I don't remember where I read this, but it was one of those books designed to "change your life." The book started with asking you to write down a description of the life you really want. Then, on a separate page, it asked you to write a description of your life right now. Then it said to put aside the copy of "what you really want," because the life you have right now is the one you apparently really DO want...it is the life you have created for yourself by doing all the things you apparently really want to do – as evidenced by the fact that these are they things you actually have done.

Who, and what, is actually responsible for your life, anyway? Is it all those extenuating circumstances? Is it all the other people in your life? Is it your education? Is it who you know?

Let's ask ourselves some questions: Could you ignore those circumstances? Do you have to associate with those people? Are you really obligated to them, or is the 'obligation' you feel something that you've created? Could you break it? Could you meet new people? Make new friends? As for your education: Take note for a moment that neither Bill Gates nor Steve Jobs graduated from college. Keep in mind that every book every college student will read is available to you in bookstores and libraries. Do you need to pay someone else before you can look up curriculums for courses you want on line, get the books and read them? What do you really need to know in order to change your life, anyway?

Since I first wrote the paragraph above, many colleges have actually made many of their course lectures available online for free. Sites like those of the Kahn Academy, Coursera and Udacity have become available - if you have access to the internet, there's really not excuse at all for not having the education you want — even if you dropped out of high school and can barely pay your rent.

We've all heard the cliché that it's not what you know, but who you know. And of course, the "who knows you, which is equally important." It has been shown that who you associate with will profoundly affect your level of income and achievement. T. Harv Ecker, author of Secrets of the Millionaire Mind, claims he can predict your income accurately if you give him a list of the 10 people you spend most of your time with, along with their yearly incomes. How does he do it? It's simple...just average the incomes of those 10 people, and you'll probably come up with your own average yearly income.

So...this will seem harsh and difficult for many of you... but don't you have the ability to leave behind those who are holding you back? Can you make new friends who are already living the life you envision for yourself? Can you consciously choose to spend more time with those people and less time with the old friends who have mindsets that may be holding you back? Of course you can.Who is really responsible for your life, anyway?

Radical Responsibility

As many of you know, I've been studying and writing a lot about real wizards lately. One of the biggest things I've discovered is the power of taking what I call radical responsibility. That means you take responsibility not only for your actions, which is what we've been talking about up till now, but for everything in your life. As it turns out (and I don't pretend to fully understand how this works or why it should be so)...the act of taking responsibility actually creates power.

How is it done? Just assume you are responsible for everything that comes into your life. Did you turn on the news and hear about innocent women and children being abused somewhere in the world? What did you do to bring that into your life? What did you fail to do that allowed the conditions for that to happen? Can you change those things? Did someone you know just get a raise and a promotion, and tell you about it? What did you do to bring that into your life? Did you recently lose (or find) a loved one? What did you do that brought that into your life? If you can't imagine what you might have done, perhaps you can at least choose to take responsibility for what you do as a response to these things. Do you simply wail and complain - or do you take steps to change yourself, or the situations that create the things you want to change?

And with all these things...whatever you did that brought those things to you, can you change them? How? When?

Responsibility for the Magician

For those of you that are performers, this principal has everything to do with the success of your shows and your careers. Who is more responsible for the experience that is had in a theater than the performer? There's a phrase that "there are no bad audiences." It's not true. However, bad audiences are created by performers. Or they are allowed by performers. Either way, it's your responsibility, and you have the power to convert those experiences, at least in part, just by accepting the responsibility, and by choosing to make the necessary changes in your own actions.

So, here's your assignment. Think of one thing in your life or your show that you wish were different. Write it down. Then write down all the things you have done to make it the way it is now. Write down a description of how it will be when you change it...then a list of the things you need to start doing differently right now in order to make that a reality. Then do it!

ReviewingMagic

I took a course in college on dramatic criticism...and one of the first things we learned was the difference between a reviewer and a critic. We all love to hate critics, especially those who review our own work – because we think of criticism as being negative. "You're so critical" usually means you have a lot of negative things to say. However, when it comes to being a critic in the arts, that's not true at all. The critic's job is to understand, not so much to judge. That falls to the reviewer.

The reviewer's job is to say "I liked it," or "I didn't like it," and then to give us a little bit of an idea of what the play or film or work of art was like, so we can figure out if we would like or not like it, as well. "It was a rollicking adventure." "A comic book turned into film," "a real whodunnit." We use reviewer's reviews to help us decide what to see, where to spend our money. They are basically reporting on their own taste and how a work relates to it. "Don't miss this one!" "to be avoided at all costs." We get a bit of experience with different reviewers and find out if our tastes match theirs. If not, we stop reading them. If they do match, we're happy to follow their advice.

We expect a bit more from the critic, though. The critic will still let us know they liked or disliked a piece – but sometimes even when they dislike something, they'll decide it is important. They are interested in things like where a particular piece fits into its genre, or how it relates to other works of art on a similar theme. They try and figure out why and how a particular moment or piece works and affects us in a particular way. What influences might have been operating on the artist who created a piece? What is the historic tradition that may have inspired this piece of art?

In short...while we might learn whether we should buy a ticket, or a particular item... from a reviewer, we can actually learn to become better artists and more appreciative audiences ourselves by reading good criticism. Each has their place – and their uses. But I think it's a big mistake to mix up the two, or expect something from one that is really the purview of the other. Of course, there are times when reviews contain real criticism, and critics offer opinions that we might have expected from a reviewer. The lines between the two aren't always clear or firm...but it's good to know the difference, anyway.

For myself, I like reading real criticism of magic and theater. Articles like the ones you'll find in books by Eugene Burger and Bob Neale, in magic, or by Peter Brooke, Clive Barnes and others in the theater. Books which talk about why we do magic in the first place...what it's for, and how different kinds of magic affect audiences in different ways. How magic can take on meaning. These are things I want to know, and that help me be a better director and critic myself.

I already have more than enough magic props and tricks – I'm not sure you can really ever have enough books – so I'm less likely to go out of my way to read the latest reviews. I suppose that's another difference – reviews tend to be of the moment: What's the latest thing, and is it any good? Critics are less bound by time. We still read Artistotle, one of the great critics, and what he wrote is almost as useful today as it was when he wrote it. The reviews of "Oedipus" when it was first performed in 500 BC...well, good luck finding those.

So...that's my take on reviews and critics. I hope it gives you some food for thought!

Secrets

I think it may be time to rethink this whole secrecy thing. I find more and more that our traditional magicians oath - you know, the 'never reveal the secrets' bit - places our attention in the wrong place. For me, at least, the fanatical dedication to secrecy leads to an emphasis on the magician's role of fooling the audience. That, for me, is not the primary job of the performing magician, though it is the role of one kind of magician – the Trickster. For myself, I really prefer magical performances that give me a magical experience. I can get that from a mysterious story told well, an optical illusion that plays with the way my mind creates reality, or a bit of fascinating body magic – as much or more so than I can from being fooled by a clever gimmick or sleight-of-hand.

Which is not to say that a good magician can't use a good trick to create that experience of mystery. They can, and many people honestly do love being fooled in that way. I'm not suggesting we should take that away from them.

But I think it's a mistake to think your primary job as a magician is to fool people.

As a matter of fact...remember The Masked Magician? While magicians were up in arms, thinking his exposures would destroy their livelihoods by revealing their cherished secrets – most of my discussions with audience members who were not magicians had to do with their hating his exposures, because they really didn't want to know. What this showed me was that audiences are completely complicit in keeping our so called secrets secret. There was nothing revealed by The Masked Magician which couldn't be found in magic books then available in any Barnes & Noble or Borders Bookstore. The so-called 'secrets' were always out in the open, for anyone who wanted to know them.

What's more, although I think many magicians do take the exposure of secrets very seriously, there are an awful lot of us that do not. The fact that we can know the secret and still experience the magic seems to me to be at least as interesting as all those secrets themselves. For myself, I am doubly delighted when, even though I know every detail of how an effect is produced, I can still see the effect and have the experience of the impossible, even though I know it isn't, somehow, real. Knowing I'm experiencing a real illusion is something that brings joy in itself.

So...here's another kind of radical thought: Like great gurus and teachers, the true magicians' job MIGHT be in actually leading our audiences to discover the secrets behind some of our mysteries. There are wondrous things in each of our lives – in the ways our own bodies and minds function, for example – of which we are completely unaware. When we are led to discover those things – the experience we have is one that is certainly akin to magic. That which we had been unaware of, or perhaps not believed to be possible, suddenly becomes real for us. For me, at least, that is the experience I want to have from a magician – one that expands my world, my possibilities.

Again – this isn't to say that our pursuit of so-called secrets is a useless occupation. By probing the multitudinous ways in which our senses can be fooled, by going deeper into the mysteries of what it means to be human, that is the real wizard's path. It is a noble thing to seek out deeper, "secret" knowledge – not for the purpose of fooling others, or gaining power over them – but for the purpose of actually finding powerful ways of awakening them to that secret knowledge. If our performances can allow them to experience real and tangible truths that provide more depth and power to their lives – well that is a true and noble purpose indeed, and one for which our magical art is uniquely qualified.

Language - Internal and External

I want to talk to you briefly about the language you use. Language is tremendously powerful – and it works on many different levels. There is the language you use when conversing with friends. A slightly different kind of language we use in letters, or in e-mail. An entirely different kind we use in text messages. Still a different kind we use when speaking before a group, or writing an essay.

While all of these are important – and some of what I'm about to tell you may apply to many of them – I really want to talk about the language you use when you speak to yourself. Wizards know that they change the world by first changing themselves – and that's a very large subject for another time – but the obvious follow up to that statement is:

Okay, so how do I go about changing myself?

There are, of course, many ways to do this. However, one of the fastest and easiest is to re-write the programs each of us runs all the time. What programs? Well, think to yourself for a moment. Have you recently forgotten to do something? Maybe it was just something you were going to pick up at the supermarket, and forgot. What phrase ran through your mind when you discovered you had forgotten it? Did you call yourself a name? "I'm such an idiot!" Maybe you blamed something outside yourself. "That jerk who bumped into me made me forget that!" Be specific as you try and think of what the phrase is that you hear inside your mind when something like this happens.

Now, think for a moment: Could you change that phrase if something big depended on it? Instead of "I'm such an idiot!" could you tell yourself, 'I know my memory is improving, but I guess I have a ways still to go". Could you give yourself a "self-program," something that would trigger you to run through your memorized or written shopping lists every time you approach a cash register?

Hypnotherapists do just that for their clients, and there's no reason you can't do it for yourself. The therapist would get you into trance, then suggest, "You know, this is really up to you – but I imagine the next time you find yourself walking towards a cash register or cashier, you'll find yourself automatically reviewing your shopping lists. No matter what else is happening around you, you will find yourself stopping and going over the list. You might even find you'll hear my voice in your head whenever you see a cash register, saying "review your shopping list!" And – the next time you approach a cash register, your mind will play the new program, and you'll remember. And if it doesn't...well, you'll have that other new programmed phrase that will tell you, "I'm getting better, but I have a ways to go. " And then you can re-run your meditation designed to set the "when I see a cash register: remember my list" program.

If you think about it, you know you already have hundreds of programs already working for you (and against you, if we're honest about it). As you're driving along the road, you see a stop sign, and your body automatically runs the program that gets your foot to the brake and stops your car. If you accidentally back up into someone as you're shopping in a store, your "Oh, excuse me" program kicks in without you're having to think about it...that is, unless you've programmed a more aggressive "Hey, what do you think you're doing?" program, in which case you may find yourself in more arguments and confrontational situations than is really necessary.

There's an important aspect of creating this kind of self-program. It is the language you will use when you 'speak to yourself.' When you're consciously creating these little program phrases, always be positive with the language structure. Your sub-conscious mind hears only the verbs and nouns – it doesn't hear "not, no, won't" or other negative qualifiers. Therefore "Don't eat Junk" comes through as "eat junk." "Quit smoking!" comes through as "Smoking!" Getting around the "no" can take creativity. Instead of "don't eat junk," you might want to "eat something that will make me feel great!" or when you feel bored or have low energy, instead of the "I'm feeling down: time for a snack" program, you might want to run the "I'm feeling down...a short run would make me feel great!" Instead of the "I'm feeling so fat! I'm depressed!" run the "I feel so much better as I begin to get my body in shape...what can I do next?" program.

So: remember, real wizards change themselves in order to change the world around them. One easy way to change yourself is by re-writing the programs you habitually run in your own mind. When you do this, be sure and use positive language, so that your subconscious will actually get the message you intend to send.

By the way: this positive languaging also works when you write scripts for your performances. The act of witnessing a performance actually affects the neurology of your audiences, and speaks to their sub-conscious minds as much or more than it does to their conscious minds. If you want to be more effective at transforming your audiences, speak consciously to their unconscious minds!

ShowDoctor

(Note: The following was written for a program celebrating the release of Jeff McBride's book, The Show Doctor.)

Tonight we're celebrating! As I sit down to write this, Jeff McBride's book with Larry Hass has just been released! It is the first magic book with a version created and released just for the iPad, which includes video, web-links and lots of bells and whistles never really possible before. I'm excited. For Jeff, for Larry, for Stan Allen, whose MAGIC magazine staff created the iPad version, for Jordan Wright who created the amazing videos that are part of the whole thing...an outstanding accomplishment!

Let's talk a bit about the magic that comes with the discipline of writing and teaching. I've watched Jeff's teaching and "show doctor" career for over 20 years. I remember when he was on tour with the Radio City Rockettes back in the mid-90's, and we decided to make life more interesting for him by booking him for lectures at local magic clubs in as many of their city stops as we could. He was just beginning to speak in his shows then – before that he had performed in whiteface, and never spoke until he had removed it during the "Mask and Mirror" piece at the very end of his shows. It was the process of lecturing each week that got him comfortable with speaking on stage, after so many years of not doing it.

I was also with him for some of his consulting – on Broadway shows like Legs Diamond, Jekyll & Hyde, and an early Houdini Musical. Later on he worked with

Lawerence Khong on his Magic of Love show, and helped him make huge strides forward.

From the first time I saw Jeff lecture, it was obvious that he loved teaching, and had a point of view that other magicians were hungry for. Having been trained through the American Mime School and at Kabuki Za in Tokyo, and then working as an opening act for major rock bands – one of the toughest gigs any performer can have, by the way – he had developed a sense of showmanship and knowledge of what it took to grab an audiences attention and entertain them which few magicians ever get. His lecture audiences loved getting those insights...albeit with a healthy dose of manipulation technique and tricks mixed in...right from the beginning. And Jeff rapidly discovered that he loved lecturing and teaching.

I've spent a fair amount of time teaching and directing myself. And there's an interesting thing that almost always happens: When you're asked to teach...or to write about...something you think you know really well – you discover there's a lot about that thing that you didn't really know as well as you thought you did. You find yourself having to clarify your thinking, adding to your knowledge – in ways you had never considered. And I got to see that happen to Jeff. I saw it as he figured out how to teach card manipulation on his first set of videos for L&L.

I saw it during our early Master Classes, as he and Eugene would spend countless hours after the students had gone home at night discussing each student...and not only how the student had done, but what we could do as teachers that would better help those students. They learned...and we learned. And now, in The Show Doctor, a great deal of that learning has been written down and shared. After thousands of students, Jeff has discovered what most of those students really needed to learn...even when they didn't know they needed to learn those things. That is what is shared in this book.

I hope you'll pick up a copy of The Show Doctor and study it. Some of you will find wisdom on every page. Others will say to themselves, "I don't need this." If you're one of those – well, I think you're the ones the book is really for. Take a chapter, read it. Twice...then try and apply what it tells you to just one of the pieces you perform. See what happens. I think you'll be surprised.

I've seen hundreds of students come through the Master Classes..many who were quite sure there wasn't much we could do for them, because they were already operating on such a high level. These were invariably the students who made the biggest leaps – who moved from doing mediocre performances that they thought were great...to moving on to the path of true excellence.

I truly hope you'll find yourself...if not right now, then soon...on that latter path. We at the McBride Magic & Mystery School spend quite a lot of our time thinking and working to help raise the overall level of our magical art. I know Jeff's book will provide a significant step along that path to excellence for many, many magicians who are wise enough to read it and heed its many lessons.

Steve Jobs: Focus

In this chapter I'd like to talk just a bit about focus and it's relationship to excellence and innovation.

It has only been a couple of years since Steve Jobs' untimely passing. Steve is one of my favorite contemporary wizards, and I believe a detailed study of his life and ways of thinking would be profitable for any aspiring wizard. Today, I want to relate a story to old me by one of my friends who happens to work for Apple.

It appears that when Jobs returned to Apple as part of their package deal to purchase his NeXt Computer company, one of his first actions was to gather all his department heads and ask for detailed reports on what new and exciting projects they had in the works. Remember, this was a time when Apple was in serious trouble, and many were predicting it's ultimate demise – but they had many talented people working on lots of fascinating projects. As a matter of fact, there were over a thousand new products in development.

Many of the new projects were good, some were really quite excellent and innovative...and a few were truly outstanding. What was Jobs' response to the reports? I'm not sure of the exact figures, but my memory is that he killed off all but 14 of the development projects. His reasoning? Better to do one thing (or fourteen) better than anyone else than 100 things almost as well as someone else. If the company wasn't leading the trends, he felt they would continue to flounder.

Later on, Jobs had some comments about how those first decisions on his return would affect the company's phenomenal success since that day:

"People think focus means saying yes to the thing you've got to focus on. But that's not what it means at all. It means saying no to the hundred other good ideas that there are. You have to pick carefully."

"Quality is more important than quantity. One home run is much better than two doubles."

"It comes from saying no to 1,000 things to make sure we don't get on the wrong track or try to do too much."

I've heard similar things from others, as well. I remember when I first met Eugene Burger over the phone while we were planning the first Mystery School. I had read one or two of his books, and had begun teaching myself to do magic again, after some 20 years away from it. I remember telling Eugene, "I've got about 20 tricks I can do reasonably well again...of course it's not like what a real professional could do."

"Oh?" said Eugene. "I've finally got my working repertory down to 15 tricks. I've been thinking of I could get it to just 12, I could be really good!"

That was 20 years ago, and I've learned a lot from Eugene and many others since then. One of the biggest things is that finding one or two things that really inspire you, and giving them your full focus is a far better strategy for success than trying to pursue a hundred different paths.

As we say in some of our advertising for the Magic & Mystery School: You probably already have too much magic stuff. Tricks, gimmicks, etc. You probably know too many tricks, have too many books and videos – and most of you are still wondering why you haven't hit the big time in terms of your success.

Why not take just one thing, one short piece, and work on that piece until it is the best version of that piece in the world. Perhaps it will have a more creative or moving story. Perhaps it will be more deceptive and magical than anyone else's presentation of that effect. Maybe you will just become the best performer of that effect, engaging with your audiences more fully and effectively than anyone else. But just one such finished, polished, "best in class" piece can make all the difference.

Think for a moment of how it feels to be that person who knows and can perform 100 tricks...all just adequately. How do friends and audience respond? How do you feel being barely good enough when performing? Do you think that is the best way to serve the art form you've chosen?

Then think of how it must feel to know you have just performed one thing better than anyone else in the world has ever done. How will you stand, talk, sleep at night, knowing you are the absolute BEST at that one thing?

There's only one way to reach that state...and it is through intense, laser-like focus on one thing.

Supporting Others with Magic

Magician's live in a strange world, indeed. We are members of a unique fraternity, eager to help one another and share – and at the same time so many of us want to guard and keep our secrets just for ourselves. I distinctly remember a day some 15 years ago when I was invited to join the SAM, and handed a form to fill out, in which, among other things, I was to swear I would not reveal the secret workings of any trick to anyone outside of magic. I had just been in a local Barnes and Noble scanning through a book on their remainders table which purported to teach the basic secrets of magic to anyone who wished to pick up the book. It had been authored by the same distinguished magician who was now handing me the paper swearing me to secrecy. I told him I thought I would take the matter under advisement, and later decided I didn't want to sign on to that particular oath.

I think we tend towards the same ambiguity when it comes to really helping one another. I am often consulted by magicians about their marketing strategies. A common question is, "should I put my calendar on line?" Making your performance schedule available on line can help those meeting planners and others who might want to book you find out about your availability, so they call you only for dates when you're available. It can also work as a kind of brag sheet - "Look at all the cool places I'm booked!" But that same calendar also signals other magicians and variety artists that "Hey...here are places you could contact to get booked, too!" In the best of all worlds, this would only lead to more variety artists getting booked – but all too often it can lead to the kind of cutthroat competition that only serves to drive everyone's prices down, and cheapens our art. The minute a booker knows he can get one performer to say "I'll do that for $10 less," the entire market for that kind of entertainment is immediately devalued in that location. So many magicians simply keep their calendars, and as much information about specific bookings as possible, out of sight. I can understand why.

The choice of whether or not you want to go out of your way to help your fellow magicians and other variety artists is one each of us should consider, and decide upon for ourselves. For myself, I'm grateful to have had personal mentors in magic, starting with Bob Fitch, and then extending to my good friends Jeff McBride and Eugene Burger, who share their knowledge and passion unstintingly. Through the McBride Magic & Mystery School, I've become friends with and helped out hundreds and hundreds of fellow magicians over the years. In almost every instance, I've learned as much as any one of them did. Each class brings new insights, new skills and, most of all, new friends. I've seen us all grow as a result of our work there. It helps us each hone our own ideas about what's really important in magic -- and in life.

Transformation - Part 1

Transformation. That's really what it's all about, isn't it? Magic is the art of transformation. We transform objects into other objects. Transform objects by vanishing or making them reappear. We transform them by demolishing or cutting them, and then restoring them. And all of these things are metaphors, in some way, for transforming ourselves.

I remember a time when I just didn't get the idea of self transformation. I thought it was only for people who didn't like themselves very much – and that it couldn't possibly be for me. I guess I must have been a bit of a self-satisfied, arrogant young prick. Either that or I was just severely lacking in imagination, never imagining what I MIGHT become if I had the courage to face change – to actually seek transformaton.

I've written before about finding a purpose for everything you do. Finding a purpose for the individual pieces you create, for the shows, for your career. When you find a good purpose, and really develop it so it speaks to and inspires you, that's a truly powerful thing.

However, when you think about it, the very idea of purpose pre-supposes the idea of transformation. If everything is perfect just as it is, the only purpose you might think of is to make sure everything stays just as it is. And that would be a useless thought, because in that perfect world there would be nothing that could upset the perfection of the world.

Happily, we don't live in such a world. We live in a world where we can imagine a thousand improvements everywhere we look. We could all be stronger, smarter, more caring. We could live in a world where it was easier to manifest shelter, clothing and food for all. Where medical care wasn't too expensive, where no one had to work at jobs they hated. There is virtually nowhere you can turn your eyes and ears that you can't find something that could be improved...with just a bit of imagination and effort. And the struggle to make those improvements – and to settle between us the issue of what are the improvements that need to be made – is the stuff of every story, every book, every movie, every piece of art there is.

As practitioners of the fine art of wizardry, we find ourselves on the front lines in the battle for transformation. In the next chapter, I'll tell you about some interesting paths to change...techniques you can use in order to instigate change, and make that transformation actually take root and grow. For now, I would just urge you to spend some quiet time on your own and consider the things you most want to change. Imagine yourself at the end of your life, many, many years from now, looking back. What changes would you wish you had been able to make in the world? How will the world be better for your having been here?

What injustices will you have righted? What new paths will have opened up for future generations because of you?

There are many ways to do this. Some people do their deepest thinking while sitting and listening to music, or while out running or riding their bicycles. Often your best thoughts will come when you least expect it...after you've asked yourself the question, spent a hard hour or two looking for answers without finding them...and then put the whole thing out of your mind for a time, only to be surprised as you're going down the aisle in the supermarket, when the answer you were seeking suddenly pops into your mind, inspired by the shape of a head of broccoli or the movement of a leaf of spinach.

Whatever you come up with...one, two...or several major changes you think you would like to make in the world during your short time here...write them down on a piece of paper, and keep that with you. You may think of additional things you'd like to improve as time goes by... just add them to the list.

In the next chapter I'll ask you to take it out and have a look after I've offered up a couple of surefire ways of actually *creating* transformations.

Transformation Part 2

In the last chapter we began a discussion about transformation – how we create change. I asked you to think of what changes...what transformations, you might like to create during your lifetime. How will the world be different because you were here? Many people spend years trying to answer the question of "why am I here," as though the answer to that was somehow predetermined and might come from outside themselves. Wizard's think differently – they decide what their purpose is, and then set out to actualize that purpose.

As I said last time we addressed this subject, all

purposes presuppose some kind of transformation..some sort of change that is to take place. I recently read a fantastic book, by the same two guys...Chip & Dan Heath, who wrote the popular book "Made to Stick." The new book is called "Switch." They are true scholars of the psychology of our culture, and they lay out the problem of bringing about change with an interesting metaphor:

Imagine for a moment that you have an elephant on a path going through the jungle. You are riding atop the elephant, and you want to make a change in the direction he is going. The brothers Heath liken the rider...you...to the rational mind. It is intelligent and knows what it wants. However, you are small, and the elephant is large. The elephant is like your emotions and emotional attachments. Researchers have shown that almost all of our decisions in life are actually made by our emotions...and then justified by our intellects, which then attempt to take credit. If you've ever tried to steer an elephant, you might well understand how difficult it will be for that tiny rider to change the elephant's path when the elephant is set upon a particular course. So...if we want to cause change, we might be better to make an appeal to the emotions...the desire body...of the entity..person, creature or organization...that we want to change, than to it's intellect. Advertisers know this.

Yet...there is a third major factor we need to consider if we want to change the course the elephant and it's rider will take – and that is the path. The elephant – our emotions – will often take the path of least resistance. Even though it may WANT to go wade in the lake, the broad path it is on doesn't go by the lake, but to a small watering hole. If the path makes it easier to go to the watering hole, chances are that is where the elephant and it's rider will end up – and eventually decide that that is where they wanted to go all along.

For example, let's suppose you want to change a bad habit you've developed. Maybe you're in the habit of having a glass of Scotch every evening when you arrive home, before dinner. It once seemed a very "grown up" and "independent" way of unwinding at the end of a hard day. But your spouse has mentioned several times that they wish you were a bit more responsive at the dinner table, and had the energy after dinner to engage in some activities together that would be fun. You've been having your 'happy hour' drink – sometimes more than one - for a couple of years, and you tell yourself you really enjoy it... but you could give it up if you wanted to.

So you make the attempt. One day you get home, and tell yourself you're not going to have a drink, even though it has been a particularly trying day. You're just not sure what else you might do during that time when you were used to having your drink. You get home, walk past the liquor cabinet, and sit down in the chair you usually sit in, turn on the news, and proceed to watch it...all the while thinking about that drink you're not having. You make it through, and are successful that day. You mention this to your spouse, and she congratulates you. You feel great for your small win.

However, after dinner, your spouse has to work on a project for work the next day, and you find yourself on your own...so you sit and read a book, watch some TV...all the while telling yourself, "I wish I'd had that drink! Now I'm wide awake and no one to play with."

The next day, you come home, go to the liquor cabinet and pour yourself a tall one. You're halfway through the drink before it occurs to you – Oh! I was trying to quit! So much for changing that habit!

So...let's analyze this attempted change the way the Heath Brothers might:

What part of your actions/ attempts might correspond with the driver? What is your rational mind telling you? Well...that your spouse wants you to stop, and you should want to please your spouse. Perhaps it is reminding you to be careful not to become an alchoholic, or that you've been putting on weight lately, and that cutting out the drinks at night might be the cause.

And what part is the elephant? Well...the elephant is the momentum you're habit has developed. You don't even have to think about getting yourself that drink any more. Your body just finds it's way to the liquor cabinet, pours it...and you aren't really even consciously aware until you're halfway through that tall glass. You like the taste of the liquor, and the way it helps you relax. You feel it is a reward for getting through another difficult day. Your elephant feels quite contented with this habit.

And what is the path? Let's look at the actual physical path that's involved: You enter your home, walk straight to the conveniently located liquor cabinet, all outfitted with clean glasses and bottles of liquor that you keep stocked. Perhaps there's even a small fridge there with ready made ice cubes. The cabinet is next to the little closet where you hang your coat...all very convenient. It is even on your way to the kitchen where you say hello to your spouse, or the TV room where you go to sit and savor your drink as you watch a little TV before dinner.

SO: How do we go about changing the habit? First: Research has found it takes about 26 days to form a new habit. Old habits don't really get "broken" so much as they get replaced by new ones. So we need to plan a way to replace your "drink after work" habit for at least a month. What can we do using the elephant and rider metaphor, that might be effective.

First, I think, is to replace your self-talk about the habit. You need to re-program your elephant...your emotions... about the habit. Instead of "liquor is my reward," you need to learn to think of it as something that is making you fat and aging prematurely...or whatever other true images of the effects of liquor might be that will work for you.

Instead of, "I'm going to reward myself with a drink," you might think, "I'm going to balance out my day (which you spent most of sitting in an office chair), by getting my body back up to speed. Each night I'll add 2 minutes to my daily workout (walk, bicycle ride, yoga regimen, tai chi... whatever works best for you), until I'm up to a full half hour. At the end of my workout, I get to have a nice hot shower, then go and enjoy dinner and the evening with my spouse. I love how this helps us build our relationship and keep it fresh.

The idea is to re-structure your emotions around the habit – replacing the old ones with new ones about what you don't like about the old habit, and what you really love about the one you are replacing it with. And then you're feeding your rider – the rational mind – the new language of the program.

And here's an additional kicker: You can change the path. If you don't have to pass that liquor cabinet on the way in the door every night, or if it is stocked with spring water and other healthy drinks instead of liquor, at least a part of your temptation to "fall off the wagon" each night will be taken away, and you'll find it much easier to pursue the new habit. Put the liquor away somewhere it is hard to get at, so you only get it out for parties and real special occasions, or get rid of it altogether if you really think you might have a problem with it. Make the "path of least resistance" one that goes through your exercise room, NOT past the liquor cabinet.

Now, by re-programming your conscious, rational mind about the old and new habits, and by really getting your emotional self on board – convince that elephant that it really WANTS the new habit, AND THEN by re-structuring your path...the path of least resistance...to embrace the new habit and avoid the old...You will find it much easier to make the change you desire.

Wands
The Wizard's Staff

One of the things that would seem to define a magician is the magic wand...or as I prefer to think of it the Wizard's Staff! The wand or staff has long been a symbol of power. King's carry a scepter, as a >symbol< of their power. Several sports use wand-like objects: In baseball we have the bat – and in this case, it amplifies the capabilities of the one swinging it. In tennis and badminton we use raquets...for the same reason. The leverage provided by the bat or raquet allows us to hit the ball or shuttlecock much harder and faster than we could throw it just using our arms.

Orchestra conductors use a wand to conduct orchestras. Again – a useful symbol, and in the conductor's use of the baton, it actually amplifies what the orchestra sees. I think the orchestra leader's baton is a particularly good analog of the magician's wand. You see...wands are meant to be more than just symbols of power. In fiction – think Harry Potter here – the wand actually holds and channels power. It is not merely a symbol, but something that actually carries a magical charge, that allows things to be done that could not be done without it. If a wand is broken, it's power is lost...or seriously changed.

Performing magicians tend to be fond of wands that look like this, or like this... [images here] and use them to tap things in order to make little balls disappear, or wave them over things to make things materialize inside – they tend to use the wand as nothing more than a slightly distracting costume prop, and their audiences tend to respond accordingly.

In the recent set of Harry Potter movies, a very different sort of wand was used. The wands looked far more organic – like living twigs, and each had something magical inside. The "sorcerers" and junior sorcerers were paired with their wands. Without the wand, the sorcerer is nearly powerless. Quite a different situation from that of the typical modern performing magician.

And the wizard's staff...well, that was used to channel lightning, to split mountains. A kind of lightning rod the wizard could use to channel the powers of nature. Now that's my idea of a wand!

So...I think it's important for a performing magician to decide just exactly what his or her relationship to the wand really is. Will it be a costume prop, symbol of power? Or will it have powers of it's own? How does your wand manifest it's power? Though pointing? Tapping? Drawing power from afar? Is it an orchestra leader's baton, or a baseball player's bat? How personal is your wand to your character? Only when you've answered all these questions will you really be able to make decisions about how your wand should look, and how you want to use it in performance. How will you treat YOUR version of the wand? Or will you use a wand at all? I've seen some performers use their fingers in much the same way others use a wand, and to great effect.

I hope you'll have some fun considering these things... and if you choose to use a wand in your performances, that you'll treat it – and all your other props – in ways that are consistent with the decisions you've made about them and their relationship to your performing persona and the kind of magic you do.

What Would You Do if...

As I write this, we just recently celebrated the year's shortest day, the Winter Solstice. For many cultures through time this has been the marker of the year's turning... the ending of one productive year and beginning of the next. And this weekend, we'll celebrate our culture's New Year.

So it is, traditionally, a time to take stock, and to consider new beginnings. There's a little mental exercise I like to run for myself...not only at this time of year, but the theme seems right.

Here's how it goes:

If you could not do the main thing that you do now...the thing that you might define yourself by: for example, Jeff McBride is a magician. Kobi Bryant is a basketball player. Angelina Jolie is a movie star... I have a friend who is a magician, but defines his role in the world primarily as "father." So, if your defining role suddenly vanished, what would you do, instead?

I once saw the actor Richard Harris answer this question on a talk show. He was at the height of his career as an actor at the time,having just starred in the title role of the movie Camelot...and his answer was, "I think I'd be a cat burglar. It's the only thing I can think of that might give me the same thrill as performing does. Since I was a young boy I loved climbing on things, and I definitely have a bit of the outlaw in my character. I need to take risks in order to fell alive, and the role of cat burglar really appeals to me."

I'm glad to say that wouldn't be the choice most of us would make...but this can be fun as a mental exercise... and give you some answers to who you really are, and ways you might find more happiness. You might, for example, be a banker who would love to toss it all over and pursue a career as a film producer. You might be a magician who decides if he could no longer perform, he would want to be a teacher, or write adventure novels. Imagine what your life would be like in this new role you've imagined for yourself. How would it be different? How the same? Who would you associate with that you don't now associate with? Where would you go? What would your days be like? Your nights? What is preventing you from doing this other thing now?

If the thing you choose as what you would do if you could no longer do the thing you do most now, but you prefer to continuing on your present path...perhaps you can find some ways to include that other thing into what you're doing now.

For example: Imagine yourself to be a magician, but you love to read and write mystery short stories. Could you include your role as a mystery writer into your performances as a magician? Or maybe you'd like to write mystery short stories about a character who is a magician, and either a detective or a criminal.

Though I started this article out with a reference to the New Year and new beginnings, in fact any time is a perfect time for this kind of assessment. Right now, for example. I hope you'll take some time to reflect, and answer these questions for yourself.

- First: What would I do if I could no longer do what I do now...and;

- Second: Would I be happier doing that thing, and can I change? And;

- Third: If I don't choose to change completely, right now...can I include that other thing in what I do now? Can I incorporate that thing into my current job and identity...and would it make me happier or more productive?

Have fun with this!

Wiz-dom

I have spent the past several years learning more and more about what makes a wizard a wizard...and one of the top things is that real wizards have wisdom. Just listen to the words...you're sure to see the connection:

Wis-dom is Wiz-dom
A Wizard is a Wise-ard

Wisdom is one of the ways someone gets to be a wizard.

"Okay, then...so what is wisdom?" That's one of those words we all think we know, but when you try and pin down the definition, it's tough to do. It is not just the ability to hold a lot of information. One must gain lots of real knowledge...and I don't mean the kind that comes in books. Albert Einstein – who I would qualify as one of the "real" wizards – wrote:

"Real knowledge comes from experience. Everything else is just information."

His point is that if your knowledge hasn't been experienced...used...it isn't useful or real to you. Books contain information – it's up to us to turn that information into real knowledge, and then to mastery, and finally into wisdom.

Think about the process of learning a magic trick. First we see it, or read the effect. You certainly can't really be said to know the effect then. Perhaps you read about the method, or view it on video. Still...you don't really know how to do it until you gather the necessary props and start practicing. At some point, you're able to "do" the trick...but you still don't have any real idea of how it will play for an audience. You've begun to know the trick, but you're still far from mastery. After you've performed the piece for a thousand times or so, you'll begin to get really good at it. You might think this is the point at which you begin to gain wisdom about the trick...but that's not always true. Certainly you could be said to "know" the trick at this point...but if you haven't reflected – considered all the aspects in detail, you really haven't mastered it. What sort of person will respond best to that trick as you perform it? How will they be affected by it? Is it best for opening or closing a show, or somewhere in the middle? What have you learned about people by performing that trick for them? About yourself?

At that point, I think, we're approaching the realm of wisdom.

Some people are naturally wise in the ways of the world. I live near Silicon Valley, the heart of the science and technology industry. There are lots of really smart people here. But many of the most highly educated ones are not the real leaders...the real world changers – the wizards. Instead, they're people like Steve Jobs and Bill Gates... people who never finished college because they realized early on that they weren't going to get the knowledge they needed out of books and college courses. The only way they would get that was to get out into the world, into the trenches, and learn to build world-class business enterprises by giving themselves the experience of actually building companies.

Thanks to the internet and our incredibly connected world, information is readily available to anyone who wants it, on a scale that boggles the mind. But even as the information, the connectivity and ability to communicate increases exponentially – so it seems our ability to actually get out and have the real experiences that will make us competent and wise individuals seems to be diminishing.

More and more we find ourselves glued to our computers and smartphones, following the latest Twitter feeds and Facebook trends. Learning to have the same limited range of experience that everyone else has. We surf the zeitgeist faster than was ever possible before - but it has become more and more difficult to step outside and have the unique and interesting experiences we need in order to develop our real selves and new kinds of wisdom.

One of the great things we get to experience as magicians — at least in part because magic really only happens live and in person – is that we get to create real experiences for our audiences. And they are very special experiences – the kind that can force them to reexamine their assumptions about the world. Depending on how deeply you are willing to engage your audiences — with story, metaphor and so on — those experiences can trigger the kind of reflection that might lead to real wisdom. Not just any old trick will do it. If you leave your audiences just wondering "how did she do that?" - well, that won't get you there. But if you use your ability as a performer to reach out and touch their hearts and minds...you might just be able to ignite a spark...that spark of wisdom which will help transform those audiences into the wiser, more responsible, more caring and powerful human beings we call wizards.

I believe our world needs more wizards, and that one of the jobs of any wizard is to help others along the path. I hope you'll join me in my quest!

Directing for Magicians

One of the biggest difficulties for many performers and speakers, both amateur and professional, is building your support team. We're really all only as good as our teams – but it's so easy to think of yourself as a "one-man show," or "one-woman business, self sufficient, proud – and ultimately worn out and mediocre. Building a team out of people who are smarter and more skillful than you are, each in their own fields, can only help you lift the level of what you can do on your own.

In this article, I want to talk about a really important member of that team for any performer: Your director. Whether you have someone who, like me, went to school and studied to be a director, or you're relying on friends, family and magic club or toastmaster's club members to direct you and give feedback, it is tremendously important that you have someone you can trust to give you helpful criticism about your performances. We all need a "third eye," with another human being behind it, even if you are recording video and watching each performance yourself. There are just things we can't see about ourselves that someone outside will see right away.

But how to be a good director, or how to know when you've found one - that's the difficult question. Remember, the reason for having a director is more than just having someone who can tell you when you're flashing. Ideally, they'll help you clean up your script, find new ways to guide your audience's attention to the points they need to pay attention to in order to "get" the story your magic is telling, and to help you structure your performance for maximum impact.

If you're a member of a group who does this for one another, you'll be called on to direct others. Even if you're not, it will be good for you to be able to help guide those who are directing you. If, like me, you've already been directing other kinds of theater, you'll want to prepare yourself to re-learn everything. The magician is not only the actor/performer, but the writer, producer, often the designer of their shows, and they have a lot of technical restrictions you won't encounter in any of the other performing arts. Things like "I can't gesture that way with that hand...it's hiding something." Or, "I can only do that production with my right hand." These are important considerations that most stage directors never have to thing about.

The first rule of directing is to get honest responses. I always like to see a show twice before I go to work on it as a consultant or director, providing the show is near being in condition to be seen. The first time through is really just for my enjoyment. I want to see it the way an audience who is there for the first time does. I don't want to be thinking about the technique behind the show at that point.

The second viewing is when I start applying my critical mind to what happens. That's when I start to understand how the performance works. That when I begin to ask and answer the questions of why I love some moments and not others. Is the opening setting up the right expectations? Are they being met later in the performance? Are we setting up the "magic moments" as effectively as we possibly can? Is the pacing doing everything it can to enhance the effect we want to create? Is everything clear to the audience, or are them confusing moments?

When you're getting feedback from people not trained as directors, this las is some of the most important information you can get. Four or five different people may give you their opinions on your performance – and they'll all have different ideas of how to "fix" it. Most of them will be wrong. However...you'll notice that most of them talk about the same moments in the act that need fixing... and that's your indication that you need to work on those particular moments.

The second rule of a director/ performer working relationship should be that you're both willing to try different ways of doing things. What seems like a good idea in the director's head often won't play as well as something else. And both the performer and director may love moments that audiences just don't get. Ultimately you need to perform before live people, and have your director see the show in front of live audiences in order to tune up the way it will actually play for an audience. The show that looks great in rehearsal may often not get the response you think it will when performed for an audience.

A third rule for directors and others asked to give feedback is to be sure and talk as much about the parts you really liked, that are working — and why those are working, as you do about things that you think can be improved. All too often, the director feels they are there to fix what is wrong, and they fail to give feedback about what really works and why. The performer is left without an understanding of what is great about their performances, and may go off and work to improve things that are already perfectly fine. On Broadway, directors typically visit a show at least once a month during a long run, to "take out the improvements" that the actors have discovered while the director was away. Things that seemed like they would be an improvement to the actor, but, from the audience, are not.

Along this same line, if you've studied to be a teacher of young people, you may have been taught the 3 to 1 rule, which tells a teacher they need to find 3 things to praise before giving one negative criticism. This makes it much easier for the one receiving the criticism to really hear that criticism. The praise lets them understand that the director or teacher is really on their side, and likes what they do, overall...but that they also see things that can be improved to make the overall performance even stronger.

Finally – as a performer, even when your director launches right into their list of "notes" for you and they are all negative, try to avoid defending your choices. We all tend to want approval for our hard creative work, and we're all sure that "we know best," what we were trying to create. So please, listen to everything your director has to say, and try to make it work for you before you begin defending your other choices and arguing with the director. When you do have a difference of opinion, it will often be because the director hadn't been able to understand from your performance what you were trying to do. We all make leaps of logic in our own minds that we assume others will naturally make...but which turn out to be completely opaque to others watching us. If you discuss with your director what you're really after with a particular piece, they may well change their notes for you in order to supply the pieces missing so that the piece will work the way you originally intended.

I obviously can't do more than scratch the surface of what there is to know about directors and directing in one small article, but I hope you'll find what I have been able to share to be useful to you. Now get out there and find someone you trust to start giving you feedback on your shows and talks. You'll be amazed how much more fun you can have, and how fast you're performances will start improving!

Knowledge is Experience

"Only Experience is knowledge – everything else is just information."

-- Albert Einstein

Wizards are, by definition, wise people. People who have wisdom. But what is wisdom? My definition is that wisdom is a special kind of knowledge that comes from experience, and reflection on that experience.

So what does this mean for you and me, as performers?

Well...to start off, it means that just watching a video or reading a book doesn't give us real knowledge. Just because you've read about, or seen "how a trick is done," doesn't mean you have the real knowledge of how to do a trick. You only get that by doing the trick – again and again – in front of a real audience. Even practicing a trick in front of your mirror or video camera won't bring you to the point of really "knowing how to perform that trick." Only getting in front of an audience with the trick over and over again will give you the real knowledge of how to do that trick.

It is the same with business. You can read a hundred

books, or attend 50 seminars, on how to run your business – but until you get your hands dirty and actually do the things you read about in the books, you won't have real knowledge of how to do them – and you won't know, in your bones, whether they will work for you or not.

I used to offer an online course called *Get Your Career in Gear.* I know it was a good course, because the students who took it and went to the trouble to send in their weekly assignments for my feedback saw huge growth in their businesses. However...only about 20% of those who bought the course actually sent me the work. I'm quite sure that those who didn't do the work, didn't see the results the course was designed to create. My idea in creating it was that I would lead the students through the different steps you need to take in order to run a business – to get themselves set up with their financial and legal obligations, to make sure their marketing materials all supported each other, to help them begin building their own strong teams – pretty much everything you need to create a strong business -- and the homework they were to send me was the actual work they would need to do in order to make the business work. The idea was that once they had finished the course, they would have had many of the experiences of running a business before they had to risk doing it 'in the real world.'

I finally pulled the course, and converting the basic information and worksheets it contained into a book. It will be out as an e-book sometime later this year – at a much lower cost than the $600 I was charging for the course! Although the book will contain lots of the information I've gleaned over my 30 years managing shows and magicians – people still won't get the real knowledge of how to run their businesses, unless they do the work and give themselves the experiences that the book suggests.

I had a similar experience with Volume 1 of this book, Beyond Deception, when it came out. I hear again and again from people who have actually done the exercises in the book that it has taken them to new levels in their work. Fortunately, those who have just read the book seem to have enjoyed it as well – but I wish they would actually do the things the book recommends, because then it would stand the chance of really achieving the goal I have when I write, which was to inspire more magicians to take their magic to new levels, creating real magical experiences instead of just continuing to present strings of tricks.

Of course – real experience is a lot of what our students get when they come to the Magic & Mystery School. From the very beginning, Jeff and Eugene recognized the importance of students' participation. Those who come "just to observe" leave having had a great time, but those who participate fully --- well, those are the folks who go on to win the competitions at the conventions and who make quantum leaps with their shows and careers as a result of their visit with us. They are the ones I think have a chance of joining the ranks of the real wizards.

Varieties of Magic

Considering that the practice of conjuring and performance magic is actually quite a small one when you compare it to that of almost any other hobby or profession, it's amazing how many different varieties of the art there are. From uncles pulling coins out of their nieces' and nephews' ears on up to the big theatrical shows of David Copperfield, Penn & Teller and others, magic has almost as many different styles and uses as there are magicians practicing the art!

My friend Eugene Burger has a phrase for this. He states, "There are many rooms in the house of magic," and every time I hear him say it, I find it a reason to celebrate. We don't have to be a performing professional to be a part of the world of magic. Some of us can be collectors, or historians. It's perfectly fine just to be a student who wants to know all the different techniques others use to fool their audiences. Some of our best inventors or builders actually never perform themselves. And yet, we're all joined in our love of this incredible art.

This section, therefore, explores some of those different varieties of the art. The list is by no means exhaustive, but a more or less arbitrary selection which was derived from different subjects that have come up over the years of teaching classes for magicians at the McBride Magic & Mystery School. The presumption is, I suppose, that if our students were interested in learning about these things over the years, you may find them to be of interest, as well.

Magic with Cards

Cards are to the magician what a piano is to the composer. They are easily available, relatively easy to manipulate, and common enough that most audiences have at least a basic knowledge of what they are and their basic attributes. For many of us, learning card tricks was our introduction to the joy of performing magic.

We've all learned lots of card tricks. As magicians, we tend to be fascinated with them, even if we don't necessarily perform a lot with cards ourselves. There are countless variations, and a wide variety of principles which are often applicable to other kinds of magic. And we find it all endlessly fascinating – whether our audiences do or not.

Believe it or not, there are people out there whose first reaction when you show them a deck of cards will be, "I hate card tricks," or, worse, "I hate magic!" They've had the experience of encountering too many similar, not particularly entertaining tricks not done very well. This presents a particular challenge for those of us wishing to do magic with cards. How do we make our tricks interesting even for those who say they "hate card tricks?"

There are, a number of ways around this attitude. Many can be won over simply by presenting card magic that is truly entertaining, in a friendly and confident manner. When the trick goes beyond "pick a card, look, I can find it," we immediately transcend expectations. Even those who think they hate card tricks are often astonished by what can be done by an expert, with cards vanishing from one location, appearing in another, changing even while being held in a spectator's hand, and so on. Some, however, cannot be so easily won over.

There are many card tricks which can be performed equally well using tarot cards, in the pretext of providing so called psychic readings. It's not difficult, even with standard playing cards, to build an interesting story that is illustrated by the trick, or to create an interactive experience such as the telling of someone's fortune. Many in your audience who have had bad experiences with poorly performed card magic are, nonetheless, eager to learn about their own future or to have some sort of "real" magical experience...even when that experience involves playing cards.

Business cards can also be a great vehicle to present magical effects that will be more memorable to many than tricks done with playing cards. Take out a stack of business cards in preparation to share them with new acquaintances, and you can not only find an excuse to perform magic you would otherwise have done with playing cards, but will also give a sort of magical "charge" to those cards for those you give them to...and thus encourage them to keep them.

One of my own favorite kinds of magic is mental magic. I know many magicians who suggest one should never use playing cards in mental magic. "Once you take out a deck of cards, it's all just card tricks," is what they'll tell you. And I think there is an element of truth in that. If you are standing in front of a group and take out a deck of cards, their first response will be "oh, card tricks." So, if you want to use playing cards in mental magic, it's important to justify their use, even before the deck appears.

I like this kind of justification: "I'm attempting to get an impression of what's in your mind...but it is an iffy thing. You could be thinking of any one of a zillion different things...from the desert you'll have with dinner tonight to forgetting a loved one's birthday, or something from a story you recently read or...well I could go on, but you get the picture. So I thought I'd take something we all know reasonably well, that is easily recognizable in a very visual way...and which is limited to a relatively small number of choices. Does that make sense? Of course it does.

I thought we might use this deck of playing cards. There's a good number of choices still available, but they come within limits – two colors, four suits, and 13 values. Isn't that right?"

Now, there is a reason for the mentalist to be using the cards...it's not about a trick I can do with the cards, but rather a feat I could supposedly accomplish with any series of objects...and the playing cards are simply a logical choice — easy to carry, easy for all to understand.

These are just a few of the ways that come readily to mind of ways to get around the "I hate card tricks" mindset. I'm sure that with just a bit of thought, you can come up with others – perhaps more suited to your own particular style of performing.

Magic with Coins

Let's think for a moment about magic with coins. A subject near and dear to me, as coin magic was where I began my "return" to magic that eventually led to my work with Jeff McBride & Marco Tempest.

I was managing a Broadway theater at the time, and part of my job involved greeting our audience members as they entered the theater each night and directing them towards their seats. We opened the doors at 7:30 each evening and the show started a half hour later. The bulk of the audience would arrive within 15 minutes of curtain time...so that first 15 minutes were a bit slow. During that 15 minutes, and the 15 minutes leading up to intermission, I found time to practice sleight of hand – and the most unobtrusive, always-with-me prop I could practice with was a half dollar coin.

You see, when still a boy of 8 or 10 years old, I had decided sleight of hand was not for me. After about the hundredth time I dropped the coin I was trying to palm, I just gave it up. I now think I was just impatient, but at the time I was sure I just didn't have the ability to master most of the sleights I tried to learn. As a matter of fact, until years later when I saw people like Jeff McBride doing them, I would have sworn that virtually no one could do some of those sleights!

At that theater...just before the show and while waiting for the intermission to come around each evening, I had plenty of time to really practice. After about 1,000 more dropped coins, I was able to master quite a few of the sleights necessary for effective coin magic. To this day, if someone finds out I'm a magician and asks to see a trick, I'll probably take out a coin and do a few simple tricks. Along with rubber band magic, coins are one of the few props it is really easy to make sure you always have available, and that people readily recognize. And people love magic with money. Money is something we're trained to pay attention to...so as soon as interesting things start happening with a coin or a bill, you automatically have interest.

As with so many other kinds of magic, though, I see a basic problem with the way most magicians perform coin magic. The coins become just abstract, easily manipulable objects. For something that people have worked thousands of hours to possess, it seems a shame not to tag into the intrinsic emotional hooks we all have around money. "I never have enough," or "I'm a prisoner to my debt," to "old moneybags" and more...money is, like it or not, something most of us are emotionally attached to.

So, wouldn't it be great to see a bit of coin magic that teaches the value of saving money? Or one that is about how a scam artist has tried to defraud you, only to be outsmarted himself? A piece about how credit card debt or failure to pay attention to our investments can destroy someone's happiness? I would certainly like to see someone doing coin magic like that...

While we're at it, perhaps we could have dove magic where we acknowledged that doves are a symbol of peace, or, escape magic being about re-claiming our personal freedom. There are a few magicians out there really using the identity, value and meaning that lies within their props to create and enhance their magic. Even if you're not among that group, I think you'll find it will pay you well to spend some time considering just what associations your audiences might have with those coins, bills, balls, cups, ropes, and so on...before you take them out and start doing tricks with them.

You've heard this from me before: One of the elements of any performance is the story it tells. Your props...and therefore the magic you do with them...cannot help but tell a story. It is up to you to decide just how meaningful or how powerful that story will be.

Rope Magic

There are many magical effects one can perform with a piece of rope. Knots can be magically tied, or made to melt away and disappear. The rope can shrink, stretch, turn color. Two ropes tied into loops can be made to penetrate one another, just like linking rings. A rope can become rigid, and then again flexible. It can be cut into pieces and then restored again. This can all be quite clever and delightfully puzzling...but like all merely clever "tricks," it can also descend into being merely clever. Good for a quick, light hit of entertainment, but difficult to sustain.

However, rope magic can easily become much more.

Our friend, the late Earl Reum wrote a book called *Communicating with Magic*, all about how speakers can use magic to help them make their presentations more memorable and exciting. One of the best ways to get and hold someone's attention is to surprise them – and magic is all about surprise. In that book, Earl listed 16 common magic effects, and how they can be used to help a speaker illustrate different points they might want to make. Of the 16, 3 are rope effects — more than for any other kind of magical prop.

Rope carries a certain amount of inherent symbolic meaning for us. It can be used to tie us up...to take away our freedom. We tie a string around our fingers to help us remember something, and there are ancient memory systems in which knots in a piece of string serve as reminders of different things. Snakes are the same shape as a piece of rope, and so the symbolism that goes along with them – for some it is fear, for others healing and enlightenment – can be associated with a piece of rope handled in the proper manner. We use ropes for climbing or descending from high places. We use them to tie other things together. We swing on ropes, use them to hoist sails and buckets...in short, the rope has many uses and associations. Perhaps the most famous feat in all of magic is a trick with rope: The Indian Rope trick, in which a piece of rope tossed into the air becomes rigid, can be climbed, and symbolically connects the invisible heavens with the earth.

Seeking the inherent metaphoric meaning of the various props we use in magic can be a good jumping off point for our creative process. Suppose I've just fallen in love with a particular effect – a cut and restored rope effect, for example. Can you think of three ways we might make that cutting / restoration more memorable? Penn and Teller did it with a live snake. Unforgettable. What other situations can you think of that would have an enhanced emotional impact? A rope someone might want to use to make an emergency escape from a high place is accidentally cut in half...or someone needs two pieces for something, but each time they look away, the two pieces keep restoring themselves to one piece before they can be used. I'm sure you can come up with a dozen more if you give it a few minutes thought. What would different kinds of people use rope for. Why would a burglar have it? A doctor? A policeman? A teacher? You get the idea.

Rope is one of the great "packs small" props. You can buy it almost anywhere, and you can perform many different effects with it.

So I would strongly encourage you to go get a piece of rope. Learn a trick...and then apply the magic of your own creativity to turn that trick into a truly magical experience – a trick that makes use of the rope as what it is, what it might mean to you. A trick presentation that's really all yours!

Family Shows

It seems to me that at least half the magicians I talk to think of family shows as something they want to "move beyond." They think, rightly, that it is a great place for them to get started as professionals. Family shows are easy to book and (they think) don't have to come up to the same standards those same magicians might set for their theatrical or corporate or theater shows. "Too simple to really worry about. Just throw a few tricks in a bag an go. I'll figure it out on the fly."

The family or 'kids' show is most often performed in someone's living room or backyard, or at events like scout banquets where the families of all the boys and girls are gathered.

I think it is important to realize that it is at these shows that most people first experience magic. They provide the kind of real magic experience that you can't get on television. Magic performed live, right before your eyes while you're in the company of friends and family. I think that makes this kind of magic especially important.

Although the family show might not pay as well, on a per show basis, as some other kinds of work in magic, it is possible to make a very good living doing this kind of show. I know at least one magician who does a dozen or more shows almost every week. He lives in a nice house, drives a great car, and has put his kids through college at good schools — and he does it by performing a consistently great show that appeals, on different levels, to all ages. The kids in his audiences see and hear one show, and their parents get a much richer experience, because they understand so much more. I'm not talking about double-entendre, dirty jokes, but just the fact that the same sentence can mean and refer to different things to us at different ages. A comment commiserating with having to pay a mortgage or tuition bill can go right by the little ones...but hit squarely with their parents, who 'get it,' even as the kids are marveling at the $1 bill turning into a $10.

So I think it's important to remember, when we're asked to do a family show, that we are likely to be introducing much of the audience for that show to the performance of magic. As magicians and fans of magic ourselves, it's easy to forget that most people have never seen a live performance by a professional. What impressions would you, as a real lover of magic, want those people to take home with them? Will it be a memory of bad jokes and obnoxious quips at their expense? Will it be the "How did he do that?" question that so many magicians engender? Or will it be the proverbial "sense of wonder," that magicians like Doug Henning spoke of as being what he wanted to create with his magic? Will you leave them thinking of magic as something practiced only by clowns, wise-guys and buffoons? Or something mysterious and a little bit spooky. Perhaps you want to give an experience that is enchanting and beautiful. I'm not suggesting there is one right answer to this question... only that it's important for you to answer it for yourself, before you accept that family show gig and just toss together a few effects that will allow you to show off a bit.

What is the experience you would really like to have had for your own introduction to magic? What will inspire your audience to want to see more? Perhaps to ask you back? And what are you doing to make sure that the show will reach all of the family members...from 8 to 80, male and female...at the same time, not ever leaving any of them feeling left out, or offended because you've said or done something inappropriate to one of the other family members? This whole "family show" thing isn't so simple, after all, is it?

Impromptu Magic

Impromptu magic is magic that you can do almost anywhere, without a big set-up, or only when you've remembered your props. And that leads me, rather improbably, to thinking about elevator pitches, which are, almost by definition, given in impromptu situations.

You've all heard the term...I've talked about it here and in my online career course extensively. "Elevator pitch" has become almost a household word, which is interesting, as it started as an "insider" term in the film industry. And my question for you is two-fold:

Do you have an elevator pitch? And if you do – does it include magic?

I really believe it should. Not a long, drawn out routine, but a magic "shocker." Jeff McBride often uses his "cards from mouth" effect for this — and it gets him both noticed and remembered. People are, on the one hand, a bit shocked – but, more important, they are then delighted by the magic moment he has provided. He has given them a magical experience in just a few seconds. A free sample, if you like.

In life, the more people you meet, the more often you'll be asked, "so, what do you do?" If you say, "I'm a magician," you may or may not get interest. May or may not be remembered. Even if you add onto that, "I perform as a headliner at Vegas Casinos and major corporate events." You'll be just another mildly interesting new acquaintance, and they may or may not remember your name in 10 minutes time. But if you give them a magical experience that surprises and engages them in a pleasant way, you've just made a new friend, a new fan for your magic. If a picture is worth a thousand words, actually delivering a magical experience is worth 10 thousand!

The effect can be something you carry with you, or just something you can always do. Part of the reason I first learned sleight of hand with coins is because, if I was caught somewhere, unexpected with "OK, if you're a magician, show me some magic," it was a pretty sure bet there would be a coin handy, and I could do something magical. Magic is an interactive art. Giving someone a description, or showing a photo or video just doesn't convey the same impact as something that happens right in front of them.

So, whether you're an amateur ambassador for magic, or seeking a career doing it, please make sure your elevator pitch – your way of introducing yourself – includes a moment or two where you actually create a magic moment for those you are meeting. And if you really want to capitalize on this, have a couple of more effects "up your sleeve" and you can extend that first experience to continue to "make friends and influence people." You'll find yourself rewarded many times over – both in your own enjoyment from practicing our art – and in the number of new friends and clients you'll gather!

Stage Manipulation

I admire those who are great manipulators, great sleight of hand artists. It's not something I'm good at myself, not having spent the thousands of hours it really takes to be a good manipulator. But I have spent many hours directing quite a few magicians and their manipulation magic acts, so I do have a few thoughts on the subject.

First is that even the best manip acts are seldom completely deceptive. It is rare to see one with no flashes or slightly awkward moves that telegraph what's really happening. Like the concert piano, a great manipulator must practice every day. As the great pianist Horowitz said, "If I miss one day, I know it. If I miss two, my audiences know." Perfection matters. One flash, one awkward "telegraphing" moment, and you're suddenly doing a juggling act, not magic. So please, if you're not going to put in the hours each day to practice, don't go inflicting your "act" on the public. Save it for your mirror and the one person who will really appreciate it.

My second thought about manipulation magic is that it takes a lot of theatrical skill and showmanship to create a manip act that is more than just showing off. While our friends and fellow magicians may be always hungry for magic, the general public, our real audience, really wants something more. Much as I love a good stage or close-up manipulation act -- the first time I see it -- they are rarely really riveting theatre for more than a single viewing. When they are, it is because the performer has taken the time to really craft a magical experience using that manipulation magic and to really connect with his or her audience. Looking good and executing the feats of skill well is great, but if you want to create art that will keep your audiences coming back, it really isn't enough, all on its own.

If, on the other hand, when you watch Norm Nielsen or Jeff McBride perform their card routines, what will strike you first may be the impossible appearances and other effects -- but the thing that will make you watch them again and again, even if you are not another magician, is the beautifully structured relationships they create with their audiences. Jeff is playful, executing a move twice, then having it not work the third time, showing the backs of his hands, making eye contact and shaking his head "no," and then producing another impossible fan... and looking squarely at you as if to to say "Gotcha!" Sometimes he is flirtatious, at other times frustrated, or demanding. He runs the full gamut of emotion during that 3 minute card act. And, that is at least one of the things that sets a great manip act apart from the rest.

So, how *do* you give a manip act that kind of dramatic flair? The answer lies in the actor's art. You are playing a character on stage, with real life desires and emotions. What desire leads you to produce that first fan of cards? When it appears, how do you feel about that? Why do you decide to try and produce a second fan? And how do you feel about *that*, when it happens... or fails to happen? Are you curious about how those appearances happen (as a character)? Or mystified? Or do you just feel powerful and certain you can do it? And if that is the case, why are you showing us, your audience, your power? When you create a script with a sub-text answering this kind of question for each moment in that manip act you're working on, you will have taken your first steps to creating something original...something worth watching more than once.

Then it's time to start in with those thousands of hours of practice...practicing not just the moves, but actually rehearsing the moves with the motivations, the physical expression of those motivations, varying timing and dynamics, eye-contact with the audience...and the hundred and one other things that go into making a great performance. I really hope, if you're into manipulation magic, that you will do this. You'll be doing a favor not just for yourself, but for the art of magic itself!

Magic and Medicine

Magic & Medicine - this world of magic and magicians certainly takes us to some interesting places, doesn't it? Of course, for eons, magic and medicine were more or less one and the same thing. The tribe's shaman or medicine woman took on the combined roles of healing, keeping and transmitting the tribe's lore, serving as an intermediary between the every day – the mundane world of the tribe – and the divine, spiritual, and mysterious. Back then, most of those things were pretty much synonymous with magic.

Then, not so very long ago in historic terms, the medical community decided it no longer wanted to share the cloak of the magician. Unfortunately, they were mostly fooling themselves and their patients. They practiced such "scientific" methods as bleeding, and often administered addictive narcotics as their primary medicines. Things which, today, we see as the height of quackery. And yet... even well into the last century, there was really very little our doctors could do to assuage their patients' ills. I recently watched a talk by Atul Gawande: How do we heal medicine? [TED talk on medicine], who told of the time he entered the world of doctoring...only 30-40 years ago... and that there were, as he put it, 'only about 40 things we could actually cure!' Everything else was about lessening a patient's suffering and hoping their own immune systems fought off whatever malady they had. Little wonder that the health care system back then was so much less expensive – there wasn't much they could actually do! Today we're in a better situation in terms of our abilities to actually diagnose and treat many, many different illnesses. But the costs of this overall increase have been monumental. And, oddly, the most effective medicine for most ills continues to be the one that served the ancient medicine folk and shamans the best. For them, magic and medicine were synonymous. We call their medicine by the name 'placebo.'

Magic & Medicine - Alternate Version

Magic & Medicine. I'd like to practice a bit of that right now...are you up for it?

When we study the way our minds work, from moment to moment, we learn that every experience we have actually changes the mind. New connections develop with every new experience...every new idea. And, in turn, our mind changes us. The nerves in the brain regulate our endocrine system — the chemicals that control how we act, how we feel, the rate of our heart beat, our breathing, our immune systems, the growth rate of different parts of our body. And so every experience we have – including the one you're having right now, reading this – actually changes us. Not just our consciousness...but our physical bodies!

And it works both ways. Change your facial expression, your posture, the rhythm and tone of your speech...and it will change the way you feel and the way your mind works!

Try it for a moment: Exhale and slump down in your chair. Let your shoulders droop. Take your hands and make the sides of your face droop. Just place a palm against each cheek and move your hands downward. Take really shallow breaths, and maintain that sad-sack look on your face In just one, two, three breaths, you'll notice your feelings have begun to change. Did anyone out there ever "pretend to be sick" when you were a kid, in order to get out of a day at school, only to discover you really did feel sick as a result? I did. If you've done what I just asked you to, you've done something similar to yourself right now — and if you maintain it, you just might get sick as a result.

Let's fix that right now. Take a deep breath and sit or stand up straight. Feel the power of your chest and shoulder muscles as your chest expands. Lift your face and smile, or even let it go into a big grin. Let your eyes sparkle. Take another deep breath and maintain that smile. In some kinds of yoga, one of the exercises is to imagine inhaling through your "third eye" at the front of your forehead towards the back of your skull, and to let a smile form at that spot at the back of your head, at the very top of the spine. When you do that, you can't help but smile with your whole face. Take another deep breath and try that. Imagine the energy comes in through the third eye and shoots right back to that smiling spot. Then send it right back out the third eye. How do you feel now?

What do you think — was that magic, or medicine?

For centuries, the terms medicine and magic were synonymous throughout many cultures. I have Native American friends who, to this day, speak of "my medicine," meaning their magical and spiritual practice – not the pills they might be taking.

Since every experience we have changes us both mentally and physically, you might want to think for a few minutes about the effects your performances are having on your audiences. Is your magic "good medicine," or bad? Will you leave audiences feeling more alive, energized and empowered – or will they be left feeling powerless and frustrated? While you're at it, you might consider what effect the experience of performing is having on you. If either answer isn't what you would like it to be – remember, you have the power to change things. The choice is yours. You can make your magic "good medicine," – or not.

I wish you all happy and healthy magic. You are the only one with the power to change your magic...and your life.

Mental Magic

The subject is mental magic. It is at once more and less theatrical than magic with props. It is more dramatic because it is more personal — what could be more interesting and exciting than the contents of our own minds? That is the material the mentalism works with. At the same time, the mental magician often finds himself limited to just the material contained within our minds, instead of the big, flashy props, dancing girls and giant illusions we are used to seeing in other kinds of magical entertainment. While sorcerer and trickster magicians can rely, to some extent, on the visual spectacle of their performances to build and maintain an experience for their audiences, the mentalist generally has to rely on a completely different set of tools in order to create and build up an entertaining experience around what they do.

I have seen different performers take this challenge, successfully, in very different directions. Gerry McCambridge has a terrifically entertaining and successful show in Las Vegas. For someone interested in how to add visually exciting theatricality to the mentalists' artform, his show provides a fantastic education. Gerry has found ways of taking basic mind-reading, prediction, mind-influence and the other basic effects of mental magic, and transforming them into large, spectacular theatrical metaphors. Attending his show is a bit like watching one of television's more raucous game-show experiences. People shout out answers, shoot basket balls at the stage, and much, much more. The show is great fun on many levels...not least of which is his very strong mental magic. That's one way to solve the problem.

My own impulse is for something that feels a bit more intimate. I like the feeling of interacting "up close and personal." The quality that comes with building rapport and trust between audience and performer – in short, of going a bit deeper. My friend Paul Draper likes to go into the audience and work with audience members in a more personal, intimate way than you will see some others do. Max Maven often brings one or two audience members onstage with him for unhurried one-on-one interactions. Many mental magicians prefer to work with smaller groups, in more or less what we might term "parlor" settings. They rely, for theatricality, on their own ability to connect with those for whom they perform.

In nearly every case, though, while the really great mentalist's interactions may appear to be spontaneous, they are actually carefully crafted. The volunteers have far less in the way of options than the audience is led to believe. As a result the mentalist is actually enacting a carefully crafted dramatic skit with each piece. If written well and convincingly performed, these can be extremely entertaining. If not...well there are few things duller than bad mentalism.

When successful, all forms of mental magic do rely on certain principles. It is never enough just to read minds, make predictions, or influence others. Just as with close-up magic or big stage magic, it is extremely important to your success that you figure out how to really "make a show" of your performances. And, just as with other forms of magic, the ultimate success, what your audiences will remember... are the stories you create for them with your magic. It's not that you have to tell a story and make the magic secondary. What you really have to do is create an experience in which your audience will participate, and which they will then remember and tell to others, after the performance has ended.

Will the story they tell be the story of a game? If so, how can you make that game exciting? And will they wind up as the winner, or will you? Will their story be one of pathos — a tale of love lost, or loved ones who are no longer with them bringing messages from the beyond? Will they be detective mysteries in which they are involved, and you, the performer, play the part of Sherlock Holmes? Or romantic adventures, told through mysterious mental interactions. "I don't know how she could have known what I was feeling (or thinking)...but she did!

I've suggested a few possibilities for you here. I hope the ideas I've suggested will help you find ways of making your presentations of mental magic as exciting and magical as they can be.

Parlor Magic Theater

This article will discuss one of my favorite kinds of magic. Magicians are fond of calling it Parlor Magic, even though very few of us actually have parlors in our homes, or even know what the term really means. The parlor was a room similar to the modern living room, but used almost exclusively to receive guests. My grandmother had one. It was the "special occasion" living room. There was another, plainer living room where the family hung out.

So when we refer to parlor magic, we're talking about magic performed in front of a small audience... small enough that the magician probably doesn't need a microphone, working in a small space or on a platform. The performer is our 'host' for the evening, and the performance is intimate. Theater for small audiences has long been a favorite genre for me. In grad school, my favorite place to work was our little black box theater where audiences generally ranged in size from 50 to 100. My first job in New York was managing *The Fantasticks* and it's theater, the Sullivan Street Theater, which seated 153, and as such was amongst the smallest official off-Broadway theaters. Theaters smaller than that were designated for showcase productions where no one was paid more than car-fare, and which were supported mostly through grants and donations, as it was (and is) difficult to make any profit doing theater in such a small space.

As magicians, we're luckier than most people doing business in this kind of space. With only one performer, it's much easier to pay the bills than when you have a half dozen or more actors, a couple of musicians, a stage manager, light and sound operators, etc. And the intimate nature of the space, with no one in the audience more than 15 or 20 feet from the performer, or from each other, creates an atmosphere that is electric in a quite different way than is available in large venues. I think it's ideal for magic.

While magicians are fond of talking about doing close-up and stage magic, I'd bet most of the professionals now actually making a living in magic actually do so in parlor settings—at birthday parties, in small theaters, at Blue and Gold Banquets, Rotary Club luncheons and the like. Small platform magic is the bread and butter gig for most working magicians. There are more gigs to be had in this market than all the restaurant close-up work, hospitality suite, General Session corporate events and casino stages combined. It may not pay as much, per show, as working larger venues... but there is a market in every town in the world for this kind of magic. In fact, magic is one of the few entertainment forms that really does work well in this market.

So: what kind of magic do you do in parlor settings? Real close-up magic generally doesn't work so well...unless you learn what Jeff and Eugene like to call "hands-up, heads up" presentation techniques. What does that mean? Simply that you no longer perform the magic with your hands down at waist level or on a table top, with everyone looking down at the cards or other props, but, instead, everything happens up next to your face. Virtually every card count, sleight, or other magic move *can* be adjusted to work as a "heads up" presentation, and that simple change can transform many of your favorite close-up effects so they'll play well for stage and parlor. Remember, in this larger setting, you need to make contact with and involve all of your audience. Close-up effects designed to involve one or two people with magic that happens "right in their hands" or "right under their noses," doesn't always play as well for the larger audience... but you'll be amazed at how many of your favorite close-up pieces *do* translate well.

Of course, there is also a lot of magic specifically designed for this kind of performance.

As an audience member in this setting, I want the option to be involved, or not. I don't want to be forced to come up on stage, but might be willing to do so. I am very happy to feel I am a part of the experience that the rest of the crowd is having...not so much as a spectator, but as a participant. The experience is somewhere between watching a play passively in the theater and being at a great party. The performer is more in charge of things than a host at a party is likely to be...but he is letting us, the audience, in on the action a bit more than we would be at a play or concert.

I think one of the guidelines that will really help magicians in this kind of setting is to think of themselves in the role of host. If you are hosting a dinner party at your home, how would you treat your guests? If you're a guest in that situation, how would you like to be treated by the host? Would you expect to be asked your name, if he or she doesn't know it already? Perhaps be introduced to the other guests if you don't know them? How would you feel about being teased, or having jokes made at your expense? What kind of host would you like to have at the events you attend? What memories would you as a guest, like to take home with you?

By answering these questions for yourself, you'll be well on the way to crafting the kind of parlor magic performance we would all like to attend...and to assuring yourself you'll be invited back to entertain at many more such events.

StageMagic

I like the idea that different art forms are defined by the different sets of questions the artist gets to answer. Different choices to be made.

The visual artist, for example, gets to answer questions about subject, size of their work, 2 dimensions vs. 3, color palette to be used, the style they will paint or sculpt in... and so on.

Composers get to answer questions about key, melody, rhythm, instrumentation, meter, harmony...and more.

In the theater: which covers any live performance on stage – we get to answer more questions than in almost any other art. That's because the art of the stage encompasses so many of the other arts. We make pictures and sculpture as actors move about the stage. We get to choose our setting – to build sets, use particular props, light it all in a particular way, etc. We choose a story to tell, a style to tell it in. We choose words, phrases, rhymes, and more. What characters will we portray? What costumes will they wear? What kind of musical or rhythmic background shall we use? In short, we get to create a complete, immersive experience for our audiences.

This is exciting territory – but can also be a bit daunting, and here's why: Every one of those choices will affect the overall experience of your magical piece. Changing any one of them can vastly alter the outcome for you and your audiences. What's more, failing to choose, say, a costume doesn't mean your audience won't experience a costume choice – they'll see what your characters are wearing, and it will affect their response to your work. Whether you've consciously chosen a particular speech pattern or phrase or not...your audience will hear and be affected by that speech pattern and those words when you speak them. So, with all those choices to be made, you also have the responsibility to make them all!

As you can see, if stage magic is your big love, you have a big job ahead of you to prepare yourself for it. You need to learn not only how to perform the sleight-of-hand and illusion magic, but also how to move on stage (take a dance class!), how to speak (take voice and acting classes!), how to design and create set pieces, how lighting design is done.

You also need to learn how to communicate with the people that make a theatrical production operate: the stage hands, light board operators, sound operators, theater managers, stage managers...the whole gamut. Because if you don't understand the basic etiquette and communications methods these people know and use regularly, you'll fail to make them an effective part of your team, and your shows will suffer.

Finally — if you want to build a career doing magic on stage, you should probably learn as much as you can about the business of operating a theater. What are the costs, marketing, licenses, etc. that are needed? Until you understand how a theater survives in it's particular community, you won't understand why they can only afford to pay you what they can, or why they can or can't charge more for tickets...or expect to sell those tickets. And you won't be able to offer them the particular things in the way of marketing you and supporting your show that will make it possible for all that to happen.

Magic onstage is my favorite kind of magic. But please realize there is more to it than buying a couple of big illusions, hiring an assistant and learning how they work. To be successful, you need to make sure you take the time to really master all the aspects of theatrical production. Not only will you find more personal success, but you'll help make it possible for this wonderful art we all love continue to prosper.

Street Magic

I've always been fascinated by the subject of street performing. In fact, I had proposed the subject as a thesis subject while in graduate school.

The history of itinerant street performers is really fascinating. During the middle ages, for example, they were the group probably most responsible for carrying culture and customs from one country to another. Italian comedia dell'arte performers travelled throughout Europe, and their influence can be seen in everything from the works of Moliere in France, to Shakespeare and the subsequent Restoration comedies that followed in the English theater.

Before that, the jongleurs, magicians and troubadours would travel from one court to another, paying their way with their performances. A large portion of what we know of the murky history of the dark ages is kept only because of the oral tradition – later written down - of these performers.

When you watch a television sitcom today, chances are you're seeing stock characters, gags and situations that, with just a few name and setting changes, could come right from the comedia dell'arte!

But none of that is what drew me to the idea of performing in the streets in the first place. What I found attractive was the sense of independence the street performer would have. No boss, no set hours, no set location...freedom! Later on, as a coach and director for a number of different variety performers, I came to realize something else about street performing:

It is the best training ground you can possibly have as a magician or variety performer. Audiences in theaters are, in a sense, "captive." They have elected to set aside time to be entertained, paid a fee, and come into a theater with the idea they will stay until the entertainment ends. Holding on to them in that situation is almost too easy. On the streets, however, you have to be able to grab and keep their attention in the face of a hundred distractions. You don't have the help of comfortable seats, stage lighting and the like. Many of those you want to keep have other things they were planning to do before you grabbed their attention, and they are standing, ready to walk away at any moment. If you give them a moment when that's possible, they will go. Street performers therefore learn very quickly, from necessity, how to grab attention, build an audience, make a group feel like an audience, and to please that audience continuously for a period of time in a way that will make the audience choose to give the performer money. A tough assignment! But if the alternative is starvation, you'll learn the lessons quickly.

Performers I have known who went this route have invariably developed into extremely competent, confident entertainers. They can work various situations, adapt easily to different settings, and usually have proven to be those who are in the business "for the long haul."

As a wizard, street performing is one of my favorite "recommended activities." It will expand your comfort zone, teach you a lot by experience, in a short time, and provide you with a way of stepping out of the mainstream of our culture. The street performer is automatically "other"— not one of us — and as such, they get to see all kinds of things you might otherwise never see, and and learn things you would never learn. It is an experience that provides an education not available in any school.

So, I'm betting most of you reading this have never done any kind of street performing. As an assignment in connection with this essay, I'd like to urge you to give it a try, even on a small scale. If you find yourself waiting in line this week, take a few moments to step out of that line and entertain the others waiting. Just one trick is enough to start. Or, when you're waiting for a bus or subway. Make sure you have a good, finished trick with you, then step up and use it to entertain at least one stranger. You'll probably be terrible at it the first time. So try it again. And again...until you start getting a good response. Just try it – it will expand your world, I promise, and, eventually, it will give you the power and confidence to affect your world in positive ways.

Restaurants & Table Hopping

I had a hopping table once. It was really annoying. There was that day it hopped up and down on my toes for two whole minutes! Another time it woke us all up in the middle of the night, hopping around the kitchen, making a terrible racket!

Seriously, though... I do want to talk about performing table-side, and I have to apologize for what you just had to read to get here. In my defense, it is April fools, day, as I write this.

I went out recently with some friends to a Mexican restaurant. Great food...we hadn't seen each other for some time, and so we had a lot to catch up on. Unfortunately, they had strolling musicians. Just as we started to chat, over they strolled. They weren't bad, if you don't mind mariachi music....but they destroyed our chance to thttp://www.mcbridemagic.com/pages/venues/corporate-meetings.phpalk for a good 10 minutes or so. And then we felt like we should tip them in exchange for our inconvenience. We won't be going back there again soon.

If you're going to work in a restaurant, or do strolling magic at cocktail parties or other venues where people have come for some reason other than to see a show, you're likely to run into a certain number of those people who really aren't interested in being entertained while they're trying to enjoy their meal or their cocktail party conversation. If you insist on seeing yourself only as an entertainer, and them as people who really don't want you to entertain them, you'll often find yourself in an unhappy situation.

However, if you take on the role of wizard seriously, you'll immediately see that there are other possible perspectives. You have most likely been hired, in these situations, to make the experience a better one for everyone involved. To make sure that even the less gregarious attendees have a good time. To help people who might feel awkward about introducing themselves to others, get introduced by someone else, or by an experience they might have in a group with those they want to meet. As real wizards we are the creators of experiences...for ourselves and others. If you look at your job as being there to enhance the experience people have, and pay attention to what each individual needs — well there are quite a few different ways you might achieve that without the risk that they may see you as an annoyance. In short, if you can get past that feeling that it's all about you, and realize that it is, in fact, all about them, you'll find much greater success doing this kind of magic (or in almost any enterprise you undertake).

Are there people waiting for tables because your restaurant is overbooked? People who regularly wait in line because your establishment is so popular? Perhaps the best way to enhance those people's experience is to make their unexpected wait a more pleasant one by offering them some magical entertainment as they wait in line or sit at the bar while waiting for their table to be ready.

Do patrons regularly wait for 8 or 10 minutes for their server to greet them, once they've been seated at the table? In that case, your role might be to bring menus and greet them in a magical way as they await their server. Servers may appreciate this, because clients who haven't been kept waiting tend to feel they've received better service and are more likely to tip the waiter.

Once you begin to see yourself as someone who enhances the overall experience for everyone who comes to the restaurant, you may well begin to find creative ways to put your talents to work. Are you the "magical greeter" who brings patrons into the space in a way that makes them feel special, and that calls attention to the fantastic ambiance the restaurant owner has created? Or perhaps your performance is the "icing on the cake," available only while a party is waiting for their deserts to arrive.

So...when you perform in a restaurant, at cocktail parties or other events...what are you doing to enhance the overall event? Sometimes the best thing you can provide is an ice-breaker — something for people who don't already know each other well to talk about as they do get to know one another.

In each situation, how do you fit in to the overall experience? Do your tricks, stories, costume and jokes all fit in with the overall ambiance...or do they clash? When all is said and done, will your audiences feel your performance was an interruption, or an integral and enhancing part of the overall experience? I sincerely hope it will be the latter!

That is only likely to happen, though, if you work closely with the restaurant manager and staff.

A hint: Don't ask "how can I help?" - that will elicit only a lot of head scratching and determination on their part that "you really can't," which is not the response you want. Instead, ask "Would it help if I..." whatever your idea is. And don't be upset when they tell you no, that you'll only be in the way, or you'll cause a traffic jam, or whatever. Keep thinking and making suggestions...you really want to make yourself useful and welcome to all. How can you can you help the hostess when she has a line? How can you help waiters do their jobs better? How can you help the wait staff get better tips? Is it better to stroll and introduce yourself, or let the maitre'D offer your services? Will someone therel tip you off to do something special for their most valued patrons?

I think you get the picture...unless the restaurant has long experience with magicians, you need to be selling them on how wonderful it is to have you there, as much as selling the patrons on your magic. And though you may feel you can guess the answers to all your questions, the staff will appreciate your asking. Once they've begun to see the advantages of having you there, they may well start actually coming up with ideas that will help you fit in better, and help you make yourself indispensable to the restaurant so you'll be able to go back and work there for a long, long time.

Another Kind of Restaurant Magic

I recently went to see Teatro Zinzani in San Francisco, starring the incomparable Voronin. One of the things that really struck me about Zinzani was that every part of the experience seemed so well thought out. From the way we were greeted when we entered the spiegel tent...by a character in costume and fully in character, to the small gift shop carrying period themed items that seemed completely in character with the ambiance and overall flavor of the experience. When we entered the main performance space and were seated at our table, waiters were immediately there to suggest drinks and appetizers, and we were left just the right amount of time to sit, take in the décor and get comfortable before things began to happen around us. When it was time for a course of the meal, in between performance pieces, the waiters crouched in the darkness just out of view as the current performance piece wound to a close, and then, seemingly almost invisibly, placed the next course in front of all of us at the same time. We never saw them get into place, and by the time we picked up our forks, they were gone.

There were ambient performance bits going on as we ate, but each one was focused on a particular table, and only lasted for a minute or so. The people at that table could give the performers their full attention and still get back to their meal before it was cold. The rest of us could pay attention to the performers, or to our meal, or to the conversations we might want to have with our table mates. The performances were a distinct but non-intrusive part of the overall experience. Performers, waiters, bus-boys... everyone was always in character, always attentive to our needs and desires. At the end of the evening, we felt we had all shared in a remarkable, seamless experience together.

Tradeshows

I don't think I'll ever forget the first trade show I worked with a client. It was CES, and my client Marco Tempest was to work for Panasonic...who just happened to have the largest booth at CES that year. Our show was not your typical trade show performance. Panasonic had built a large stage, backed by a giant LED screen – about 12' high by20' wide. This was before such screens were common, and just having the screen there pretty much guaranteed we would draw a lot of attention. We were doing a virtual reality piece in which Marco popped up on the giant screen – a "visitor from the near future," and walked out onto the stage. He proceeded to select a volunteer from the audience who would go into the virtual world where they could experience the new Panasonic totally integrated home...all made possible by their new technologies. This was at least a dozen years ago, and a lot of what he was demonstrating was really only a dream at the time...some of the products wouldn't be released for 5 or 6 years. Things like being able to shoot video and have it transferred wirelessly to a computer enabled TV where you could edit using touch gestures, and e-mailing the results to your friends...you know, the kind of thing you can do on a smart phone today, but which seemed kind of unbelievable back then.

Well..we created the piece, and went through a multitude of endless meetings with the marketing people from Panasonic. Every detail was questioned, re-done, and then re-done again. When the show finally opened, I was amazed. At 9am on that first day, the convention center in Las Vegas was mostly empty. Between then and 10am all the booth staff arrived...and then suddenly, at 10am exactly...a wave of some 40,000 people swarmed the floor. We did one 10 minute show every 40 minutes for 8 hours... and every show was jammed! With our 120 seat "theater" space, we made up only about 10% of what Panasonic was offering that year. I'm sure they moved a lot of product, but the amount they spent on that booth was mind-boggling. Trade shows can be big business, indeed.

Of course...we weren't the only magicians there. Several booths had magicians with much smaller set-ups. Mostly a guy standing on a low platform behind a table, with a microphone so he could be heard, and kind of playing the role of a magical carnival barker. They were there for the same reason we were: to get attention, repeat their client's name loudly and often, and, hopefully, draw potential buyers into the booths. Magic at CES can be kind of a losing game, since you're fighting for attention with whatever the shiniest new "miracle" technology is that year. We were glad to have all the bells and whistles of a giant screen, full theatrical lighting, a seating area, and a great sound system to help us.

Fortunately, not all trade shows are so tough. Most aren't as noisy or bright as CES, and at most, magic is one of the more novel things the attendees will encounter.

So...what do trade show marketers want from you? It will vary, of course, but for the most part the want three things:

- First: They want you to draw a crowd and get attention for their products.

- Second: They want you to represent their company and product in the best possible light.

- Finally: They want you to send the qualified members of the audience you have gathered into the booth to talk with their salespeople, and buy, buy, buy!

If you can't do at least those three things, you probably won't be terribly successful as a tradeshow magician. Remember, you are not there to get attention for yourself – but to get attention for the company and their product. Your performance is essentially a commercial for that company...and, as with all commercials, if you draw a crowd and entertain them, but when you're done they don't know about the product, and don't enter the booth to learn more, you have failed the folks paying your fee.

I remember one particularly brash fellow who kept selling himself at a very high price. He could draw huge crowds, but at the end of his show, none of them knew anything about the company he was working for or any of their products, and none of them came into the booth when his show was over. I'm sure he couldn't understand why he was fired after just one day of a 4 day show, but it was pretty obvious to those of us who saw him work.

So, as with any other kind of magic, when you work trade shows, remember to turn the tables and put yourself in the shoes of the folks hiring you. What are their concerns? How will they measure your success? (I can tell you that if they sell significantly more with you working for them than without, they'll think you're being successful).

And then, know your audience. What are they there for? How will they judge what you do, and your contribution to the show as a whole. Did they learn more of what they came for as a result of seeing you work? Did you make it easier for them to meet the people from the company you are there to represent?

If you can pay attention to all those things, deliver on all those expectations, you may well have a career ahead as a trade show entertainer. Be prepared to work long, hard hours, and to let go of your own ego in service of your clients...and then it can be a most rewarding way of earning a very good living with magic.

Trickster

I've been re-reading something from Bob Neale and Eugene Burger's "Magic & Meaning" on the Trickster:

"Tricksters are merry mess-makers whose ridiculous and outrageous nonsense is dangerous dirt generated for the creation of new life... They make mischief with meaning. This play reveals the limitations of our being human, especially the arbitrariness of life that lies concealed by our determined coping. It also exhibits and promotes an exuberant joy over the nonsense of what is, and an unquenchable hope over the novelty of what can be attempted."

And later:

"The trickster is clown, magician and confidence artist. These three images are about creativity – trickster creativity. To explore tricksterism is to investigate the possibilities and limitations of creaturely creators, and the connections between creativity and earlier understandings of inspiration and revelation."

So...

Let's examine the kind of magic we might expect from this Trickster – and the shape of our our work when we take up the role of the trickster.

I have a question for you: Can you remember a time when you were tricked? Perhaps someone played a practical joke on you. How did you feel? Or perhaps a magician fooled you with a trick. How did that make you feel?

When I was about 7 years old, I went with my father and some friends to be a clown in a parade. I was a sad clown who walked with a flower. I would look sad, walk along, and offer the flower to someone along the parade route. When she reached out to take the flower, she was left with just the straw that served as the flower's stem. I walked away with the flower itself, putting another straw from my pocket where the stem should have been so I could go and find another victim. Lots of people laughed. I kept my sad face on. Today, I wonder how those women who got a straw from me felt. There was a real human interaction happening – more than a trick. I was a little boy offering a flower, apparently to brighten her day. Instead, I tricked her and left her standing with a useless piece of plastic. The sweet little sad boy turned out to be a jerk.

Or perhaps you've been the victim of a scam, and actually lost money to a con artist. How did that make you feel? While we're tempted to jump in and assume it made you feel awful, and would never do that again – I recently read a book on con artists in the early and middle part of the last century – and one of the facts that struck me was that some of the biggest marks – those who lost the biggest amounts to con-artists, were often most likely and willing to be conned again, sometimes by the very con-game that fooled them the first time!

I keep asking you how it made you feel to be fooled, and of course there's no right or wrong answer. Sometimes, for some of us, it feels great. Other times, it makes us feel awful. It always affects us, though. And that's what I think is important to think about.

When you fool someone with a trick, you're doing more than just fooling them. You're making them feel something. If you're in character as a clown, you're fooling them in order to make them laugh. If a magician, you want them to feel entertained and perhaps a touch of wonder. The con artist wants their money – and sometimes wants them not even to feel they've been tricked at all, but simply had bad luck.

Whenever you trick someone, you will make them feel something. They'll feel something about themselves, and something about you. Tricksterism can be extremely powerful. You can shatter someone's whole world paradigm with a trick. You can change minds. Open people up to ways of thinking and feeling they might never have imagined. You can also make them feel taken advantage of, or embarrassed at having been made to play the fool. These things are likely to happen whether you intend it or not. So...please take a few moments when you're crafting your piece of Trickster magic to consider what effect you would like it to have on those who experience it. While you're at it, consider what effect it might have on you, as the performer. You'll be using that trick to create experiences between yourself and others that may be very powerful – whether you intend that or not.

The child playing with his father's loaded gun doesn't really mean to kill his friend – but that doesn't change things after the fact. Just because he doesn't intend the effect doesn't make it less real or permanent. And it doesn't really make him less responsible. So it is with your performances. As Trickster or in any other role.

So...for this week's assignment, I hope you'll take a second look at a piece of Trickster Magic you might be doing, and imagine the tables have been turned. You are now the unsuspecting audience member having just experienced the trick – how did it make you feel? Is that what you, as magician, wanted? If not...it's time to make some changes!

Sorcerer

Where the Trickster's magic happens through interaction with others – the sorcerer is master of the world of things. Sorcerers command the powers of nature: Earth, Wind, Fire and Water. All that can be very exciting – for the sorcerer. All too often, though, the performing sorcerer forgets that his or her performance also needs to engage and entertain others.

This is a purely personal prejudice, and one that is likely not to win me a great many friends among illusionists... but I find myself bored by most big illusion shows. After the first 5 minutes, I don't really care that you can make the girl float in the air, cut her into 8 pieces, restore her, and then vanish yourself from a box only to appear in the back of the theater. I – and every adult who has gone to a magic show or watched a TV special – has seen that. It was amusing once. Twice – well, not so much. One often has the feeling the sorcerer illusionist's show could go on equally well if all of us in the audience were suddenly transported out of the theater...which is something I've very much wished for as I was sitting through yet another illusion show.

And yet...it is possible to engage an audience with this kind of magic. As human beings we make meaning, and thus emotion and caring, through the creation of stories. Events by themselves are like those too often repeated meaningless illusions. Mildly interesting, once. But place events within a context. A story with a hero and villain, where great principles that we all hold dear are at stake, and then those events begin to take on real interest.

So, how does the sorcerer create something that will hold an audience, that will make audiences who have already seen other manipulators and illusionist sorcerers, sit up and take notice? How do you make them want to tell their friends all about your show?

One big way is to find another character to interact with. Dramatic action is usually based on conflict..and as a story teller, in order to tell an interesting story you need conflict. You need another character who can challenge you, who you can interact with. This other character can sometimes be your audience as a whole (think of Lance Burton dividing his audience in half and getting them to applaud and scream, to "see who gets the free drinks"). It can be a single volunteer – think of Jeff McBride's "Sorcerer's Apprentice" coin routine with a boy from the audience. It could one of your assistants, suddenly given a role in a story – again we look at Lance Burton and the "evil masked character" he duels with. Sometimes, the other character can even be the props you are using. The little ball that WANTS to be under the cup, and no matter where else you put it...just keeps going back there.

So...if you are, or want to pursue your magic in the role of a sorcerer, please take your audience into account, and find ways of enhancing the story of your magic so it will engage and enchant the audience. The too typical show-off sorcery magic is fine for the beginner...but it won't take you beyond the lowest rungs on the ladder of magical entertainers, and it won't help you build a lifetime in the art of magic.

Your assignment from this article? Take a piece of magic you already do and write the story of that piece from the viewpoint of one of your audience members. Who are the characters? What motivates them (what do they want?). What prevents them from getting it? (conflict). How does this get resolved? When you've written that story out, go back and read it. Is it a story you could tell effectively without the magic props and effects? When that audience member tells that story to their friends, will the friends want to see you for themselves? How can you improve the story? Do that...and improve your piece of magic.

Oracles & Character Truth

Magicians taking the role of Oracle are a bit rare. We define the oracle loosely as the fortune teller, empath, prophet or mind reader. The powers of the oracle are being in touch with the unseen currents of emotion, time and deep spiritual matters. This covers quite a range. Everything from the gypsy fortune-teller to the psycho-therapist.

The role of oracle allows the performer to engage with his or her audience in their own favorite pastime: thinking about themselves. I remember at an early Mystery School, Paul Harris was a special guest. We did a session on tarot readings, and one of his comments was – "Ah, yes. When I get hired to do walk-around at parties in Vegas, I usually end up working the line of people waiting for the fortune-teller." People love to be the center of attention, love to talk about themselves. If you want to be thought a great conversationalist, just ask someone else to talk about themselves, then listen actively.

All this can make a "mind reading" piece extremely attractive to many magicians who are not naturally suited for it. If you're primary mode is "alpha male, super-sorcerer, master of the elements," or "super trickster, Mr. Practicle Joker" - chances are strong that your audience may find the shift into mind-reader, empathic oracle to be a bit of a stretch. The result: They'll see your sensitively developed, deeply nuanced piece of mental subtlety as just another magic trick, and one that's not terribly spectacular.

It is certainly possible,, come times even desireable, to play different roles within the course of a single show or even within a single piece, and this may seem a contradiction to that. On some level, I suppose it is. But it brings up the subject of character, which is kind of the underlying subject of this whole series on the different varieties of magic and magicians. Some characters can encompass all of the different magical archetypes, but others cannot.

It might be that the trickster/ gambler guy who delights in showing you how he runs his 3-card monte scam, or demonstrates ways to cheat at poker...sometimes "gets a hunch" that proves true...and can use that as an "in" for him to demonstrate his uncanny ability to forecast the outcome of something...a foray into the world of the oracle. That same guy probably is not equally suited to doing a sensitive card reading for someone who wants to know if his relative is going to make it through their current medical crisis, though. Should he attempt that, it will ring false.

One of the things some actors do when preparing a role is to sit down and write up their own short character biography and analysis. Where was my character born? Raised where, and by who? What was my childhood /

college/ job history like? Am I more optimist or pessimist? What are my core beliefs? What special talents does my character have? Do I like others? Am I quick to anger, or not so much? Does my character fit into a "type"? (I.e: alpha male/ jock, mousey accountant type, professor... trickster, oracle, sorcerer or sage)?

The more fully the actor can understand the character, their background and what drives them, the better equipped they are to create that character in a way that is interesting, engaging, and, above all, believable. I think it is equally important for you, as a magician, to present a character who is all of those things for your audience. "Dropping out of character" is the actor's equivalent of 'flashing' for a magician...and when you are performing, you are automatically held to the same standards as an actor.

So...your assignment here is to sit and write up the short biography and character analysis for the character you currently play when performing. This will give you a baseline for choosing and developing new material. In addition, once you've written it out, it gives you a way to go in, have a look, and find places you can make bigger and more interesting choices that will help you build a more interesting character for your audiences.

On Performing as a Magician

Magical performers find themselves in a different relationship to audiences than most other performers. No other art form challenges audiences to "catch" them as they deceive. Few other performing arts actually interact with their audiences in the direct way that magical performance does. And few require skills designed to be hidden from their audiences. All of these things make the performance of magic unique, and bring with them a special set of demands.

This section is specifically for the performing magician. That courageous being who stands before a group of people and seeks to enchant, fool, and astonish them. If you choose this path, you must master not only the skills of creating illusions, but also the showmanship of a PT Barnum, the story-telling skills of a Stephen Spielberg...and more.

As a director who works with many different magicians, I have the greatest respect for the abilities and discipline they must have to succeed.

StageFright

Imagine the performer, standing in the darkness backstage, preparing to walk out in front of a thousand people, all there just to see them. Ask him how he feels, and you might hear something like this:

"I have to tell you, tonight I'm a little nervous. I mean... just the idea of all of you out there...all the thousands of eyes on me right now...just staring at me, listening to the sound of my voice...will I screw up? What will you think of me? It's enough to make anyone a little nervous, don't you think?"

Well..yes, and no. If you think of it from that self-conscious point of view – with your focus on yourself and how you must appear and sound to others, on how they'll judge you. Then yes, stage fright can be paralyzing.

I heard a great story told by Tony Robbins, of a time when he was engaged to coach the singer Carly Simon, who suffered from stage fright so badly that she gave up performing live concerts for quite a long time. Tony wanted to understand the nature of her stage fright, so he asked her to go into some detail of just how it manifested. I'll paraphrase the story here:

"Well, I get up late in the morning on a concert day, and enjoy a nice brunch. I start thinking about the concert and what I'll be singing. My manager usually calls to tell me we're sold out about that time, and make sure I'm feeling OK to go on, and I tell him yes. That's when the butterflies begin. Right here in my stomach. Sometimes I get a little shaky for a few minutes, but I go on getting myself ready to go to the venue. I get dressed, pack my costumes for the evening, and get ready to travel to the theater. On the way there, I often start going kind of all hot and then cold all over, and I begin to feel a little nauseous. I try to calm myself by thinking over the running order, what we need to rehearse and stuff. Once we're at the theater I check in at my dressing room, have some spring water, and go to the stage to work with the band a little. That usually stops the shaking, but I can feel the tension building as curtain time comes closer. I start to get nauseous again, and my whole body goes hot and cold, and sometimes my hands start to shake uncontrollably. I hear the crowd starting to come in, and I feel my heart start to race. My palms get all sweaty....and sometimes I just freeze up. I can't move at all. It's just terrible!"

Later that same week, Tony was invited backstage at a Bruce Springsteen concert. Apparently he's a big fan of the Boss, and while he was hanging out with him before the concert, he thought about his conversation with Carly and asked Bruce what his day was like on a concert day:

"Well, I get up late in the morning on a concert day, and enjoy a nice brunch. I start thinking about the concert and what I'll be singing. I imagine the hall I'll be playing and all the people who will be there. My manager usually calls to tell me we're sold out about that time, and make sure I'm feeling up to go on, and I tell him yes. That's when the butterflies begin. Right here in my stomach. Sometimes I get a little shaky for a few minutes, like I'm plugged into an electrical socket, but I go on getting myself ready to go to the venue. I get dressed, pack my stuff for the evening, and get ready to travel to the theater. On the way there, I think about what's in store, and I often start going kind of all hot and then cold all over. I go over my running order in my head, you know, what we need to rehearse and stuff. Once we're at the venue I check in at my dressing room, have some coffee, and go to the stage to work with the band. That gets me warmed up, and I can feel the excitement building as curtain time comes closer. Sometimes the butterflies come back then for a few minutes, but I hear the crowd starting to come in, and I feel my heart start to race. My palms get all sweaty....and I just have to start moving around. They start chanting in the audience and I just get so pumped...by the time I hit the stage I'm all wound up and just can't wait to get out there and feed them what they're waiting for. It's fantastic!"

You see...The experiences are same, but the interpretations are completely different. While the nerves and energy and anticipation fed Springsteen's excitement, Carly saw them from a different perspective, and they worked as stage fright for her!

I think the real distinguishing factor is your perspective. If you're focused on yourself and what people will think of you – you're bound to experience stage fright. If, on the other hand, you focus on your audience and the experience you're about to give them, then you'll experience excitement and anticipation. The choice is really yours to make – and it can easily make the difference between failure and success. Incidentally, if you take that same choice one step further, and focus on the specific experience you want to give your audience, your purpose for performing – that can make a huge difference in every other aspect of your performances (and career) as well.

As with all the choices you make as a performer – this one really only makes a difference when you put it into practice performing in front of audiences. Making it in your imagination, or in front of your mirror, won't help at all.

Guilt and the Magician

In the world of magic and magicians, there are a lot of reasons many of us probably *should* feel guilt. Things like performing without having sufficiently scripted or rehearsed our magic. But misleading your audience in order to provide them with a truly magical experience is not one of them.

I know magicians who go to great lengths in structuring their routines so that they never tell an outright lie. While I applaud them for taking such care with their scripts, I have to confess I think their magic would probably be better if they put that same time and care into making their scripts more interesting.

Many magicians appear to feel guilt about using sleight of hand. This brings on what Jeff McBride calls "the blinks," that condition that comes at least partly from practicing before a mirror – where the magician invariably blinks just at the moment he or she is executing the questionable move. As a result, they never actually see the flash that their audiences will all see – because their eyes are closed when it happens! They give lip service to the idea of using misdirection, but fail when it comes to directing their own attention to something other than that guilty move.

When an actor goes onstage, he is pretending to be

someone he is not. Every gesture he makes, every word he speaks is, on some level, a lie. And yet he is able to do so, for the most part, without feeling any guilt at all! So why should magicians feel guilt as they perform what amounts to physical lies, all for the entertainment of others? They should not. This is, effectively, not a moral judgement, but an aesthetic one.

If you, as the performer, fully believe the reality of what your character is doing and saying, then so will your audience. If, however, on some level you cannot really "get behind" the character, and feel a subconscious need to "let us know" that you are not really what you're pretending to be – well then the audience won't believe that performance, and it will fail to move them.

How can that help you as a magician? Well, it will help you to think of yourself as an actor, acting out the pieces you are performing. Like the actor – if you truly believe, if you're totally committed to your own belief in the reality of what you're presenting – then your audiences are far more likely to believe it, too.

If, when you pretend to place that coin or sponge ball in your hand, you really believe it's there, so will your audience. But if part of you is thinking "did I get away with that?" instead of being fully in the character's reality, where that ball is actually in the hand where you appear to have placed it – then you will, on some level, telegraph your own disbelief!

There's a phrase about impossibility that is variously attributed to Henry Ford, Goethe and several others...but bears repeating no matter who it was who said it first:

"The man who says he can, and the man who says he can't, will both be correct."

I think it's similar with guilt and the magician: The one who feels the guilt, probably should feel it, and the one who does not, should not. Because the one feeling the guilt is telegraphing that guilt and destroying the very experience of magic he or she is trying to create! And the biggest reason for feeling guilt? Not enough practice. Not enough rehearsal. If you haven't rehearsed your presentation to the point you no longer have to give conscious attention to the secret moves, and you get in front of an audience with that presentation anyway – well that's when you deserve to feel guilty!

Learning to Act

I spent most of my college and grad school careers learning to act, and then teaching acting. I was actually better at the second, as I was only a fair actor, myself. The subject is worthy of a lifetime of study, so an attempt to encapsulize it here would be silly. Instead, I'll just touch on a few of the high points in what I've learned:

First: You can only learn to act by doing it. There are some great books out there on acting – but you won't have a clue what they're talking about if you haven't actually spent the time in rehearsal and onstage in front of an audience. So, please: get out there and audition for school plays, or community theater. Take classes in acting and improv. Get on your feet, in front of others, and with competent teachers.

That said, please be aware, when it comes to acting teachers, only about 1 in 5 is actually competent. Many are wonderful people, and will put you through exercises and scene study that will be lots of fun. But very, very few actually know enough to be considered really competent. The sad thing here is that you probably won't recognize the incompetent ones until you've found one or two of the really competent ones. But go and study anyway. When you finally find that one really brilliant teacher, it will change your life.

I mentioned that books can't teach you to act – it's kind

of like reading books about becoming a race driver. They'll inspire you and give you some of the jargon – but you won't really have a clue about driving a race car until you're behind the wheel and on the track. So, here are the books to read, once you've appeared in a couple of shows: First, these three by Constantin Stanslavski: *An Actor Prepares, Building a Character,* and *Creating a Role.* Don't make the mistake many do of only reading the first one – it's inspirational but in many ways misleading. Then read Bobby Lewis' books, *Method or Madness?* and *Advice to the Players.* Then, if you're looking for a good set of step-by-step things to do and learn, try *The Actor at Work* by Robert Benedetti. I've read quite a lot of books on acting, but this list gave me more than all the rest combined.

Remember: acting is lying, much as is magic. So, how good a liar are you? Ask your friends to give feedback on your performances. What did they believe and not believe? When did they get the sense you were not being honest with them? You can practice in public. Try becoming someone else next time you're shopping. Lie about your name (if you're not using a credit card or paying by check), dress in ways you would not normally dress. Speak differently than you normally would. Can you carry it off?

Acting is whole-body, whole-mind. It's really good for you, but only if you fully commit with all of yourself! Because it's a whole-self proposition, your warmups need to involve your whole self, too.

What works for you is what works for you. There is no one right way that works for everyone. Some actors use inside – out methods. That means they construct the inner life of their character first, and hope that will inform their external performance. Others work outside in. Lawrence Olivier once said he would only really "get" a role when he got the false nose right. He would sit in front of his make-up mirror and manufacture different false noses from make-up putty, and there would come a point when he saw

– and got – the character he was trying to create, looking out at him. Only then, by inhabiting the physicality of that character, was he able to take them on and perform them with truth.

Acting is called acting because it is all about taking action. Until you do it, you won't know what it feels like. Until you do it right, you won't know what that feels like.

You can read and read and read – and never learn a thing. But read anyway. You can take a dozen classes and learn nothing, or the wrong things. When you find the right teacher, you will know it. And it will be worth all the effort.

As magicians, we truly are "actors playing the part of a magician," and as with any other kind of acting, if we are not fully committed and completely truthful, our audiences will know it. Even if the character you portray is 99% the same as you – if we, as an audience, don't believe that the character fully believes what he is saying and doing – we won't believe it, either. And the performance will fall flat. On the other hand, inspired acting can make the simplest trick truly magical!

So, please, if you're going to perform, get out there and learn to act!

Rehearsal

If I don't practice one day, I know it; two days, the critics know it; three days, the public knows it.
— Jascha Heifetz

Want to know two of the biggest keys to being a great magician? They are practice and rehearsal. Don't mix the two up — they're similar, but not the same thing.

Both involve repetition – a lot of repetition. But practice is where you repeat a skill you are learning, again and again and again — until you have mastered it. In *Outliers* by Malcom Gladwell, *The Talent Code* by Daniel Coyle – both highly recommended – it is said that mastery of a subject – magic for instance, or a sport, comes after 10,000 hours of practice. A single skill takes 10,000 repetitions. Sounds like a lot, doesn't it? But it really isn't, when you're thinking of something like learning a new sleight. A couple of hours a day can get you 250 – 500 times through most sleights. And at 500 a day, ten days gets you 5,000 and 20 days the necessary 10,000. To master the technique, you just need to put in the time practicing.

Rehearsal is something a bit different. That is when you repeat a whole performance piece, or even a show. This rarely happens 10,000 times, even when you're a professional performing several times a night. Broadway plays typically rehearse for 3 weeks before opening, and are lucky if they can get 20 "run throughs" completed before audiences start seeing the show, and maybe another 20 before their official "opening night." However – the *skills* that the performers in those shows use to create their performances have often been perfected through well over 10,000 hours of practice.

Professionals will know well enough that it is rehearsal, and then rehearsal before an audience (also known as performance), that creates mastery of the performance situation. More than anything else, rehearsal is where a live performance discovers its shape, and where the performer develops his mastery of that shape. Things which look great written out in a script, or even in storyboard or the imagination – often don't work so well when they are "up on their feet." Sentences that look great on the page might be difficult to say, or sound stilted. Pieces that seem like poetry on the page might have difficult pacing when they are actually performed. As we perform the piece "live" we discover moves, timing, phrasings — and alternative ways of doing things, different from what we had imagined. We learn from doing. Our bodies give us feedback we can't get without actually performing.

Once we think we've mastered a piece by rehearsing it, beginning to end, again and again – then it's time to actually look at the piece, on video tape and through the eyes of test audiences. When you actually see yourself performing, you will most likely be amazed at how different you look and sound from the way you imagined you looked and sounded. When other people look at your performance, they'll see even more things that you were unaware of "from the inside."

So: Rehearsal is the great separator of the amateur, the dabbler, from the professional. Here are a few simple rules for rehearsal:

- A mirror may be okay for practice, but not for rehearsal. It can actually be detrimental. Recording on video is much better, without watching a monitor as you're rehearsing. Go back after the fact and watch and make notes.

- Rehearse as if you have a live audience even if you don't.

- When you make a mistake in rehearsal, cover and continue as though you had an audience. Do not apologize or stop when you make a mistake. If you do, you'll be training yourself to that behavior, and will find yourself doing it in live performance.

- If you've made errors during a rehearsal – and you will – go back when you are through rehearsing, and then practice the moments where you made errors. Start a few beats before the spot where the error occurred, and continue for a few beats beyond it. This trains your body to do the correct thing, in context.

- It is possible, once you know a piece, to rehearse in your mind. Sit down, close your eyes, and imagine going through the piece, moment by moment, as though you are actually doing it. Olympic athletes do this, and it has proven to be nearly as effective as actually rehearsing 'on your feet.' This tends to work only after you've rehearsed the piece live for a few dozen times, though.

- Don't expect instant mastery, or beat yourself up when you make mistakes. The more you beat yourself up, the slower you will be to reach mastery. Instead, compliment yourself for your successes, and go back and practice the parts where things went wrong, and then rehearse some more.

Note: There is never a time when you no longer need to practice, or to rehearse. Skills need constant reinforcement. And you can always get better. That's what sets the true performing artist apart from the craftsman, hack and amateur. Commit to becoming just a little better with each performance, every day.

The Fine Art of Accepting Applause

Applause – the knowing of how to get it and how to accept it gracefully – is another one of the things that sets the experienced and professional performer apart from the rest. You would think it would be easy, and for some performers, their relationship with their audiences and with applause is something that comes fairly naturally. But not for most.

First off: We never want to beg for applause. Audiences hate performers who beg for or demand applause. I've seen performers gesture to demand applause, and – if not part of a joke – that's a sure way to alienate your audience.

On the Other side of the coin – audiences do want to applaud. Part of all dramatic interaction are the creation and release of tension. And applause is the necessary release for your audience. If you don't allow the release, there's no point to building the tension -- and you'll frustrate them. Not allowing applause can be just as bad as demanding it. It's a delicate relationship.

This is one of the areas a good director can most help you with: We often need an outside sensibility to see things like: Where are the natural applause points? What's the best way to let the audience know about them? What do you do when they don't work – when the audience doesn't respond as expected? Even more important – what will you do when they do?

When it comes to applause moments: not all are created equal. So, how do you acknowledge different kinds of applause – in mid-piece, at the end of the piece, at the end of your show? And, while we're on the subject – laughter is a special kind of applause – and needs to acknowledged, as well.

Sometimes just a pause is sufficient to acknowledge a laugh or applause moment. Sometimes a pause and a "take" to the audience is better. Other times, a full stop with a bowed head is the thing. And there are times when that full circus performer or opera star's grandiose multiple bow with arms flung wide is what it takes to fully satiate the audience's need to applaud. May you all be so successful!

Going back to the idea of having a director's help: Please be aware that there are many, many ways a director and lighting designer can help you with your applause cues. A slight bump up in lighting levels can send a subtle cue that "it's time to applaud." There are postures that automatically cue applause. Facial gestures. If you have other performers on stage with you, their reactions to whatever you've just done can cue applause. Pacing can help build tension to a release point that will cue applause. Done right, a blackout followed by a slow fade up of the lights on stage can help build applause. My friend Jeff McBride likes to slap his hands together in front of himself once as he takes a bow. His single clap suffices as a subtle cue his audiences that it's time for them to applaud. House lights coming up at end of a show, done with right timing, can boost the applause and almost cue a standing ovation.

Whatever methods you've use to generate it and cue it, however you decide it's most appropriate to accept the applause and laughter your performances generate – please be aware of just how important that applause is to the overall experience – both for you and for your audiences.

Timing

There's a quote in a book by Penn & Teller – I think it was How to Play in Traffic, about Buddy Hackett talking about comic timing on the Johnny Carson show (some of you may remember those two).

Buddy says, "Ask me what's the biggest secret of comedy."

So Johnny comes back, "OK. What's the biggest secret..." and before he can finish, Buddy shouts in his face, "Timing!"

In comedy, as they say, timing IS everything. And it's a valuable – though not always predictable tool – in any kind of a performance. In magic, your timing can make so much of a difference in so many different ways.

It can help with misdirection – if you don't use some time to separate the revealing of your magical effect from the move you used to create it, you're much more likely to get caught!

Dramatically, timing is just one more of those tools you can use to create different effects. Things like building excitement by slowly accelerating the rhythm of the performance. Or creating great anticipation by doing that kind of build up, and then [pause, pause] a long pause. You can use different speech rhythms to delineate different characters in a story you are telling.

But how do we learn to do this? The problem >I< have with timing is that it is really difficult to know how it really works. What works for one joke or stage bit might fall flat with another.

As a director, I know just how important the timing can be for the delivery of a particular line or how crucial the rhythm of a particular scene can be. But I find I'm often wrong about the way I think it should be. Oftentimes the timing trick I think should work in any given situation, doesn't...or it works just great for me and for the performer, but winds up not playing well for audiences. No matter how sure I am about a piece, or the performer is...if it's not working for the audience, it's time to try something different. Only lots of experimentation – on your own AND in front of audiences – can really give you assurance that you've got it right.

One of the great difficulties many beginning performers have is the ability to feel comfortable during moments of silence. Too many beginners think they must fill every moment with activity, with sound, or the audience will lose interest. In fact, the opposite is true. When your performance becomes one long run-on stream, the audience has difficulty following you – and you lose them.

Taking a moment to breathe at the right place in a performance can help you give the performance shape... and help calm you down and get you back in control when your energy is starting to get away from you. Use different pacing, taking time to pause, time to take a breath, and so on...and you'll do much better at keeping their interest. You'll probably have more fun performing, too!

The great playwright Samuel Beckett was famous for writing pauses into his scripts. He would use three dots to indicate a short pause, and the word "pause" to indicate a longer one. Actors who ignored those directions to pause did so at their peril, because the delivery of Beckett's lines took on a whole different context depending on whether the pauses were played correctly or not!

This is one of those subjects far too vast to cover in one short article like this one. In fact, timing tends to be a really personal thing. If you work with a good director, or if you come work with us at one of the master classes in Vegas, timing is one of the crucial elements we will help you with – and you'll be amazed at just how much of a difference some simple adjustments can make!

Magic with Apparatus

I suspect you all know what I mean by 'apparatus,' but here is Merriam Webster's definition:

a: a set of materials or equipment designed for a particular use

b: a group of anatomical or cytological parts functioning together <mitotic apparatus>

c: an instrument or appliance designed for a specific operation

Origin of APPARATUS – Latin, from apparare to prepare, from ad- + parare to prepare

First Known Use: circa 1628

So what do we learn from that? Well, for one thing, I find the root – that *ad parare* – to be interesting. To have apparatus, then is to be prepared. Cool.

I wrestled a bit with what I wanted to talk about on this subject, because as someone who seldom actually performs magic, I don't deal a lot with apparatus.

Except, of course, that I do. I recently spent nearly $1,000 of Marco Tempest's money just shipping some of his apparatus – in this case a one of a kind set-up he uses for *Magic & Storytelling*, an Augmented Reality performance — from one side of the country to the other. A recent Jeff McBride show in China cost upwards of $20,000 just in shipping expenses! As magicians, more than most other kinds of performers, we rely on apparatus.

We carry it with us, ship it, spend hours setting it up and tearing it down – one might say we depend on our apparatus. Without it, much of the magic we do would be impossible. When it breaks, especially during or just before a performance, it's a big deal. When we can't replace something, that's a big deal. And so, I decided, maybe the most useful thing I could discuss with you in this essay is how to build systems to organize and take care of your apparatus.

When I was in graduate school, I used to spend a fair amount of time in the scene shop. I wasn't studying tech theater, per se... I was a directing student. But in my mind, I was studying to become a director/producer and therefore needed to be able to undersand everything that made up a production. So I needed to understand all I could about scenery, props and lighting, about the technical side of theatrical production. I expected to learn things like how to build and paint scenery – but I think the biggest and most important lesson I took away from that scene shop was one about having a clear system, and living by it, to take care of the apparatus of the shop – the tools and supplies we used to create the scenery.

The guy who ran that shop had some very strict rules. They were designed to promote good habits in the shop... habits of safety and of efficiency. Every tool, every can of paint, every piece of lumber and hardware – had its place. And the places were clearly labeled. If the tool was to hang on a pegboard, it hung within a painted silhouette shape for that tool. If a particular kind of hardware belonged in a particular drawer, that drawer was labeled with the name of that hardware.

When we walked into the shop for a session – whether it was a class or a work session building things for a show, everything was always in its place. We quickly learned that when we were doing a job, whatever that job was, the tools we had been using were to be returned immediately to their proper place when we were through with them. No one left the shop at the end of a session without everything having been stored in its proper places, floors having been swept — in short, before everything had been returned to the way it had been found when we started.

At first it all seemed like we were just being forced to cater to the teacher's anal retentive whims. At first, many of us found ourselves late for our next classes, not quite believing he was serious that we couldn't leave until everything was back in order. Before long, though, it became clear that this shop was far more efficient than most of the other shops I had ever worked in. No one wasted time looking for a tool. That tiny bit of time we were required to spend when finished with one tool, to put it back where it belonged...saved hours of time we (or someone else) might have had to spend to go looking for it later on. When we were nearly out of some kind of hardware, someone noticed and reported it, and replacements were ordered, so that we never actually did run out of most things.

I think that may have been my first introduction to the strength of building systems... in that case, it was a system to manage the apparatus of a scene shop. Since then, I have developed clear systems (which I often update) for running my office, for organizing a kitchen, even for organizing my e-mail. And those systems save me hundreds of hours of work each year.

So, how will you go about building your own system, to manage your apparatus? If I were you, I'd first try and get a handle on what I had. Make a list, maybe in a spreadsheet program, or lay it all out on a table, or if you have too much for that, on the floor of your garage. Move things around so they seem to go together. Maybe you keep all your decks of cards in one place, thread props somewhere else, coins in another area. Or perhaps you have different kinds of performances – your kid show, a restaurant show, etc., and want to group your various apparatus that way. Once you have a basic organizational idea for the apparatus, consider how best to store it so it will be easy to find, and so that you'll know at a glance if you have everything. Some people like to use cases with cut-out spaces for each piece of apparatus. Others just keep them in labeled zip-lock bags, organized into boxes or bins. No one system would be right for every magician – we all have different kinds of shows, and our minds each work differently...so what works for me might not work for you.

However... having a system to manage your apparatus is something that works for everyone. It only works, of course, if you actually use that system. Discipline about your systems is essential for making them work. Having a system you don't use conscientiously is a bit like having a bottle of pills you never take – neither one does you much good. But if you can first build that system, then accustom yourself to using it all the time, you'll be amazed what a difference it can make in your life. As magicians we all depend on our apparatus, and the usefulness of that apparatus will be greatly enhanced by the use of systems to organize and care for that apparatus.

Gimmicks & Gaffs

Our subject tonight is gimmicks and gaffs. I know magicians who take great pride in not using any gimmicks or gaffs in their magic. "I'm a purist, I only use sleight of hand," they'll tell you. Others are perfectly happy to produce their magical effects by whatever the easiest way to produce them might be... and that is often through the use of some sort of gaff.

For myself – well, whatever floats your boat. I don't really care how a magician produces a particular effect so much as I care about whether it is effective, and what they do with the effect. If you're doing magic that does little more than raise the question of "How did he do that?" – well, for me, you're relegating yourself to the role of a glorified practical joker, presenting nothing more than a series of tricks and puzzles.

If you're great at that, have a good sense of humor and stage presence, well then you can do well as that kind of magician. But not so much with me. I want the magic I see to do more. I want it to transport me to a magical place, wake me up to possibilities I hadn't considered, or to inspire me in some way. As such, I find myself far more interested in what a magician does with a particular effect than whether or not it is produced with a gaff.

Of course, an effect that fools me enough that I could possibly get myself to believe it has actually happened as I saw it probably has a better chance of leading my imagination into that "magic zone" where I allow myself to have a magical experience.

So: If you really love doing sleight of hand, if you love it that you can do your magic anywhere, any time that a deck or cards or some coins are available, without having to make sure you have your 'magic stuff' with you in order to perform...by all means, use sleight of hand. But don't let your imperfect mastery of sleight of hand prevent you from doing magic. And if a particular effect turns out to be more deceptive for your audiences using a gaff...please use one!

Pick up some great packet tricks that do use gaffed cards and minimal sleight-of-hand, or other magic with small gimmicks, and keep them with you so you can perform anywhere. And if you are a stage performer, don't hesitate to use any means available, whether through sleight of hand or supplemented by various gimmicks, to amaze your audiences. Whatever means you choose, please, please make sure you are using the effects you create to deliver a real experience of magic. Strive for a reaction that goes beyond 'How did she do that?' Go for giving your audiences magic with a purpose, with a message... magic that causes real emotion. That is the kind of magic that will leave your audiences always wanting more. The kind of magic that will leave your audiences thinking "Wow, I love magic!" and looking forward to their next magic show.

The Talent Code

I recently read a fantastic book called The Talent Code, by Daniel Coyle. It's all about the importance of practice and its relationship to talent, genius, and mastery — all things I think we all aspire to.

The author makes a strong case that all talent is really the result of a special kind of practice. He suggests there is a moment of "ignition" when a person develops a passion for something, which then drives them to a special kind of practice which then results, after about 10,000 hours, in their mastery of that thing.

Coyle brings up the question of child prodigies – children like Mozart, who, by the age of 10 or 12, was composing and playing music at a level that has seldom been surpassed. What most people don't know about that 'child prodigy,' though, was that he was the son of a piano teacher, who had easily put in over 3,500 hours of practice before he reached the age of 10!

The process by which practice builds mastery, the author argues, is a biological one. Each time we repeat a particular pattern in our body —which means through the neurons that control that process — we add a miniscule amount of myelin to the sheath surrounding those nerves. Myelin in the substance that coats and insulates our nerves, much as rubber or plastic insulation insulates a common extension cord. So the more myelin there is, the better shielded that particular nerve is. As a result there is less 'cross talk' between that nerve and surrounding nerves. The signals are actually stronger and faster in that nerve, and they become increasing stronger and clearer as more and more myelin builds up around the nerve. How does the myelin get built? By repeating the action, the skill one is trying to develop, again and again.

So as I write this we are at the beginning of a New Year. I'm sure many of you have made resolutions, and many of those resolutions will be broken and forgotten before the end of January. However, here's one I would urge for everyone. Make it now, even if you're reading this in July.

Plan to take at least 20 minutes each day to practice the one thing you most want to master. This could be something you do in the course of your job. It might be sleight of hand skills if you are a magician, or it might be your ability to write fiction, your abilities as a computer programmer. Spend that 20 minutes each day practicing whatever you want to develop as an exceptional skill. Choose something you love – you're going to be spending a lot of time mastering it. If you can practice – in a concentrated, passionate and fully present mode – for 20 minutes just once or twice a day, within months you'll begin to see improvements of a magnitude you can now only imagine. By consciously choosing this habit of daily rehearsal, daily practice – you are consciously choosing to build myelin, consciously chosing to change your life...and that's what wizards do!

Playing Big

Magicians seem to love the phrase "pack small, play big." It's almost a mantra. I suppose because so much of magic depends on props, and we've all found ourselves mired down with far too many props to transport, many of which don't seem to deliver the requisite "bang for the buck" when we get them in front of an audience.

In most of this article, I'll talk about what it really

means to 'Play Big,' but before I get to that, let me relate a recent anecdote to give you a reason for learning to 'pack small.'

Reasons to Pack Small

We recently had a request to take Jeff's three person illusion show to Japan for a month. They wanted a "small" illusion show — only 40 minutes and a couple of smaller illusions, or about half the size of what we might do for a large theater, or a long run at a casino. Our shipping list came to 6 cases, weighing about 2500 pounds altogether. It would almost fit in a full sized van. That was for props, costumes, two of his smaller illusion props and so on. The round trip shipping estimate came to nearly $25,000!

Imagine you wanted to ship the larger illusion show. Do you think the shipping costs for that show, added on to airfares, our performance fee, and so on, might have made it difficult for our promoter to see his way to booking the show?

There are two basic ways you can handle shipping and transportation when you negotiate an engagement – you either wrap them into a "package fee," or quote a performance fee PLUS the airfares, hotel, shipping and so on. Imagine the package fee, where you have to quote a minimum of $50K just to cover your expenses – and if they say yes to that, you're >still< not making any money. Better to learn, as Jeff has, to do a spectacular 90 minute show using only what you can carry on the plane with you. You'll stand a MUCH better chance of actually making a living as a performer! And you'll avoid the expense of maintaing a huge storage space, year in and year out, just to store that big show.

Thoughts on how to make it play big

But let's move on to the other side of the equation: Let's talk about what it really means to 'Play Big.' All too often, I think, magicians feel they need to put a lot of stuff on the stage – bright colors, flashy costumes, big set pieces, and so on — in order to play big. And there certainly is something to be said for the pleasure of the 'really big' production. Ringling Bros. Barnum & Bailey Circus is one of the 'biggest' shows in the world, and it has been wowing audiences of all ages for almost a century. Their kind of 'Big' involves sensory overload. Spectacularly costumed, death defying acts in all three rings, sometimes all at once, so you don't have even a chance of taking it all in at just one sitting. And today, Cirque du Soleil has upped the bar for circus spectacle with a whole new aesthetic. They present old fashioned circus acts in a highly designed and choreographed format, in a sophisticated artsy aura that is designed to really wow the arts crowd. It would be tough to compete with that kind of 'Plays Big,' where millions and millions of dollars get spent on each new production. What's more, unless you're Siegfried & Roy, your magic — the wonder, the story, the fine points of your carefully crafted performances — would be swallowed up by those 'too big' production values.

The good news is, you don't need to go that route. There are other ways to make your magic play big — ways that those big-top showmen can't touch. Ways that don't necessarily involve large illusion props, dozens of scantily clad dancers, or even fancy lighting.

My client Marco Tempest seldom travels with more than one or two cases, of a size which can be sent as checked baggage. And yet, he performs regularly for audiences of 4, 5 or event 10,000, often providing the biggest impact of anything on the bill for those events. How does he do it? By making use of something that is already going to be provided in the situations where he performs — mostly large corporate meetings, where the entire front of the room is made up of large video screens. Marco uses those screens as his illusion props and scenery. He programs spectacular video backgrounds to what he does, and designs his performances so that the live and video portions interact in ways that make the entire space come alive with the experience he provides. A 'big' show indeed...even though it travels in the equivalent of a couple of suitcases.

Another way to making a show 'play big,' is to find ways of expanding your otherwise 'small' magic. At the Legends of Magic conference a few years ago, Ormond McGill gave a demonstration of how to take an otherwise small trick and make it play big. Ormond took a simple card location trick — "Pick a card...was it the queen of hearts? Yes!" and turned it into a 15 minute, dramatically spectacular event. I don't remember all the details, but I do remember several audience members on stage and standing in the audience holding different cards, Ormond blindfolded on stage, and a story. The story created a situation in which the stakes for him being able to find the card were high. And I clearly remember the standing ovation at the end of the trick. How often can you manage a standing ovation while performing a simple card location?

The keys to Ormond's success that day were these: Make use of your audience. Involve them both emotionally and physically. A magician standing alone on stage makes a much less interesting picture than a magician flanked by a couple of audience assistants, each doing something interesting. An audience sitting back in their seats watching is a very different audience from the ones on the edge of their seats participating. And an audience watching a simple card trick, done as such, is in a completely different frame of mind from one involved in a cliff-hanger story where the fate of the hero hangs in the balance.

Combine all of that with your abilities to build the tale using your voice, body, pacing, physical actions and your own deep passions, and you, too, might well manage to achieve that very big response that Ormond McGill did — even just doing a simple card location.

Don't just do tricks. Make a big impression, but creating

a big experience for your audiences. And then, like Jeff McBride, Marco Tempest and Eugene Burger, you too may be able to travel the world, doing your very big shows, all out of a single suitcase!

Technical Mastery

This essay's subject is 'technical mastery.' When we wrote it down, I suppose we meant the mastery of sleight-of-hand. I could be wrong.

Anyway, I thought I'd use this article to talk about the technical mastery involved in any kind of art or performance, not just magic. When I was a much younger man, I trained as an actor and dancer. We would spend at least 2 hours each day in the dance studio, working to perfect our technique as dancers. Two or three times a week, we would spend an hour or two in voice classes, working on our speaking voices. Some had aspirations toward performing in musical theater, and they would take at least one voice for singers class several times a week.

That was just the basic training — the conditioning of the body and voice. Beyond that, we would take courses in dialects, so we could reproduce the accents of different characters proficiently. Courses in pantomime to further train our physical expressivity. All in the pursuit of technical mastery. Why? Because that's what it takes for anyone to become an accomplished performer.

Real creativity can't begin until technical mastery has been achieved. There is a popular notion that "talented individuals" – Mozart the child prodigy is an example often put forth – are "gifted" with their creativity. Not true. What they HAVE been gifted with is a passionate interest in their art – which in turn drives them to relentless pursuit of technical mastery. That "child prodigy" Mozart had, at the age of ten, already been practicing and playing his various keyboard instruments for many hours each and every day since he began at age 4. Let's see...6 years times 360 days, times 6 hours...that's over 70,000 hours of practice before the age of 10! And his early works are, by all accounts, no better than others of the time. It wasn't until he had continued that rigorous schedule for another dozen years or more, until he had made thorough studies of many other great composers who had gone before him, that he began to show real mastery as a composer, and the creative genius for which we remember him today.

So, my question to you for this evening is this: How serious are you about mastering the art of magic? Not everyone has to become a master...there is plenty of room in our community of magic for amateurs, fans and dabblers at all levels. It is fun to learn a few simple tricks and share them with friends. It is fun to read books about the great masters, and books filled with new tricks and sleight of hand techniques. Sometimes the rankest of amateurs can make a significant contribution in the form of a new trick or idea. But to truly master the art of magic – you must put in the time to achieve technical mastery. There are no shortcuts. A good teacher or teachers can help you avoid wasting time on the journey to mastery – but you still have to get in that 10,000 hours of dedicated, conscious practice.

I think it is only then...once the artist has reached mastery, that magic can become a true art. Just as the young piano student practicing their scales and etudes isn't yet much more than an apprentice, or the 4th or 5th year student who has become good enough to play in the high school orchestra can really not be said to be at more than the journeyman craftsman – and so it is with magic. Until you have mastered the craft – the technical mastery of the sleight of hand, vocal nuance, ability to misdirect using your body and so on — you can't really claim to be a true artist. Once you have mastered all those things — well, then you will know it, and so will everyone who sees you perform. There is a reason we call performers like Jeff McBride, Lance Burton, Eugene Burger, Mac King and

Penn & Teller "Master Magicians." It's not a title easily – or quickly – learned. But I think it's one worth shooting for, if you're really serious about your magic.

Spontaneous vs. Rehearsed

One of the disciplines wizards practice is that of living each moment as though every action, every thought, every expression had an effect on every part of the universe. Kind of an overwhelming idea, when you think about it.

Here's an interesting experiment for you: set yourself a goal that you will live one or two minutes a day with this mind-set. Even eating a snack becomes quite an experience: Where did the food come from? Was it produced in a way that was good for the people working to produce it? Good for the land on which it was produced? How much pollution was created getting that food to you? What will become of the containers you received the food in? Where did they come from? How will the food affect your body? Will it increase or decrease your overall level of health and happiness? How will that affect your friends and family? There must be a thousand possible considerations of how our choices made around something as seemingly insignificant as a single snack affect the world around us – it's enough to make you wonder how anyone live with total responsibility?

Most of the time, we don't know ahead of time what the world will throw our way, and we have to respond to those things as they happen, in real time. The best we can hope to do is respond in a way that is consistent with our principles and what we do know about the situation.

So the answer, of course, is that we can't do this all the time, and we can't even be 100% conscious of everything we affect even in a single moment...but we can make an attempt to live consciously, as though each moment mattered, at least for a short time each day. And doing that will change US – which will have an effect on the world around us.

There is one time we don't have the excuse of not knowing what will happen next – and that is when we are performing. Most performances are planned well in advance, and there is a tried and true method for making sure we CAN execute them almost without flaw.

That method is the magical process known as -- rehearsal. The results of rehearsal can be nearly miraculous. It gives us the ability to deliver an experience almost precisely as we have designed it. Every word, action and expression can be just as planned. We can even plan on what we want to do in the event that something goes wrong, or our audience responds in some way other than the one we think most likely. By planning carefullly, writing out our script, and then rehearsing the show, again and again, we can train our minds and bodies to re-play our end of that experience in a very precise manner.

The performer who finds that his or her performances aren't going as they planned is the performer who has not rehearsed sufficiently. The performer who sees a video recording of a performance and finds themselves unhappy with what they see, is under rehearsed. In today's world, where practically every cell phone has a video camera built in, there is really no excuse for not rehearsing in front of a camera so that you know how you look and sound, and make the adjustments you find to be necessary.

Performers who have not rehearsed enough never get to experience the feeling of mastery that comes with getting your performance "into your muscles" so that you can do all that is required almost without conscious thought. Only then, when there is no longer any need to think of what your next line should be, or of what you must do next with your hands, does a performer move on to that point where the performance becomes a true interaction in which you get to 'play' your audience like an instrument, making the small adjustments necessary so that each moment can play with maximum effect.

I've heard performers who said they chose not to rehearse extensively, because it hampered their freedom on performance. Oddly enough, the "freedom" one gives up through rigorously rehearsing and perfecting every action and inflection, actually winds up giving you a greater freedom. If a particular moment isn't getting the response they have imagined, they now know exactly what they were doing at that moment – from having rehearsed it so many times -- and they can consciously change and re-rehearse that moment for future shows. There comes a time when the performer has already rehearsed his or her 'outs' for every part of a piece that can go wrong - and so whatever happens, they are ready.

Perhaps the more exciting level of freedom the performer gains, though, comes from the ability to completely forget about the details of their performance, and to concentrate on the real back-and forth interactions between performer and audience. Only then does the performer reach that "wizard moment," when you truly feel completely, competently in charge, completely responsible for the effect of the experience your performance is creating. That's the moment when tricks can turn into real magic.

I hope I've inspired you to go rehearse your magic. Start with the smallest segments, and rehearse them to the point you could do them in your sleep – and then put them in front of an audience again, and enjoy the new experience that you'll have — shaping your performance moment to moment, and really connecting with the people you are performing for. Enjoy their laughter, their wide-eyed gasps of astonishment – their delight as you create a real magical experience, just for them.

Rehearsal and Creativity

We've talked a bit about how we can use rehearsal to perfect our ability to give our audiences the magical experience we really want to create for them. To get our performance – words, actions, expressions – to a point where we no longer have to think about them, and can then begin concentrating on being present and interacting with our audiences.

There is also another kind of rehearsal – one that needs to happen before the kind I talked about above. This is the kind of rehearsal where the performer explores all the possible choices available to them, for each and every moment of a performance piece. During this kind of rehearsal, perfection is not the goal at all. This is more of an exercise, in which we explore whether an action should be bigger or smaller, faster or slower, done with one kind of attitude, or another. And we do that exploration not in our imaginations, not on paper, but live, on our feet, using the props we will actually use during our performance. We allow ourselves to 'think with our bodies,' and learn from the experiences we give ourselves trying out the various different ways of doing the bits. If you do this, you will rapidly discover that your body will teach you which ways are best – but only after you've made the body actually do the bits in different ways.

For example, we might try performing our piece 'in character' as someone (or several someones) very different from ourselves. We might try performing it in rhyme, or to different kinds of background music. We might imagine performing for just one person or for an entire stadium full of thousands of people, and find what would be different in each situation, as well as what parts of the performance seem like they would work in different situations. As artists, we are called upon to make decisions about every aspect – every moment – of the works we create. While it seems possible to make these choices 'on paper,' or in our minds, many are made far more effectively by actually rehearsing the actions of the piece we are creating in real time, using our body, mind and voice all together.

Oh...and when you try this, don't try the new and different ways of doing things in a subtle way. The more overboard you go, the further out past your own norms and comfort zones, the more your body and voice will teach you. The more 'over the top' your playing, the more chance you'll have of discovering things that are really special and unique.

Some performers like to return to this kind of explorational rehearsal even after they have been performing a piece for a long time. Great performance pieces are never really 'finished,' – they can always be improved. We can always go back and look at each of the choices we've made – and consider how we might make changes in order to make the overall piece more meaningful, more exciting, more logically and emotionally coherent and moving than it is now.

Of course, after going back to this kind of exploratory rehearsal, and making changes, a performer must rehearse the piece all over again in order to reestablish the perfection in their delivery of the performance that they had previously, and to get the new version of the piece 'into their muscles," just as the older version had been.

I hope this will encourage you to take out a piece of magic you've been thinking was 'finished,' and try out some exploratory rehearsals on it. You might find yourself with a breakthrough that really makes a piece that's already good, or even one that was just okay, into a really great work of magical art!

Making Magic More Convincing

We are practitioners of an interesting art form. One where some of our members like to call themselves "Honest Liars," stating that they are paid to tell us untruths. In the process, of course, they are making their prime theme a "bet you can't catch me" kind of relationship with their audiences. At the other end of the spectrum are those like The Amazing Kreskin and Uri Geller, who attempt to pass off their work as "the real thing." While the first "challenge magic" situation seems limiting, the second, where we really try to pass off our work as "real" can seem dishonest to many of us.

Personally, I think we're best ducking the whole issue. If people want to believe in magic or mind reading, that's their prerogative. I prefer to place primary focus more on the story the magic is telling, or the experience the audience gets to have. In these situations, it is important that the magic be convincing, but not essential, because "being fooled" is no longer the center of the experience.

I should point out – this is my personal bias, not something I feel is "the right way" to do magic. I'm certain many reasonable and intelligent people will feel differently.

That said: What do we need to do in order to make our magic more convincing?

First, we need to direct our audiences' attention strongly to where it needs to be for them to have the strongest experience of the magic possible. That means looking at the piece you have created, and seeing it completely from the point of view of your audience. Each moment of "the story" you are telling needs to be illustrated in a particular way so that the audience will derive maximum impact from the experience, and not be distracted by extraneous and non-supportive information. Perhaps the strongest statement I've heard of what a director's job is, is that "the audience can only focus on one thing at a time. Your job is to make sure that focus is in the right place at all times." It is all too easy to confuse an audience, or to allow them to miss essential parts of your performance so that they'll fail to get maximum impact from it.

Of course, as a by-product of this, we have the concept widely known as "misdirection" – the fact that when we structure a performance of magic properly, the focus of attention will be somewhere besides where the gimmick might appear, or the sleight of hand is taking place. I think it's important to realize that, just because the audience isn't looking at the place which will help them figure out how the trick is done, that doesn't mean they are looking at the place they need to in order to get the full impact of the story your magic is telling. Go for the right direction - not just the misdirection.

Another consideration is what not to do. These are things that pull audiences out of the story or experience you are creating for them. Magic props that look like magic props often do this. They practically shout "I'm a trick prop" "Don't believe your eyes." Magicians who perform with such props and don't provide an explanation of why they look the way they do often fail the test of believability.

To take this a step further, any prop or costume piece which does not fit the story you are presenting can be jarring for your audiences, and bump them out of the magical world you are attempting to lead them into. For example, the obviously plastic wallet, when telling a story about "my grandfathers wallet," detracts measurably from the experience of the story. Or the magician in period dress, presenting elegant "golden age" magic, who uses a Bic lighter in the course of his show. The obviously modern prop sends the signal that "this is all false."

Language that is out of place can do the same thing. I often see young magicians performing using patter they have learned from a book, which was obviously intended to be spoken by someone much older, or from a different era. Their performance has no chance of being believable, because the audience is too busy being amused by the incongruity between language and performer.

Making magic believable could be the subject of a whole book, or course in magic — or even a whole career. The two specifics I offer here really only scratch the surface, but I hope they'll be enough to get you to start thinking seriously about the subject yourself.

Consider: What sort of magical experience do you want to provide? How believable do you need your magic to be in order to get you to that point? Then, for each piece of magic you perform, for each moment during that piece, ask yourself, "Where does the focus need to be at each moment?" and "Do I need to change the structure here, so that the place they need to focus won't give away the secrets behind the magic?"

Finally: Look at each of your pieces to see where there are inconsistencies that might draw your audience's attention away from the story you want to tell, the experience you want to provide. Do the props you are using belong in that story? Does the language fit the character and time you want to portray?

If you've done all that, you're at least on the road to creating more convincing magic.

Masks

Let's think, for a few moments, about the power of the mask. If you're watching this, you know Jeff McBride, the real king of masks and magic. But the masks I want to talk about today aren't separate physical props you can put on and take off, manipulate and discard the way Jeff does on stage.

The masks I want you to consider now are the ones you wear, day in and day out. They are the expressions you have on your face when you're not aware of the expression that's on your face. And the expressions you use when you want to convey a message to everyone around you. "I'm in control," they might say, or "I'm mad as hell!" or "I'm feeling a little sad today." They are the ones you get caught wearing when people snap candid photos of you without your awareness. These 'masks' are the habitual expressions you wear while walking on the street, or working at your job. And they affect your world in ways you might never have imagined. Initially a product of your emotional life, the 'masks' become habitual over time. Then, they affect what goes on in your mind – your every thought. And your thoughts affect your emotions, your actions – and ultimately your place in the world.

Think for a moment of people you know well. Can you mimic the expression they carry on their faces most of the time? Try it. Use a mirror, and see how close you can get. Notice how the expression on your face can change your feelings. Carry a big grin on your face for awhile – even in the face of the different reactions you'll be getting from all those who see you – and see how that changes your experience of your day. Conversely – get a good 'angry' or 'grouchy' expression going, and carry that around for a few hours. You'll soon notice that the world around you has changed - those around you will treat you quite differently when you're projecting "grouch" than when you were "happy."

Oh...and a "mask" in this sense refers to more than just your face. Your entire body sends a message – both to yourself and to others – about your internal state. You can make yourself feel either great – or terrible – by changing your facial and body postures. Try it.

Want to feel terrible? Just slump in your seat, contracting like a porcupine in full defense mode, and put an expression of terror on your face. See how long it takes before you start to feel awful.

Then try the opposite. Put a great, ecstatic smile on

your face, sit up straight, open your chest and take a few deep breaths, stretch arms and legs out, luxuriating in the joy of being alive – and see how quickly you begin to feel terrific!

Actors learn early that pretending to have an emotion – whether that be joy, anger, sadness or hysteria – will cause one to actually feel that emotion. And – here's a secret: The emotions you feel and express will be mirrored by those around you. We are hard-wired to reflect back the emotions of people around us. It's partly how we know what they are feeling, part of how we learn to understand one another. Taking conscious control of the masks you wear can be a powerful way of influencing the world around you. It gives new and deeper meaning to the idea, I believe from Mohandas Gandhi, of "Be the change you wish to see in the world around you."

So...your wizard assignment today is this: Go and consciously 'try on' some different masks. This will take some courage – it's difficult to try on a mask – a habitual expression – that's different from the one you are accustomed to. It will feel strange. People will respond to you in ways that you aren't used to experiencing. You can either chose to be embarrassed by that, or you can choose to learn from it. Try several different new masks, each for a set period of time – at least an hour, and see what you learn. I think you'll be surprised at the remarkable power you find in this process of consciously altering the masks you wear.

As a performer, it's always useful to be aware of what your 'mask' is projecting. It ca also be most useful for you to learn to read the masks your various audience members are wearing. How is the performance going? That will be reflected in their faces and postures. Who will make a good volunteer, or not? Learn to read the masks, and you'll know.

Attention - Part 1

In life and on stage, controlling attention is really the key to almost everything else. If the teacher doesn't hold the student's attention, no learning occurs. If you fail to pay proper attention when driving your car down the road – accidents happen. As a performer, if you fail to guide your audiences' attention precisely, your performance will be confusing and lack power. On the other hand, if you learn to focus your attention like a laser, there's virtually nothing you can't do.

Our minds are amazing things. They would seem to be able to handle many, many things at one time. They regulate heartbeat, breathing, digestion and body chemistry. They manage to incorporate sound, light, motion, temperature and more into creating the experience you think of as reality, and they do it during every waking moment! Right now it seems fashionable to think we multi-task while we're at work. Exciting times — except it's not really true!

While the subconscious mind can do a hundred things or more at once – the conscious mind – that is, the one we're really in control of – does only one thing at a time with any degree of competence. When we think we're multitasking at work, it's all an illusion. What we're really doing is focusing on one thing, then shifting and focusing on another, then shifting and focusing on another — and each shift takes up a bit of energy, which is why you find yourself exhausted by the end of each day. It is actually tremendously more efficient not to multi-task. Focus on one thing at a time, because that's what your conscious mind is designed to do.

This is the primary reason we need directors in film and for live performance. The director's number one job is to control the audience's attention so they will see and hear all the specific things they need to see and hear in order to follow the story line. When the story line is lost, the overall effect can only be confusion. Most of us are unaccustomed to tracking the line of attention to the degree that is really necessary to create a great work of performance art...but directors spend most of their time doing just that.

You may be one of those who think such direction will just "take care of itself." You've seen hundreds of tricks and performance pieces where no one used a director, and they were just fine. Sometimes, that's true. Other times, the performer has learned how to direct themselves, or to take the subtle cues audiences give them in order to refine their work to a point where it is clear and concise. Sometimes it's just luck that they've come up with something that people can actually follow and have the experience they want.

In any event, let me give you and simple illustration of how things can fail. This is drawn not from performance, but from everyday life. I'm sure you've had the experience, for example, of talking with someone and suddenly noticing they had a thread on their shoulder. A small thing... but you noticed it, and finally felt compelled to reach out and take it away. And during that moment, you completely lost track of what your friend was saying. You had to ask them to repeat themselves. Why? Because you allowed the focus of your attention to shift away, just for a moment.

Sometimes that can be a good thing. One of the first things we learn as magicians is the principle of "misdirection." It refers to causing an audience to focus their attention on one thing, so they won't see another. However, the positive side of direction – the guiding of attention -- is less spoken of.

Here's a little assignment: For one of your magic pieces, or if you're not a magician, for any kind of presentation you might be working on – a paper for class or work, or whatever. Go through the presentation moment by moment and write a list of what you want your audience to pay attention to. What are the things they absolutely need to know in order to understand, first, what the trick is that they are experiencing, and, second, what the larger story of that performance really is. Once you know the things that attention must be drawn to in order to create an effective performance, you can begin finding the best way to make sure people's attention is actually going to focus where you want it to.

In the next chapter we'll talk more about how attention can be directed, and the kind of things that may become distractions and work against you.

Attention - Part 2

In that last chapter we talked about the importance of guiding the attention – both our own attention and that of our audience's, and how our conscious minds can only really deal with one thing at at time. Now we'll discuss some techniques you can use to guide the attention.

As magicians, we learn that "the large action covers the small one." This means, essentially, that the audience's eyes will follow a larger action and ignore a smaller one happening at the same time, even though the smaller one may be in full view. As an example: If I'm apparently transferring a coin from one hand to the other, the audience will see the large action of the hand holding the coin sweeping across my body, and will not notice the smaller action of the coin being moved into my palm as that larger action takes place.

Our brains are programmed to notice movement and to notice different kinds of movements in different ways. An object coming towards you will command more attention than one going away. Sharp actions (such as you might see from someone attacking you) command more attention that soft, flowing movements. One object moving in a different way than the objects around it will often claim attention through contrast. Change in the way something moves will grab your attention. And so we see that movement can be a powerful tool used to guide the attention.

This is true, until we are told to watch for the smaller action – and then we can't help but notice it. Our attention has been directed to that smaller action – and we may notice it even as we miss a change in the larger action or milieu. Our conscious attention can focus on only one thing at a time. So, telling people what to pay attention to – or asking a question that draws their attention to one particular aspect of something that is happening – can mask all the other aspects of that happening.

Another rule for guiding attention is that our audience will tend to look where we (as performers) look. If I look at my hands, you look at my hands. If I look you in the eye, you'll probably look right back at me. If I look off to my left... well...you get the picture. This tends to work for magicians and con-artists, as long as the audience is not aware that their attention is being intentionally mis-directed.

Actors learn early in their careers – mostly while they are still members of the chorus, whose chief function is sometimes to do this – to do something called "giving focus." You give focus, first, by looking where the director wants the focus to be, but also by the line and form of your body. You might lean towards the point of focus, or actually point to it with your hands. That way, if an audience member's attention strays to you when they should be looking somewhere else, your body language will cause them to go back and look where the director needs them to.

When I work as a lighting designer, a large part of my job is to help "give focus," by making the point where the director (often also me, when working with magicians) wants the focus to be stand out from other parts of the stage by making it brighter, or by making it be the one place that is a different color from the rest of the stage, or by having visible beams of light swing in and 'point' to the area I want the audience to look at.

One of my favorite ways to learn about how to direct focus is to visit an art gallery and have a look a the works of the masters. You'll find that items the artist most wants you to see are either in the exact center of the canvas... which can make for a rather boring composition, or on one of the "thirds" points. Thirds points follow "the rule of thirds," and you can find them by drawing lines across the rectangle of the canvas at thirds, both horizontal and vertical. Where the lines cross will be the best locations for an artist or photographer to place the main subjects of their pictures. It has been shown that a viewers eye "enters" a painting from the viewer's upper left, and traverses on a diagonal towards the lower right, until it reaches that "thirds" point, at which point it travels to the viewer's left to the next third point, and then diagonally upwards to the third "thirds" point, and finally, if nothing has arrested the attention by then, to the last, thirds point at the upper left. Things NOT at one of these points tend to be less noticed, and the viewer tends not to think of those things as being as important.

Reading Myster novels is another good source for seeing how a story teller can direct our attention. Mystery writers often use misdirection as part of their technique for building their mysteries. They actually tell their readers exactly what they need to know in order to solve the mystery – but the ones engaged in the actions leading up to the crime are incidental players in the scenes where their actions are described, so the reader simply doesn't pay attention until the mystery is resolved, and suddenly the solution becomes inevitable and obvious.

Even close up magicians can use this principle of contrast to help guide the attention. If one particular prop is a different color from all the others, or significantly larger, smaller or otherwise "different" from all the others, our attention will tend to go to that prop.

So, you see, there is quite a range of methods one can use to direct the attention of others. Movement, language, contrast and layout all affect how our minds allot attention

– and as a performer you have the ability to use all these things to make sure your audiences will actually have the experience you intend to create with your performances.

In the last chapter I suggested the performers among you might want to make a list of points their audiences need to experience in order to lead them to the overall experience you want them to have as a result of one of your performances. Now you can take that list, and then use the various methods discussed here to figure out just how you will make sure the audience actually pays attention to each of those points – and only to those points – in order that they can have that magical experience you want to create for them.

History

In any art form, we stand on the shoulders of those who have gone before us. Here are a few small lessons learned from some of the great magicians of the past.

Robert-Houdin and the effects of Magic on History

In this piece, I want to talk about Jean Eugene Robert-Houdin and how he and others have used their magic to change the world. I can remember one of my own first encounters with the history of magic as a child, when my father brought me a present upon his return from a business trip. A comic book — and comic books were generally frowned upon in our household. This one was called *The Illustrated Classic Book of Magic.*

The book taught a few simple tricks, and revealed some illusion secrets — but it mostly told the history of magic and famous magicians. Of course Robert-Houdin was included as the "father of modern magic," and I remember particularly the story of how he outwitted the Marabouts in what is now Algeria, helping to put down an uprising there by putting on his own magic show and demonstrating that the magic of Imperial France was more powerful than that of the Marabouts, who claimed to have "real" magic powers.

Of course, Robert-Houdin didn't normally claim such powers for himself. He was a rationalist — a clock maker famous for the quote that a "conjuror is an actor playing the part of a magician." However, once out of his rationalist home country, it seems Robert-Houdin was willing to release those qualms. Performing unique challenge magic — things like his own *Light and Heavy Trunk* and the bullet catch (particularly dangerous in a country where much of the populous regularly carried firearms), he sufficiently impressed locals with his magic so that the influence of the rival Marabouts, and thereby the uprising they had inspired, rapidly dissipated.

Magic history is filled with times that wizards, magicians and other magical practitioners have been called into political and military service. In *The War Magician*, David Fisher tells the story of Jasper Maskelyne (grandson of John Neville Maskelyne, partner of David Devant), who was called into service during the 2nd World War in order to assist the allies by developing modern camouflage, create fake armaments to confuse Nazi intelligence, and much more.

Not long after, magician John Mulholland found himself working for the army, writing *The Art of illusion*, for them, and then for the CIA during the cold war years. During that time, he invented a number of super-spy gadgets and sleight of hand methods for secret agents.

As a student of true wizardry I find these historical incidents and tales to be of particular interest, partly because they give the lie to our claim that "magic isn't real, or at least is only for light entertainment." Even as Robert-Houdin and others were making such claims, they were using their tricks and illusions to actually alter the course of history. To me, that smacks strongly of "real" magic. What is magic, if not the transformation of reality through unseen means?

As performing magicians we're accustomed to thinking of our art as light entertainment, but I would contend that, with just a very slight shift of perspective, we might learn to think of it as a profoundly and effective means of changing our world.

Our training as magicians allows us to see what others do not...and to make use of the knowing we gain in that way to truly change ourselves and our worlds. As the stories of Robert-Houdin, Jasper Maskelyne, John

Mulholland and so many others shows...we all have the potential of becoming REAL wizards. I hope at least a few of you watching this will take up that challenge and the next time you hear someone say of magic, "there's no such thing," - you can start an interesting discussion by telling them, "oh, yes...there is!"

Houdini

Let's a a look at Harry Houdini, and his place in history. Since we're talking about Houdini, I thought it might be appropriate to talk about something Houdini was famously good at: focus and your professional identity.

You see, although Houdini loved all aspects of magic. He also loved being the most famous magician of his age. For much of his life, he wasn't the best magician or biggest name in magic. Howard Thurston's show was bigger and better known for many years. Maskelyne & Devant were much bigger in London.

Early in his career, Houdini struggled. He started out going from tavern to tavern with his sister and a beat up sub-trunk, performing *Metamorphosis* for tips, trying to break into the big time. Later, he put together a show with all kinds of magic. I imagine many of you have seen his "King of Cards," poster...and yet he was never really famous as a great card magician. What we all know Houdini for was his escapes.

Houdini paid attention to his audiences and to his press. He understood the importance of building his name, and he noticed that the thing which got the biggest response from audiences was his handcuff escapes. This also happened to be an aspect of his show that was not a big part of other magicians' repertoire at the time he started doing it. It was something that he could, as they say, "own."

Houdini stopped billing himself as just another magician, and started building the myth that he was "The

Handcuff King." He focused on the theme that "no cuffs can hold him," and later expanded that to different kinds of escapes. He turned his whole life into theater, accepting outlandish challenges and delivering stunning public spectacles of his escapes everywhere he went.

The theme caught the popular imagination, and Houdini worked it for all it was worth. Did it mean that Houdini stopped doing magic in his shows? Not at all. In fact, although the handcuff and escape magic was the thing he banked on to set him apart from his competition, it was never the largest part of his shows. He continued to love magic in all its forms, and to perform them. The celebrity he earned through that laser-like focus on maintaining his title as handcuff king and master of escapes bought him the ability to experiment with illusions, close-up magic... and even in the early days of film.

So what is the take-away lesson from all this? I think it is to pay attention to your audiences. What do you do that gets the most positive response? What is the one part of your show you get asked about the most? What do reporters tend to focus on when they cover your shows? Once you have figured that out...spend some time and think of how you can "spin" that thing into a phrase that will be your hook, in the same way that "handcuff king," was for Houdini, or "The Man Who Knows" was for Alexander, or "Master of Masks & Magic" for Jeff McBride. Then focus all your marketing around this new identity. You'll find you can probably continue to do much of the magic you are currently doing – but refocus its presentation to fit the new theme. Who knows...you might well become the next Houdini!

Sam Sharpe -- Classifying Magicians

S.H. Sharpe was one of our great inspirational writers on magic, and especially on the artistry and poetry of magic. He was deeply concerned that magicians learn to treat their art with the same kind of respect that other artists do. In one of his books, *Neomagic - Artistry,* he discusses different roles that those involved in magic might take up. Sharpe's descriptions included the following (the following is paraphrased):

Originators – who create (and often perform) new works of magical artistry. They may or may not actually invent new techniques, but they do create new works. An example might be with Jeff McBride, who took existing principles and techniques already in use in magic, and applied them to magic with masks, thus creating a whole new kind of magical performance.

A second category would be that of **Inventors** – these are those wonderful folks who actually come up with new ways of creating magical effects. For example, once upon a time the only kind of magic with some cups and a ball relied on sleight of hand and misdirection. Some great magic ensued. Then someone invented the chop-cup. A magical device that vastly increased what could be done with just a cup and a ball. A new technique upon which many creators have built even more amazing magic pieces.

And then we have the **Manufacturers** – those who actually manufacture and distribute the works of the inventors and creators. These range from the Johnny Gaughan's and Bill Smith's who build large stage illusions, to those like Alan Wong who we work with to arrange for the manufacture of many of Jeff McBride's creations. In a mostly secret art, it can be difficult to find competent craftsmen who fully understand what it takes to manufacture the props and gimmicks conjurers rely upon in order to create their magic.

Next we get to the **Performers**, who Sharpe terms "The Executive Conjurer." If an Originator is analogous to the playwright or screen writer, the Executive Conjurer is like the Actor. He or she is the one to step in front of the audience and present the magical performance – using the products invented, created and manufactured by the others we've already discussed. There are many magicians who adopt this role – with or without also being creators, inventors or manufacturers. This is, I think, especially true in the world of amateur conjuring. One of the ways of moving up in the ranks of magic is to add the abilities of creator or inventor to one's repertoire.

Next, there is the **Producer** – a category I would fall into myself, more than the others. This category includes supplying the "third eye" of the director who helps the Originator and Executive Conjuror mold their work into a convincing and emotionally satisfying show. It also includes all the functions of getting that performance in front of an audience: the staging, lighting, surrounding framework of set, lights, sound, etc. It includes the art of generating publicity, advertising, and balancing the accounts so that the show produced will actually form the basis of a successful business. Sharpe comments that this is the area where magical artists are most likely to fall short...largely, I think, because it is such a large and little understood subject. For me, it has been a greatly rewarding role in magic – I get to be the one standing in the back of the auditorium who sees both the performance and the audience's reaction, and to know just what I've been able to contribute to the overall experience, even though my clients get most of the credit!

Finally, Sharpe talks about what he terms to be The Critic. A dangerous term, I think, because it makes us think of negative criticism. What he means by the term, though, includes the enthusiastic audience, the aficionado, the fan... all those who truly appreciate experiencing the art of magic from the non-performer's point of view.

Most of you reading this, I suspect, fall into more than one of Sharpe's "types."

Of course, there are many different ways to think

about types of magicians. Jeff McBride is fond of using his Trickster, Sorcerer, Oracle and Sage terminology. Someone else might use Shaman, Alchemist, Mystic and Technologist. Whatever categories make sense to you... I think what is important is that each of us, if we're at all serious about our work as magicians, take the time to think about just what kind of magician we want to be. What are your personal proclivities? Strengths? Weaknesses? When you're doing work in different areas of magic, which ones get you most enthused? What parts do you love, hate or feel indifferent to?

I hope you'll take a few minutes, perhaps with a piece of paper in front of you, to sit and consider for yourself, "What kind of magician do I want to be?" Write down the things you love, don't love, etc. What are your favorite moments when you perform? Do you enjoy designing and making your own props? Figuring out new techniques? Making audiences laugh? What really floats your boat in the world of magic?

And, once you've done that... what will you choose to do with it? Remember, focus is power, and this can help you hone in and focus on the things in magic which will help make it a more exciting profession or pastime for yourself and those with whom you share it.

DaiVernon

Let's take a few minutes to consider The Professor — Dai Vernon. I must confess, I don't know a lot about Vernon. Oh, I knew he was a great mentor/ teacher for many top magicians, and spent his last years at the Magic Castle. I know there are some great books and videos of his material, but I was never clear about what kind of a career he had or the kinds of places where he worked. So I did a quick bit of research online, and found out that for much of his career, Vernon wasn't actually able to make a living as a magician. Instead, he worked cutting silhouettes and selling them for 50 cents apiece, or as an inspector in the construction business. During these years, Vernon continued to study and practice his magic, and became one of the foremost experts on many areas of close-up and small stage magic.

Not long ago, we made "Diversity" the subject of one of our Monday night shows, and I mentioned then that there was a great diversity of roles a magician could take. Vernon is a good example of one of the greats who took on the roles of researcher and teacher and excelled in those roles just as much as he did in the role of performing magician.

There are many today who make similar large contributions to our art, without being headliners, or big name performers, themselves. Some never perform for the public at all. There are builders – the Johnny Gaughans and Bill Smiths of the world, who the general public might never hear of, but without whom the great illusion shows of our time could never have taken place. There are philosophers and trick inventors and writers, people like our friend Bob Neale, who strongly influence many top performers, but are seldom seen performing themselves... and many more.

I know I've been sitting with Jeff McBride or other friends at some of the major conventions over the years, and had someone completely unknown to me come up and show us a new trick they've created that completely fools us both. Come to find out, they don't perform a lot outside of their magic clubs – members of the general public never hear their names — but they soon become "underground legends" among other magicians.

So, if you love magic and work hard at perfecting your own special area of the art, but have no ambitions toward building a career as a performer, that's okay. Even if you've tried performing and it hasn't worked out for you, don't despair! By pursuing your passion fully, putting in the time to learn and perfect your work, you, too, stand a chance of making a real contribution.

Dai Vernon spent his later years performing and teaching at The Magic Castle, building the legend that has come down to us, and positively influencing a whole generation of great performers. His contribution to our art was huge — probably larger, in the long run, than many of the better known "headliner" magicians of his time.

So, remember – there are many kinds of success in the world of magic. Choose the ones that suit you and your personal talents best, and pursue those with all the dedication, enthusiasm and hard work that Vernon did. You, too, may well be remembered as making major contributions to the art of magic!

Harry Blackstone

One of the great illusions the Blackstones (both Harry Sr. And Jr.) were known for was The Floating Lightbulb.

Why, one wonders, did this particular effect catch the public's attention so vividly? Other magicians did magic with light bulbs. Others floated objects – Okito's ball comes to mind as one elegant and beautiful example. But somehow, Blackstone's floating lightbulb struck a chord that the others lacked.

First, I think, we must realize the effect was never simply a lightbulb that floated. This lightbulb lit itself, impossibly, without any connection to battery or chords. It appeared to light up by magic itself! That being the case, the presentation of the lightbulb had a built-in dramatic enhancer – a logical reason for the lowering of the theater lights. It was necessarily presented in a dramatic half-light – a sort of magical twilight, if you will. When Blackstone Sr. first presented the effect, the very fact of electric light was still in its infancy, and therefore still seemed a bit magical in and of itself. Apparently Thomas Edison himself built Blackstone's first floating bulb, now in the collection at the Smithsonian Institute. So the effect used an object everyone knew as familiar...but which was still new enough to hold a bit of mystery for them. And of course, everyone knew that a lightbulb had to be connected to the electric mains in order to light, so the lighting of the unconnected bulb and subsequent darkening of the theater created a very strong magical moment in and of itself.

Blackstone built upon that moment by first floating the bulb before him...close in to his body. He was building the drama. First a light, then one that lit itself, and now one that floated in space all the while lighting itself!

Then, to provide a change of pace and take away any element of "I know how that's done," he would move into the audience and hand the bulb to an audience member to examine. Nothing to find! This interlude over, he would return to the stage...and remember that only one audience member had been able to see the bulb up close — and so then he would float it once again, but this time out over the heads of the audience and up towards those in the balcony. The bulb would slowly return to him, passing through a small hoop on its way. Impossible. He would take the lightbulb as it arrived, along his standing ovation, as the stage lights returned.

Blackstone's Floating Lightbulb was a beautifully crafted bit of theater which took full advantage of so many of the tools and tricks a theatrical presentation can provide. From the use of the familiar but exotic prop, to the fact that it was, in fact "a light in the darkness" – a powerful symbol – to the way he built the piece, one effect atop another, to the grand climax of the lighted bulb floating out over the upturned faces of his rapt audience, and then, upon his command, returning to his hand. Brilliant magic, brilliant showmanship – and that is why the name Blackstone is still remembered with such reverence today.

Creating Material

Those of us who make our living through magic know that if we want to succeed beyond a certain level, we need to establish ourselves with unique material. We need to be creative - and that can be daunting. Many have convinced themselves that "I'm not the creative type." Fortunately, that's not true, and if you're thinking otherwise, it's time to change that thinking.

The following pieces are all about ways you can bolster your own creativity. I'll discuss what it means to be creative and provide a number of techniques you can use that are guaranteed to help you create magic that is original and that uniquely fits you. Beyond that, I talk about how you can use the impetus of having to create for a particular situation to help you come up with more ideas for building your own magical stories and pieces. Creativity and imagination are mental muscles, and just as with your other muscles, the more you use them, the stronger they'll get and the better you'll feel. Conversely - the less you use them, the more they'll fade away.

So, by all means - please try the things I've recommended below, and create something new every day. That's the way to assure you continue to grow and become more, not less, creative as you grow older.

Artistry

I have a question for you: What is the difference between an artist and a craftsman? Both might have great skill. Both work at their "craft," as it were. Coming from the world of the theater, I found many actors who were proud to think of themselves as fine craftsmen. What are your feelings about that?

For me, at least, the difference is that the artist has something to say. A good artist is also a good craftsman. The craft is the means by which they express their vision.

But you can be a very good craftsman without ever becoming a real artist. If you never discover your own vision, your own mission, your own stories — chances are you may never breakthrough and become a true artist.

In some ways, the artist is to the craftsman just what the wizard is to the rest of us. Where the craftsman is content to go from making one thing on to the next — whether those things are wooden cabinets, jewelry, a role in a play or movie, a piece of magic — the Artist has a need to express something. Something uniquely their own, about which they feel a great passion. It is, therefore, the artist who creates great performance pieces with their magic – some of which get released to the community of craftsmen so they can enjoy performing them, and spread the beauty of that work of art, created by the artist, to a larger audience.

There is no shame in being a craftsman. Skilled craftsmen keep our world going. But it is the artists who move it forward. In a like manner, there is no shame in living a good, mundane life well. Only a minority are called to be true artists — or true wizards. But it is the artists and the wizards who move the world forward, who inspire the rest, and who get to determine where we are all going. I suppose that's why I've never been particularly interested in working with performers who aspire only to becoming good craftsmen. I do respect them and their work, but it doesn't excite me to work with them. And I do believe most performers do have the ability to move into the world of true artistry. That's why I wrote my book "Beyond Deception," why I work with Jeff McBride and the faculty of the Magic & Mystery School, and why I continue to conduct workshops and write books — to inspire those of you who might be "on the fence" about making the leap into true artistry, and to help you to develop your vision and discover your real passion.

Alternative Views

One of the things that makes real wizards the wizards that they are is their ability to see things from several different points of view. When you can look at situations from more than one perspective, you can often see solutions to problems where others do not.

I love the story often told of two English shoe salesmen in the early part of the last century. Their different shoe companies sent each one to one of the emerging countries in Africa.

The first salesman got to the country and noticed that none of the local tribesmen wore shoes. He immediately cabled the main office: "Situation hopeless. No one here wears shoes."

The second salesman arrived about the same time, and to the same situation. His telegram home had a bit of a different tone, though: "Hallelujah! Situation most promising – no one here has any shoes yet, and there is no competition!"

Two men in the same business, facing the same situation – one took the standard point of view: "Look at the current level of demand, look at your competition, and assess your ability to take away their market share." He saw no market and no competition – and passed up a huge opportunity. The second man saw an infinite potential market, a way of turning it into a real market, and went on to create a hugely successful new business.

Steve Jobs operated in a similar manner. While his competitors in the high tech industry engaged in endless focus groups, marketing research and the like, Jobs said, essentially:

"Why would I ask them what they want? They don't know what they want until we show it to them."

Jobs had a vision – and alternative point of view – about

how to create products that consumers would want.

So: Here is your exercise. Pick a small problem from your life that needs a solution. Perhaps you're having problem with cash flow, or a conflict with a co-worker or family member. Maybe you're involved in a creative project, and are facing some kind of obstacle that is blocking it's completion. This will be something different for each one of you.

Whatever the problem, take a few minutes and get a blank page in front of you. First, define the problem as you see it. Be as brief as possible: Write one paragraph if possible, three at most. After you write it out, go back and make it shorter. This should only take a few moments. Read through what you've written.

Now, imagine the problem from someone else's point of view. If you're problem is a conflict with another person, put yourself in their place and write about the problem they are having with you. Really make an effort to see things from their point of view. Chances are you know more about that than you are at first willing to admit to yourself. Writing it out will help you get a sense of just where they are coming from.

After writing the problem out from the other person's point of view, add one sentence, that begins this way: "If only Tobias (or your name) would... whatever it is they think you should do to resolve things, everything would be better." Write it and forget it.

Now, write a third telling of the problem, from the point of view of someone completely outside the problem. Maybe this third party is compassionate towards you and the problem. Maybe they want to mock you. Maybe they are in the position of mentor or arbitrator, and are just waiting for you to wake up and see the problem they can see so clearly. Or perhaps they are, somehow, helpless bystanders – affected by however you resolve the problem, but feeling helpless to influence that outcome.

Whoever you choose: Now write up the problem as viewed by that person.

You can take this exercise in different directions. Write it up from the point of view of an inanimate object which is involved in the situation, as though that object were somehow aware and able to think for itself. How does the chair feel about this? The salt-shaker?

Try describing the exact situation you are seeing as a problem, as an opportunity, instead. What changes?

Finally: Have a look at the problem through time. Go back to a time before it arose, and see how it developed. Try looking back on the problem from a time months in the future...after it has been resolved or forgotten.

When working with performers on new performance pieces, one of my favorite tools is to write up an account of the piece as though written by an audience member who has experienced it. How were they transformed? What did they love? What moments really worked, or failed, for them? What was their big "take away." And that helps me create a piece that will be more effective for that audience.

All of these different viewpoints will give you insights into whatever you've chosen to apply them to, and will give you at least a taste of the power you can gain by examining things from alternative perspectives. I hope you'll play with this idea over the coming weeks, and will discover it's power for yourself.

Faces of the Magician

Trickster, Sorcerer, Oracle, Sage. Sometimes we like to see these as a sort of "stages in the life" of a magician, but I don't think that's always necessarily true. There's no reason one person can't play all the roles within the course of a single performance or even within the course of a single trick. Although it's easy to see ourselves passing through the roles at various stages of our lives, I don't believe we all do so in any particular order – with the possible exception of sage, which requires a certain experience of life that may be less necessary for the other roles.

We haven't the time to go into a lot of depth with this here, but let's just look at one creative aspect the idea of the four archetypes might open up for you, and little exercise you can do with them that is likely to spark your creative impulses.

First – sit and write the four names down the side of a single piece of paper: Trickster, Sorcerer, Oracle and Sage. Think about yourself in each role. How would you be as a trickster? How would you hold yourself, speak, express yourself? How would you interact with others. Write that all down in just a few words. Then move on: Sorcerer. If you were the Sorcerer, what would that mean? How would you move, stand, speak and relate to others? What would motivate you to perform? Do this for all four roles.

Now pick a trick. Let's say the trick is a simple one... perhaps The Ambitious Card, in which one selected card, placed into the center of a deck, rises to the top. The effect is typically repeated several times, gaining in impact each time. How would your Trickster character perform the trick? A trickster delights in fooling you, and this trick seems ready made for that. "Betcha think it's in the middle where you just saw me put it, don'tcha? But NO...here it is on top. Watch me more carefully this time." You get the idea. The trickster's message is often "the world is not as you think it is," or, "look how easily you are fooled!"

How would your Sorcerer character perform the same trick? It is important for the sorcerer to demonstrate their magical power and prowess, so the trick might well take on a different tone. The sorcerer might say, "For most people, things tend to stay where they've been put. For example this card. Place it here in the center of the deck.

Please help me by pushing it in flush, perfectly lost. Now, for you, for example, that card will stay right there in the center until you go in and physically move it. (That's were you show the card is NOT at the top of the deck) Not for a magician, though. I just give a wave of my hand, utter the secret word, snap my fingers and, voila – the card rises to the top. You might imagine that to be just a trick so I'll do it again." Where the trickster shares 'a trick,' the sorcerer uses his 'powers' to make the effect take place. How would your version of the sorcerer do that?

Let's move on to the Oracle. Oracles predict the future, read minds... they are empaths and seers. So how would you convert the same effect and present it as your Oracle character? A bit tougher, as the trick doesn't include, on the surface, any of those things an oracle does. Still, there may be a way. I once performed a similar trick as part of a tarot reading: "The cards actually seem to arrange themselves according to who they are working for. For example, in doing a reading, I might shuffle the deck, rest my hand on it a moment while asking "who am I," and then take the top card it has given me to represent myself for the reading...ah, a King of Hearts. I replace the card. However, when YOU hold your hand atop that same deck.... then turn the card...it's the Queen of Diamonds! And it doesn't matter if we put your Queen somewhere else into the deck. Just hold your hand atop the deck for a moment, thinking "who am I?" And now...turn over the card." It is the Queen of Diamonds. "See what I mean? The cards know you!" Now the trick has quite a different flavor, don't you think?

And then there is the Sage. Sages share their wisdom. They've learned a great deal, and often use stories to pass on the wisdom they've gained. So in the hands of the Sage, perhaps this becomes a story trick. "You know, when I was younger, I had the terrible habit of smoking cigarettes. I knew they were bad for me. I knew other people found them obnoxious. I must have quit a dozen times. I would tell myself, "No more," and toss away my pack of cigarettes — or more likely hide them away where I wouldn't have to see them. Like this (places card into the deck). But you know, that was the wrong approach. I thought I was quitting cigarettes, and thought that thought in just those words, "I'm quitting cigarettes," many times a day. The universe works in funny ways though, and every time I thought the word "cigarette" it was as though my mind was calling them into being. I'd go to lunch, and there would be that pack I thought I'd tossed away. Lying out, right in front of me! I would hide it away again, and a few minutes later glance at someone over at the next table. They would be enjoying a cigarette after lunch, and when I looked back, that pack of cigarettes would be right there in front of me again — right on top of the table! Eventually I'd break down and have a smoke. Obviously the universe had decreed I should be a smoker.

And then I met someone and they gave me the secret – don't think of quitting smoking. Every time you say the word "smoking" or "cigarettes" in your mind, your mind will call those things into being for you...even if you've put the word "not" in front of the word you're trying to leave behind. Instead, train yourself to say the thing you want to gain by not smoking. Instead of "I'm not smoking," tell yourself "Im growing healthier every day." And before you know it, instead of that pack of cigarettes appearing before you all the time, an image of health and well being will be the thing which continually presents itself to you, no matter how many times you cast it aside. And that's the key."

I hope you can now see how you can use these archetypes to help you create your own, personalized presentation for tricks you already know, or for new ones you are developing. The examples I gave were very simple, staying in the same archetypal character for the entire presentation. You don't have to remain "within" a single archetype for a whole trick presentation. It can be fun to arbitrarily "let your oracle out" for a few moments, then go back to being whatever your main mode is. Sometimes a trick can be a story with characters who fit the different archetypes, as well.

I'm suggest you take a simple trick you already perform, and create a presentation for that trick in each of the different modes. See what you come up with! And don't forget to have fun with it!

Audience Participation

Magic is a very special kind of theater. All theater is made up of performances before live audience. That's one definition of what makes it theater in the first place. But that relationship can take many different forms. In what we think of today as traditional theater (think of that Tennessee Williams play your local high school or community theater just put on) the relationship is something we call 'representational' theater. Although actors are aware of the audience and do respond to them on some level, there is an understood, invisible '4th wall,' which separates the audience from the action on the stage. The experience is a bit voyeuristic, as though we are peering into a box where these people live and interact, but they cannot see us, the audience. This kind of theater tends to be naturalistic, and to 'represent' real life.

In a different version of the audience relationship, we find 'presentational' theater. In this type, there is action on the stage portraying a story, but the actors are much more likely to turn and acknowledge the audience. Some Broadway musicals, comedia del'arte plays, and many forms of comedy fit into this category. It is characterized by characters who, at any given moment, might do a take to the audience, so the audience can share their reactions, but other characters in the play behave as though they don't see the take. There is a dual thing going on. That imaginary fourth wall gets broken, and the experience is a different one for all involved, but only for part of the time.

Stand up comedy and magic are extreme forms of this presentational style of theatrical experience. I think of them as 'participational' forms of theater. In these forms, we, the audience, are equal characters in the story of the evening's entertainment. While the characters in a Tennessee Williams or David Mamet play act on one another, in magic and stand-up comedy, the audience is just as much a part of the action as those characters. We laugh, or not - and our responses become part of the story. We ooh and ah at the magician's feats, or not. As often as not, in magic, the performer will actually invite an audience member to interact directly with the magician on stage. This is a very different experience from that of the presentational theater. Instead of playing out a story in front of an audience, we are involving them as characters in that story.

Now, story is an extremely powerful concept. It is the way our minds make sense of our world, and all performances, even circus acrobatics, have stories. (I know, you've heard this from me before. I repeat it often because it is so important.) The story of the act is what an audience member would relate to a friend about the act after the fact. "First she took out these three rings (or whatever your props are). Then she explained how A, B & C worked. And then she came into the audience and..." you get the idea. Even magicians who insist they are *not* storytellers, are creating stories. The question is – what kind of stories are you creating in the minds and memories of your audiences?

Sometimes the story the magician experiences is not the same story that the volunteer experiences, and is yet again different from what the audience experiences. Sometimes audiences viewing a performance from different angles might have different experiences. As the performer – you are responsible for all these stories. The different participants don't have to have the same stories when it's all over – but they should have all good stories... stories in which they got to have interesting experiences, witness interesting things, and feel entertained.

When you use a volunteer, or ask an audience to participate in some way, what kind of story are you creating for them? Have you considered it? I would urge you to sit down and write out the story of your favorite pieces from a volunteer's point of view, and from your audience's point of view. What sort of experience does each of them have? How will they tell the story of that experience? Once you've written that all out — are these stories you would LIKE to have them tell? If not, what do you need to change?

Brainstorming - Creating New Material

A lot of my first book, "Beyond Deception" is about ways of creating with new material and making it more entertaining.

I've read in business books that any company's main job is innovation. Innovate in production. Innovate in marketing. Innovate in the ways you work with your team. Innovate in ways to handle your finances. We live in a fast moving, fast changing world. Those who fail to change, fail to create, or do so too slowly, are rapidly being left behind.

Remember Woolworth's? Remember Atari? Remember Montgomery Ward? Pan Am? Eastern Airlines? TWA? Digital Equipment? American Motors? These were all huge companies when I was young... and they're all gone. All for the same reason. Markets are still there for all their products, now being sold by Virgin America, Walmart, Amazon, Apple, and others who either came later or continued to innovate and change, while these giants failed to see the need to innovate. It's the same with magic and our other performing arts.

So, you must innovate today if you are to survive... but how? Many of us think "I'm not the creative type." In fact, though, you must have at least some creativity, or you couldn't function in the world. If a street you use everyday is closed one day, you find a way around it and still make it to work. Anytime something you expect to be some way suddenly changes, you find a way to get by with the new way of things. This is being creative. What many of us fail at is being creative without first experiencing the discomfort of having our current way of doing things turned upside down.

So one way of inspiring yourself is to pretend that some aspect of your world has been taken away. Did you learn a particular magic trick using coins? Suppose you visit a culture where they have no coins. Would you give up that effect, or find a way to do it with some other kind of prop? Seashells, buttons, poker chips... whatever. And what would the significance of that change of props mean to the piece you performed?

Or suppose you use a particular story as part of one of your performance pieces. Let's say it is about a popular celebrity, but that celebrity dies unexpectedly in highly uncharacteristic circumstances, and so telling the story you have been using would suddenly be inappropriate. What would you do? If you substitute another lead character what would be gained or lost? How else would the story change with another character at its center? As you answer these questions, you are exercising your own creativity.

Or suppose you're a stage illusionist invited to appear on television, and you must perform in a very small studio where your illusion props and assistants would never fit. Can you translate your favorite large illusion – that showstopper that has become your signature piece – into something that can be performed on a tabletop before an audience of 10 people in a TV studio? Sometimes this process of translating very large effects into miniature versions of themselves, or translating close-up magic for the large stage, can be a way of discovering new and exciting performance magic. I remember a few years ago seeing — I think it was The Gamesters — do a stage illusion based on the cups and balls. For cups, they used oil drums, and for balls, dancers. It was fun!

What else might you remove, in your imagination? Imagine you could no longer walk. What would that change about your performances? Or that you have lost your voice, and must perform without speaking. What changes would that force you to make?

These are exercises of the imagination, and doing them will strengthen your creative muscles. You may never have to face these loss situations in real life – but by pretending they have happened, you can force yourself into that creative mindset you might otherwise have left sleeping.

There is a saying that geniuses don't necessarily have better ideas than the rest of us, they just manage to have more ideas. If one out of a hundred ideas is good, and you only have 90 ideas, you're unlikely to have a lot of good ones. However, if the ratio is one in a hundred and you manage to generate several hundred new ideas every week, you're very likely to have a few good ones!

If you're afraid of having bad ideas, you won't have lot of ideas, and very, very few good ones. But if you use techniques like the one I described above to help yourself generate lots of ideas, including many that will be bad, you'll have a much better chance of generating a few great ones.

Character Development

I suspect some of you find the subject of character development to be fascinating, because you've always wanted to "do characters." There's more to it than that, though.

Like it or not, each time you step on stage, your audiences see a character. Far more than in everyday living, they expect that character to have a certain consistency. When you do something they don't feel fits the persona they think they see, it registers as false. As phony. And as magicians, whose every other action is phony, but must not seem so, that can be deadly.

There is another thing about characters onstage. Have you ever seen the jokes about actors who continually ask "but what is my motivation?" It is practically a cliché in the world of acting, but one born out of a certain artistic truth. Watching a dramatic piece – and make no mistake, any time you're in front of an audience you are part of a drama, a piece of theater — we expect to be able to understand the story of what's going on. We also have a right to expect that it will be an interesting story. The way stories become interesting, and dramatic, is through conflict. And conflict arises out of different characters whose inner motivations are at cross purposes. So that "What's my motivation?" becomes an important question.

Take a popular movie. In Star Wars, for example, Luke wants the Empire to leave the independent planets their freedom – and Darth Vader wants the Empire to rule everything. A big cross purpose. Han Solo wants Princess Leah as his sweet heart – and perhaps Luke, not knowing she is his sister – wants the same thing. Another conflict of underlying desires, all fully suited to the characters who have them, but working against one another. And it is through the working out of those conflicts that the story develops. If one of the characters starts playing out a desire we can't imagine that player actually having, the story loses credibility.

So, as a magician performing on stage, one of your prime considerations must be to make sure your actions are always motivated. "Why does this character (me) pick up this object? Why do I put it there? What am I trying to accomplish by that action? Is there a way I can add a sense of conflict to that action? If I have a desire that the action is carrying out, then who, or what, might have a different underlying desire? How can we use that to create drama?

Character work can be difficult to do on your own. Much of what might be jarring for an audience are things you won't see yourself. They are part of your own everyday character and don't feel wrong at all to you, but a good director, can easily spot incongruous, inconsistent or otherwise 'out of character' moments, and help you discover ways of resolving them. Sometimes the creative solutions you come up with to these moments can take your magic to whole new levels.

I've seen some miraculous transformations using this approach — magicians who took hackneyed pieces they had performed for some time, and turned them into beautiful and moving works of art. If you're willing to put in the work, you can do it, too!

Costumes

I remember the first day of costume design course when I was in grad school. The teacher put on a slide show. We had to look at photos of various people...much like this (show slide montage)...and tell her as much as we could about each person shown, just from looking at them. We were amazed at how much we could know about a person just based on what he or she was wearing.

We could often even tell what their jobs were. Waiter, bank teller, professor, lawyer, doctor, Mom...magician! And magician...and magician. Looking at these...you almost know what the show is going to be like before they ever pick up a prop or utter a word, don't you?

What we wear sends messages to our audiences – and to ourselves – and those messages are loud and clear, even when we're not conscious of them. So what do your costumes say about you? When they see you, will your audience expect simplistic children's magic, filled with site gags, or sophisticated, poetic magic? Will they see you as friendly and open, or mysterious and a little frightening? Have you thought seriously about how you want them to see you?

The clothes you choose send one message, and the way you take care of them and wear them also sends a message. Are they frayed and in need of laundering and repair? We'll expect sloppy magic, maybe a clownish or 'street style' performance. Or are they carefully cared for, regularly laundered and pressed, thus sending a message that we can expect a controlled and meticulous performance?

As a magical performer, your primary job is to give your audiences magical experiences. Your costume or costumes are a larger part of that experience than you might imagine. So here's my thought for you: make yourself a list of how you wish you and your act to be perceived. Are you, "a gentleman magician from the golden age, stylish and witty... a bon vivant you would be pleased to invite into your parlor to entertain your high society friends," or "just one of the guys... I hang out on the street, (or around campus), and I want those I perform for to feel I'm just like they are," or "I'm a mysterious wizard out of a fairy tale..." I think you get the picture.

Then do some research. Find artwork and photos of characters like the one you've described, and then begin designing your costume so it will send the message you really want to send. Use your costuming to send a message that will prime your audiences for the kind of experiences you intend to provide for them.

Designing Experiences

There's a cliché that it's important for an act to have a clear beginning, middle and end. Because this is so obvious, it would be easy to overlook its importance...and it's a principal that holds true not only for your performance in front of an audience but also in terms of your relationship with someone who hires you for a gig.

In fairy tales, which are for many of us the earliest stories we come to know – the experience often begins with "Once upon a time." This phrase serves to let us know that we are entering what I think of as 'story space,' an imaginary world where almost anything can happen. And those stories often end with that other stock phrase, "and they all lived happily ever after." On television, shows have their theme musical openings and closings, letting us know clearly when we enter and leave worlds they create.

I think this is just as important for a piece of magic. How does the opening for each of your magical pieces 'set the stage' for that particular piece? The opening line not only lets the audience know a new piece has begun, but sets up the tone and expectations for that piece. Will it be cerebral or silly? Comedic or terrifying? Are we to be participants or spectators? And the all important 'tag' line lets them know the piece is over – and often what they should think about it. "The moral of the story is...."

This is an easy enough concept as it relates to a show or a particular piece of magic – but I wonder if you've considered that your clients overall experience with you also has a beginning, middle and end. You're crafting of the overall experience they have with you can be almost as important as the experience of the show itself. When they first write you and e-mail or contact you on the phone, what is the first impression you give? Have you considered whether you want that experience to be formal, elegant, fun or zany? Which of these best fits the tone of what you offer them in your shows? Which one best suits your own personality? What is the first impression you give when you walk in the door at the party location, corporate event ballroom, or theater? Is it congruent with the overall experience you want the clients to remember when everything is over?

How about the end of your experience with the client? Does it end at the end of your performance? When you leave the venue? Or a few days later when they get a follow up thank you note? In each case, does the experience clearly wrap up the event and summarize it for the client in a way that fits with your intentions for that experience?

If you think about it, every interaction you have with the public is an experience – a show of sorts – which you can craft to suit your needs, intentions... and to deliver your personal message to the world. Remember – these are choices that others around you will experience whether you make them consciously or not, and if you don't make them consciously, the ones made accidentally may not convey the message you want them to – or lead to the results you desire.

Magic as a Designed Experience

When we do a trick or a show for someone, we're creating an experience for that person, and for ourselves. Experiences transform people. Sometime the change is small - we get them to smile, for example. Sometimes it is large. People have have been known to fall in love, or change their religion, for example, as the result of a single experience.

So your first step, if you're going to be creating an experience for someone, is to decide what do you want the experience to achieve. This is crucial, and failure to do so is the reason, if you're in business, that you attend so many awful meetings. No one thought to design the experience they wanted that meeting to provide. It is the reason we all have bad experiences with so called "customer service," and so on. So...to get started, choose an experience, and decide what you want it to achieve.

Experiences you might want to think about, if you are running a businesses, would include: The experience of a visit to my web-site. The experience of calling my business on the phone. The experience you have when you decide to make a purchase. In our personal lives, we also create experiences all the time. What experience will you create when you're introduced to someone new? What might you like that experience to achieve? In this case, your purpose will alter depending on the other person. With some it might just be "I want to make them go away," with others, "I really want to get them to stay as long as possible." Those are only two, somewhat oversimplified possibilities, of course.

Once you've chosen a purpose for the experience you want your magic to create, how will you go about designing it?

A good place to start is by thinking of the parts of that experience. All experiences have a beginning, middle and end. Sometimes it's better to think of more than three parts: A common way of thinking when creating a sales experience, for example, is the AIDAS formula. AIDAS is a acronym to help you remember the parts of the sales experience:

Attention: First you must get your prospect's attention

Interest: Attention alone isn't enough. You must now generate interest in what you want them to consider.

Desire: Once they are interested, how to make them really want what you're selling.

Action: This is the place most beginning sales people fail: You must ask the customer to take an action. Sometimes that means buying your product now – sometimes it is just agreeing to take another meeting with you. Really large sales seldom get made in just one meeting...and in those cases, the sales team will plan out the complete buying experience for the client, sometimes over a series of meetings that will go on over days or weeks, with separate goals for each successive meeting.

As a creator of shows, I'm accustomed to thinking of a show as having at least 5 parts: Exposition or Set-up, Rising Action, one or more crises and climaxes, an overall crisis and climax, and a denoument or wrap up that gives the experience a feeling of completion. If you think about that some, you may find that these stages aren't that different from the stages of a sales process. In fact...it doesn't hurt to think of ALL experiences you design as being a sort of sales process – it's just that sometimes the "sale" is only something like "I want to get this person to smile," or "I want her to agree to have dinner with me," rather than something involving a monetary transaction.

So we break down the experience we'll design into parts – and sometimes break those parts into smaller units. And then we define the purpose of each of those units, as each one can be thought of as an experience in itself. In a magic trick, the purpose of it's introduction might be just to get the audience's attention and interest. Another moment might be to make them understand what the props are or represent. Another might be to build up their sense of what is impossible about what is about to happen...or to build up an emotional charge around it by telling a story.

The purposes of each moment will, eventually, create an overall experience which will, if designed well, achieve the goal you've set for yourself with your audience.

Let's go one step further. We've talked about choosing a purpose and breaking up the overall experience you want to create into its constituent parts...but then what?

At some point you just have to dive in and start doing this. Here are some of the tools you might be able to use in order to design more effective experiences yourself:

Color. You can use color in order to "color" the emotions your experience will create and send messages about that experience.

Sound: Speech and music are the most obvious uses of sound...but there are others as well. The sound of tapping a coin on a glass, or riffling cards, for example. By all means consider the kind of sounds you will use to create your experiences. Animated, fast speech has a quite different effect from slow, measured speech, or from monotone speech. It's the same with music. A loud experience affects us differently from a quiet one.

Emotion: We create emotion partly through the attitude we convey — the feelings we have ourselves as we perform. But we can influence audience emotions even more powerfully through the use of stories. Human beings make sense of their world through stories, and the use of story in creating an experience can be a powerful tool.

Character: Every actor, director and writer knows the power of character to influence our feelings and actions. I recently watched the film Who Framed Roger Rabbit again with some friends. It was amazing to me how differently we responded to things that happened to the 'Toons' and things that actually happened to the 'real' human beings in the course of the film.

These are just a few of the thousands of things that can affect the way an experience might play out, and either succeed or fail in creating the response you want. I hope you'll have some fun playing with them – and others you that you come up with yourself – to begin consciously designing experiences yourself.

Oh...and remember, the first time you create one of these experiences you've designed, it may not play exactly as planned. Don't be disappointed if your carefully designed experience doesn't work out quite as planned the first time you run it. In life and in art, the design process never ends. Every experience can be improved somehow, and if we're careful to observe the effects the experiences we create have, we can make those adjustments and keep making things better: day by day and bit by bit.

Comedy & Magic

Comedy is a bit of an enigma. I remember taking a course on comedy when I was in graduate school, and reading quite a few books about the subject. I came away having learned a great deal, but with the conclusion that no one knows for sure what it is that determines whether something is funny or not.

If anyone ought to know what makes people laugh, you would think it would be standup comedians, and yet, they try out new material night after night in comedy clubs around the world, only to find that a large portion of what they try just doesn't work. What one person finds hysterical may just offend someone else, or leave a third with no reaction at all.

I suppose that's one of the reasons some teachers of public speaking steer their students away from comedy. It can be dangerous. You can just as easily lose an audience with a joke or story as you can win them over with something that makes them all laugh. One person can tell a joke and leave the room in stitches, while another telling the same joke can elicit blank stares. Even the same person telling the same joke can kill with it one night and bomb the next. Comedy is tough!

Still, the payoffs for truly funny performers can be huge. Acts like Dave Williamson, and Mac King are always in demand. Performers like Jerry Seinfeld, David Letterman and John Stewart build careers and become household names... but usually only after long, hard years of working out all the glitches in their acts, and honing their comic edge in front of thousands of audiences.

With that disclaimer, let me see if I can tell you a little bit about what is likely to make something funny to an audience.

One thing is incongruity. Punchlines to jokes are often exactly the opposite of the line you would expect in a story that's not a joke. They surprise us, and, if it's a good joke, delight us at the same time. We laugh.

Outright silliness can also elicit laughter. Think of John Cleese's "ministry of silly walks," or watch Jim Carey mugging his way through any one of his films. Silliness can be doubly funny when it is out of place... incongruous within a specific situation.

Embarrassment can be very funny, as well. Jeff McBride gives a talk about creating original magic (I've included it in the first volume of Beyond Deception), where he talks about "Embarrassment plus time equals comedy." As long as you're talking about your own embarrassing moment, or re-creating it for an audience, and not creating an embarrassing situation for one or more of them in the here and now, it's likely to be funny. This is the situation and source of merriment, I think, for the "Magic gone wrong" situation presented by so many successful comedy magicians.

The bottom line on all these sources of comedy, though, is, none of them can really be relied upon. Not every incongruity, not every embarrassing moment, can be made really funny. Only experimentation with comic material, only the fine tweaking that comes with performing it again and again, before audience after audience – and often failing -- can bring the comic act to a point where it reliably elicits the responses you want.

As I say, comedy is tough. If you don't come to it naturally, and don't have a real passion for making people laugh, it can be a dangerous path to travel. If you find yourself drawn to comedy in your magic, that's great. Just be aware you'll spend a lot of time with lots of little failures before you get to a point where you succeed regularly. The rewards can be huge, so don't be discouraged, but do be ready for all those little failures before you find that big success!

And know your territory. Watch movies about stand-up comics. Read their books, so you'll know about what you're in for, both highs and lows. And when you do succeed, be sure you take the time to enjoy it!

Halloween

As I write this it is mid-October, and I find my mind turning to Halloween – our spookiest of holidays, and one that comes at the end of what has become "national magic month," – at least for magicians.

Why do you suppose, it is that we think of Halloween as a 'most magical' holiday? It is, traditionally, 'the time when the veil between the worlds of living and dead is the thinnest,' and therefore the time when it is easiest for living humans and to communicate across that veil with spirits and other supernatural beings. That's magical, I suppose.

It is also a time when "guisers" - young people dressed in masks and disguises, would go "guising" or "souling," — telling poems or singing chants in hopes that householders would give them "soul cakes" – small baked treats made for the holiday. Often the guisers were poor, the householders were the rich. The tradition has come down to us today as "Trick or Treat," in which masked children knock on doors hoping for candy or other treats. It also seems to be the reason masks are associated with the holiday — and though most magicians don't perform with masks (some do, of course) we often associate the process of transforming ourselves through masks and disguises with magic.

For myself, I really think it is that 'thin veil between the spirt world and the mundane,' that causes us to associate the holiday with magic and magicians. Think of all those posters from the golden age of magic, with little demons sitting on the magician's shoulder, or ghosts hovering about the stage. Or go back even further, into medieval and renaissance texts on ceremonial magic, and you will see sorcerer's creating and enchanting their magical circles in order to call forth spirits and demons to do their bidding. Even today, a fair amount of even our mainstream magic makes use of stories about "haunted tables," and "spirit writing." Spirits are often the explanation we give for those "unseen" forces that make our magic happen... and so the holiday when it is supposedly easiest to contact those spirits is naturally associated with our magic & conjuring.

What does all this mean for you, as a performing magician — even if you never make a reference to ghosts, spirits, masks or the supernatural? For one thing, it provides you with a great opportunity for public relations. Halloween lies at the end of 'National Magic Month,' and that fact alone makes being a magician newsworthy. It also happens to be the birthday of Harry Houdini – and the day of his death. So if you can perform a piece of spooky or Houdini related magic that lasts only one or two minutes, and can handle yourself competently on camera – that may be enough for you to land a spot on your local morning TV show on Halloween. If you've learned two or three spooky mental tricks that will work by voice alone – you could be a special guest on your local radio stations. This kind of appearance is very much worth going for, even though it won't pay you a penny...at least right away.

By being a guest on these shows, you establish your credibility. If you are good and what you do on the shows is memorable, then they serve as free advertising. This kind of exposure is more effective than the advertising you could afford to pay for on those same stations, simply because, as a guest performer, you get the benefit of an unspoken endorsement by the station. Everyone knows that a paid advertisement is paid for, and therefore it doesn't carry any implied endorsement. So by all means – get those press releases ready, call your local news teams, and do whatever you can to take full advantage of Halloween, our most magical holiday!

Magic for the Holidays

As I write today, the end of December is coming on fast, it seems we all have holidays of one kind or another. Whether you celebrate Yule, Hanuka, Christmas, Kwanzaa, or just the New Year... there's something for just about everyone to celebrate.

But let's talk about something more than just a particular holiday. Let's talk about how you can take some piece of magic you already perform... an effect you already know and love, for which you've already mastered the mechanics, and turn it into something original just for the occasion, and something that is uniquely yours. Most of you have more than one of these, so let's pick one and create something new. Here's how.

Let's start by breaking the effect down into it's most generic parts.

First, what are the objects used? A deck of cards, a chop-cup, ball and a close-up mat. Three sponge balls. Make the list.

Next, what are the basic parts of the effect (not your current routine with the effect, but the effect itself). "A selected card rises to the top of the deck several times." is good. A description of the three different methods you use to make it happen is less helpful at this point. Break it down into a logical beginning, middle and end. "I show the deck and have a card selected. The card is placed in the middle of the deck. Then I do something mysterious, and it re-appears on top of the deck. I do it again. And then once again. I say my tag line and take a bow."

Good.

Next, pick a holiday. I'm going to use Christmas as my example, because its the one I know best. What associations do I have with that holiday? Is there music associated with it? In this case, there's lots of that, list your five favorite pieces of Christmas music. Then list five objects commonly associated with it (Evergreen trees, Christmas cards, candy canes, presents, reindeer...you get the idea). Is there a color scheme commonly associated with the holiday (red and green in this case). Are there particular messages that are associated with the holiday? (Love, gift giving, if you are Christian, the birth of Jesus, celebrating family, Santa Claus, candles, wreaths... what else?)

Can the action of the particular magic piece be associated with the message or action of the holiday? In this case, I'll chose gift giving and receiving. Can I have the selected card be something that represents a gift someone wants? Or a gift someone doesn't want (for example, a lump of coal). Can I build an interesting, touching or funny story around the action (in this case, the card / image returning again and again, no matter how hard we try to hide it?) Hey, look...I've just come up with a dramatic holiday story for The Ambitious Card!

What do I associate with this holiday that would fit that story? It might be a gift I don't want, but that people keep giving me. That eternal fruitcake that my aunt and uncle insist on sending every year, which I can't stand. Or maybe I'm trying to lose weight, but because of the holiday, everywhere I turn there are cookies, or candy. No matter how many times I hide that cookie card... there it is, right in front of me again!

Do you see how defining the central action of an effect can inspire dozens of different possible stories that get acted out through your presentation of that effect? By keeping all those different holiday themes and actions in mind, it's not too difficult to come up with associations that will work between different themes and your effects.

Finally, ask yourself "Can I change or decorate the props that are part of the trick to reflect the colors, objects common to this holiday?" Can you find "holiday" playing cards? Probably. Or maybe red and green backed cards, for Christmas? Are there games out there using cards that could be reinterpreted to fit your story? I remember a game from my youth called Candyland, in which many of the cards showed the image of a candy cane. I wonder if they might have been the same sized as a bridge sized deck of playing cards? H'm.

And so, you see, it's really not that difficult to take a theme, such as a those associated with a particular holiday, and to adapt magic you already know to fit the occasion. In many cases, you might find you've developed a piece that is stronger than what you had originally been doing. And once you've adapted a few pieces in this way, it will become easier and easier to be more creative, and to create that more meaningful, powerful magic whenever you want to do.

Building Creativity

I read a lot about systems for cranking up your own creativity. As a writer, director and coach, I need to keep my own creativity in good shape – and creativity is really like a muscle: the more you exercise it, the stronger it will get. But if you let it go and don't use it for awhile, it will grow flabby and start to waste away.

I've recently been working my way slowly through a terrific book on creative thinking techniques. You may have seen it: Michael Michalko's ThinkerToys. Even the title displays creativity! While there are lots of great techniques in the book, the best one I've come across yet, is also the simplest: It can be summed up simply, too: "Just do it!"

If you want to develop your creative muscles, do your creative exercises just like you would do if you wanted to build up any other muscle. If you want to build your biceps you find a series of arm exercises and do them every day or every other day. You repeat each one for a specific number of times, then go on to the next. It's the same with your creative muscles. Pick one or two exercises and do them every day.

Here's one way to live up to the 'Just do it' prescription:

Every morning before breakfast, sit down with a pad of paper. Force yourself to write down 10 original ideas before you're allowed to eat anything. They don't have to be great ideas, just original ones. They can be completely off the wall, or as useful as you can make them. Here's one way to make it easier at first:

Pick a theme. Depending on the kind of magic you do, this might be a party theme — Masked Ball, Pirate Party, Sweet 16 Party — it doesn't matter. If you're a corporate performer, pick a company and hypothetical product as your theme. Now think of two tricks you either already know how to do, or want to work on. Write down five different ways each trick might be made to fit the theme you've chosen. Go into as much detail as you can for each one. Now put away your pad and go enjoy your breakfast.

Here's what you'll find, if you're like most people. The first few days, this will seem like a struggle. Then it will get easier and easier. By the end of the month you'll have 150 new ideas for new presentations. Most of them will be awful.

Remember, there's nothing that says the ideas have to all be good ideas. Geniuses don't necessarily have better ideas than anyone else, but they have lots more ideas. Out of the 150, there might be 10 or more that ARE good. And that's 10 more than most of the magicians you know will ever have!

Remember, the more you exercise those creative muscles, the stronger they will get. Before you know it, you'll be creating amazing new pieces on a regular basis, just like my friends Jeff McBride & Marco Tempest do!

Improvisation

The ability to improvise is one that can be useful for any performer, and in several different ways. We use it when creating new material, or when we are presented with an unexpected situation which performing. Often, the training of a performer includes lots of exercises in improvisation.

The comedia dell'arte players of late medieval and early renaissance Italy are often referred to for their amazing improvisational theater works. And yet, they used a very structured kind of improvisation. The stories were outlines. The characters were stock... there were always a pair of lovers, a conniving servant, a greedy old man, and so on. Each actor in comedia specialized in one or two characters. Those characters were known for their lazzi, or set comic bits. Each one had a repertoire of character foibles and comic gags they could insert into different scenarios. Those bits were highly worked out and highly rehearsed over time. And so when a troupe wanted to do a new play, they would outline the story, then insert the different characters with their set bits into the story, and could very quickly put together a whole new entertainment piece, seemingly improvised. But it was actually made up of bits and pieces that had been around for a long time.

That's one level of improvisation, and one I think we can learn from. After a thousand or so performances, most magicians will have encountered most of the situations any particular piece of magic is likely to get them into... from audience members shouting out when they think they see you flash to the dubiously 'funny' comments hecklers might make. After each has happened several times, the performer thinks up the best possible response, which then appears to be improvised at the moment when that situation next happens in performance.

With better performers, these are original bits and responses. Be careful not to follow the path of the hacks, who just draw from the 'tried and true' lines you've all heard too many times, or from other performers' bits without their permission. In a like manner, you may have a large repertoire of set pieces at your disposal, which you can quickly assemble in different formats, with different introductions, to quickly create shows for different situations. You could (as some of our faculty do) even more or less improvise a whole show for a particular situation.

There's another level and use for improvisation, though, and that is to help you create and develop new material. This kind of improvisation is much like the play of children. One object can stand in for another. We can pretend to be different characters in different situations, and see what happens. One of my favorite improv exercises for magicians is to have them perform a piece they already know – in a completely different persona. How would Arnold Schwarzenegger's Terminator perform your favorite Ambitious Card routine? Try it out... improvise, and see what your version of Arnold would come up with. Or how would Britney Spears perform the same piece? A rap star? President Obama? It's fun to imagine these... but even more fun to actually improvise your way through them. This is one of those places where the actual experience 'in the body' usually far surpasses whatever you might be able to imagine.

Improvisation is one of the best ways to challenge ourselves move outside our normal comfort zones – and that's a place you want to be if you're serious about growing in your art. If you've read the first volume of Beyond Deception, you'll already know that I suggest many exercises and games for creating and improving your magical performances there. I also recommend a couple of other resources you might wish to check out – two books by a woman named Viola Spolin. One is Theater Games, and the other Improvisation for the Theater. Both are meant for training actors, but the activities they suggest will help you stretch and learn – and to develop new material, no matter what branch of the performing arts you're in. They are also great fun if you have a group — at a party or at a magic club — just as games. They will help you get to know yourself and your friends much better, very quickly.

I hope you'll try the exercise with the different characters performing your favorite routines. Have fun with them!

Innovation

I've read that the one real job of any corporation is innovation. We praise innovators, especially in the arts, but more and more in business, design and manufacturing. But what is innovation, really? On one hand it just means coming up with new stuff. But I think there is more to it.

I've encountered magicians who thought themselves innovative because they changed the color of their props from that of the most commonly marketed version. Or because they traded in their sponge bunnies for sponge squirrels, and added a line about "That's really been driving me nuts" at the end of the routine.

Innovations, yes — but without much depth. That's the kind of innovation people come up with when they are just seeking to be different, but don't have anything to say with their art beyond "Look at me. I'm cool." On the surface, there is a difference, but the basic piece of magic hasn't really changed. It continues to be done in the same situations, and with the same overall effect.

Another level of innovation comes into play when the magician weaves a piece of magic into a story he or she wants to tell, with the magic somehow enhancing the story... providing an illustration of the punch line or moral of the story. This kind of magic can be innovative in the same way a play or novel can. It takes a tool – the trick – that already exists, and uses it to create a new experience for the magician and their audiences. This approach can transform light entertainment into something that is both more personal and more effective.

When Jeff McBride created the original Mystery School, and more recently his Wonderground magic nightclub experience, that takes us to yet another level of innovation. In these instances, the artist is creating something bigger than just a single performance piece... or even a show. They are using magic to create a whole new kind of experience for their audiences. This is quite a leap, and one that takes us to new and deeper levels.

Another level or kind of creativity is the kind my friend Marco Tempest regularly uses: He combines forms not generally thought to go together. Marco started doing magic when he was very young, but he also had a great love of technology. Over the years he began doing magic with computer screens and video as the back-up, and combined the illusion techniques with the technology to create a whole new kind of magic. More recently, he has become fascinated with the power of story and ideas, and his latest works, like The Magic of Truth & Lies, told with three iPod's, and A Magical Tale and The Electric Rise and Fall of Nicola Tesla, all available for viewing on the TED.com site... actually seem to be exploring a new and exciting art form which transcends it's parts – it is bigger and has more depth than either the magic or technologies that it uses.

Well...here is the good news. You can innovate, too. We are all naturally creative, even though many of us have been convinced by others that we're not. Here's one way you can begin:

Choose three things that you love. Let's say performing magic is one of them. What else? Tennis? Swimming? Science fiction? Old Movies? Those are just a few of my passions...but what are yours? Make a list of at least three of them. Then figure out how to combine them. I've been talking of how Marco combines his love for magic, technology and story telling. If you're watching this, you know Jeff McBride's work, which combines his passions for sleight-of-hand magic with pantomime, masks and learning about other cultures. By combining your passions, you can come up with something that is just as uniquely your own as Jeff and Marco's work is for them. By the way... this works especially well when they don't seem like the different passions could go together... the harder you work at making them fit, the more likely the result is to be a real mind-blowing experience for all!

Now, go forth and innovate! And please try do more with it than changing the color of your sponge bunnies.

Magic Spells

When we think of witches and wizards, one of the first things that pops into mind might be that they use magic spells. What is a spell?

Websters defines it as "A verbal formula believed to have magical force." A magic word, like "Abracadabra" is a very short spell. "Abracdabra" translates as "It is created as it is spoken."

So, to cast a spell is to use a verbal incantation in order to influence events, or to gain power over something — or someone.

To be under a spell is to be enthralled or enchanted – controlled – by the power of the magician's spoken words.

Are spells real? Well... like all of magic, that really depends on your point of view and how you define them. A magical incantation is certainly one way of getting into contact with your own or someone else's subconscious mind. In a sense, every story we tell is a kind of spell, taking us into a magical world where everything is possible. Affirmations are kinds of spells... and so is a lot of marketing. Heard any interesting ads on the radio lately?

Whether or not we call them spells, it is certainly true that words have power. The words we use to describe ourselves to ourselves and others have a great deal of power to influence how we see ourselves, and how we are seen in the world. For that reason, in my workshops on building a magic business, we spend a considerable amount of time defining something we call an 'elevator pitch'. The term elevator pitch comes from Hollywood, where a scriptwriter might have a brilliant idea for a new movie or TV project, but needs to get it in front of a major producer or network executive before it can get funded or produced. The producers have very little time to meet with screenwriters pitching new projects, because there are hundreds — maybe thousands — of them out there. The only time a writer may actually get to talk with a producer is sometimes an accidental ride in an elevator. The time will be only 20 or 30 seconds. If the screenwriter hasn't distilled his pitch for his project into a compelling 20 seconds, he may be out of luck. But, if he has... well his film may be the next blockbuster.

So, that's where the term comes from. How is it useful to each one of us? If you're a magician, or anyone who has a product to sell, or who sells their services in any way, believe me, having a great elevator pitch will serve you well. You'll find you can use it when you meet someone at a party or business gathering to introduce yourself or your business. It can become the basis of a description on a web page or in a flyer. Some people actually put their elevator pitch on the back of their business cards, to help people they've given the card to know why they have that particular card.

What's more, by creating a great elevator pitch — one that makes you or your product sound great to whoever hears it, and by practicing that pitch aloud at least once a day, you'll succeed in selling the most important person you know on the contents of that pitch – that person, of course, being yourself!

I've been reading a lot about Mohandas Gandhi, the father of modern India...and one of my favorites of his quotes goes:

"A man is but the product of his thoughts; what he thinks, he becomes."

So, if you spend time each day thinking, "I'm an okay magician. My tricks aren't that good yet, but they're getting better," you'll always be "not that good, but always getting better." On the other hand, if you think, "I create miracles that help others transform and break through the barriers that keep them from their dreams!" well...that's who you'll soon become!

I urge you to spend some time writing your own magical spell – your personal elevator pitch – and to practice delivering it out loud several times a day. Make it a friendly commercial for yourself and your services. Tell yourself and others who you really are, what you really do, that makes you special. Don't be afraid to be different. You need not brag, but don't put yourself down, either. In the process of creating the script, you may well discover that you really are quite a special person. By rehearsing it aloud each day you'll find yourself growing more and more confident that this is the real you... and you'll be right!

Magic & Tragedy

When I saw this subject in our list of subjects for our Mystery School Monday show, I was a bit baffled. 'Magic and Tragedy,' is a rather strange subject, I must say. Tragedy, translated directly from the Greek, means "Goat Play," or "Song of the Billy Goat." Go figure.

If we go back to Aristotle, we find that there are some things that go into making a play a true tragedy. Among them are the hero or heroine's suffering, the fact that some trait they have (their "tragic flaw,") which they often see as a strength, is the very thing that brings about their tragic downfall and suffering. There must be an element of inevitability...and a fall from grace.

The point of tragedy is to affect a catharsis – which is a kind of climactic 'over the top' experience which cleans us out, emotionally speaking. By vicariously experiencing the suffering of the hero, we, the audience are somehow able to cleanse our own psyches, and, it would seem to follow, to avoid having that same experience ourselves. Greek tragedies are often driven by the will of the Gods — beings that are larger than life, and somehow beyond human. There is a certain magnitude of experience associated with tragedy, because small misfortunes don't have the juice to drive us all the way to catharsis.

Today, we often use the term tragedy to mean any sad story – but in fact, most sad stories fall more clearly under the heading of melodrama, or drama, and don't follow the fairly strict dictates of what constitutes a real tragedy – either in their structure or in their true effect on audiences. Bathos – deep sadness – is not catharsis.

All of which is to say, the subject of real tragedy is probably not one most performing magicians need worry about. There's not a big market for it, or even a clear understanding of it except amongst academics and aficionados of grand opera, and of Greek or Shakespearean theater.

Sad stories, are, on the other hand, very much possible in the realm of performing magic. One of the most moving pieces of magic I've experienced was by a magician named Mundaka – a long story told about himself and his partner, Tiko – a bird. The story was of their travels together, their adventures traveling from island to island, telling tales and performing for the locals. One night Tiko flies up into the trees... and then off into the sunset, never to return. Tiko has passed on, out of Mundaka's life, and he is left to mourn. We, the audience, mourn with him. His great love for Tiko made Tiko's passing sad for all of us. A sad story.

But wait... beneath that tree where Tiko had perched before flying off into the sun, Mundaka found a single feather — a souvenir by which he could always remember his friend. And sometimes, when he sits very quietly with the feather in his hand, he can still almost feel Tiko's presence. At this point in the performance, Mundaka sat in silence, holding the small feather lying on his outstretched palm. And, after a time... the feather twitched. Then it rose up and danced above his hand. We all felt chills run up and down our spines, tears began running down our cheeks. Tiko's spirit was in the room! Mundaka asked would we like to experience Tiko for ourselves? He moved around the audience, and the feather danced above each one of our hands.

That was 20 years ago, and I remember it like it was yesterday. Truly moving magic!

It was a sad and joyous story, and one made all the more so by the addition of magic. Almost any emotion we might experience in the theater can be enhanced, can be made both more real and more magical by the use of bits of magic. But only if all of the elements of great performance, of great story-telling, are incorporated. Only if you, as performer, are totally invested in the story yourself. If you don't care, if the story doesn't bring a tear to your eye – it won't work for the audience. If we see you faking it, the sad story becomes just another cheap trick, and that will not endear you to your audiences.

A Magician Prepares

The theme assigned that led to this article was a bit cryptic: "A Magician Prepares." When I first saw it in our schedule, I thought, "Prepares for What? A show? A career? His props? A script?"

However, the phrase echoes the name of one of the most influential books ever written on acting: An Actor Prepares, by Constantin Stanislavsky. This one book formed the foundation of what came to be known as "Method Acting," as taught at the famed Actors Studio in New York. "The Method" relied heavily on internal emotional work for the actor, based on the idea that if you could make yourself feel the emotions accurately and deeply, then you could express those emotions powerfully in your acting. Method training teaches techniques for accessing the emotions you have felt in your own life, while performing a character on stage or before a camera.

Stanislavsky never intended the internal work to be the whole of his system of acting. In fact he was horrified when students informed him later that it was being propagated as "The Method." Nevertheless, it became a standard for modern American actors, and is probably the basis for much of the great American film acting of the last half of the 20th century. Stanislavsky himself went on to write two more books on acting: Building a Character and Creating a Role, about the physical and analytical methods actors need to use to create their art. The three together give a very good overview of the actor's art, though Stanislavsky himself stated he never intended them to create a particular method, but rather as a chronicle of the experiments he and his students performed while learning their art.

If we are, as Jean Robert-Houdin put it, "actors playing the part of magicians," it stands to reason that it would be good to learn a bit about acting. Stanislavsky, the master teacher, seems a good place to start — especially if you take the trouble to read all his work.

First: That inner emotional work we need to do in order to learn to act "as if" what were happening while we were on stage, in character, was real. The point, you see, of developing an emotional technique for acting was so that actors could deliver consistently strong work night after night, whether the were visited by inspiration or not.

When audiences are paying top dollar to sit in the theater, the performer needs to be able to deliver a consistently high level of performance, no matter how he or she feels that evening. If you see live performance regularly, I'm sure you have had to sit through a few times when the performers just seemed to be "phoning it in." Having a strong emotional and physical technique, with a full analytical understanding of what you are performing, can help you avoid delivering that kind of second-rate performance.

The subject of acting and performance technique is, of course, too large to do more than outline in a short talk like this one. Actors study for years to develop their craftsmanship to a point where they are really ready to work professionally. And the great ones never stop working at it. But I'll try and at least point you in the right direction.

A good beginning is the three books I named above: An Actor Prepares, Building a Character and Creating a Role, all by Stanislavsky.

First, lets talk about the emotional techniques underpinning the performer's art. They include understanding action: what is the character's motivation at each moment they are performing? What do they want, expressed in verbs – actions? Then, how do they feel about what they want and how things are turning out? There are many ways of recapturing and expressing the feelings your character would express, but the best is to understand and "play" their motivated actions, and then react in a real manner to what is happening as a result. If your character really wants an audience member to change their mind about the card they've chosen, for example, how do you feel when that doesn't happen? (Take note here...I'm talking about the character you are playing as the magician/performer, not yourself as you are. If your routine is well constructed, it doesn't matter whether the audience member changes her mind or not, but it does matter to your character). If you're really "in the moment," you will respond in a real manner to whatever happens... and if you're really "in character," the response will be true and believable. If you're not, well, then the illusion of that character, of that moment, will be broken, as surely as being caught in a secret move or revealing a gaff will expose the magic illusion you're trying to create. The audience will experience that false moment, and the effect of your performance will be diminished.

When it comes to the physical part of performing, we must think of things like your body and voice. To be an effective performer, you need to study expressive movement and voice. If you are serious about a career as a performer, it's really not an option – you need to get out there and take classes in dance or martial arts so that you develop an expressive body. And you need to train your voice, through speech or singing lessons. Beyond that, you really need to rehearse your act again and again, each time exploring ever more expressive ways of delivering the performance. Then you need to set (finalize) those performances, physically as well as emotionally, so that your timing, inflection and quality of movement becomes second nature. For the serious professional, work on our bodies and voices is every bit as important as practicing sleight of hand.

It is as I predicted: I have barely scratched the surface here of what you need to do and learn in order to become not just 'an actor' playing the part of a magician, but a good actor, playing the part of a really great magician. I hope I've at least piqued your interest. So go, get the books, enroll in the classes, spend some time each day training your voice and body to more expressive, and you'll be amazed at how quickly that new knowledge will help you improve your magical performances, no matter what scale you perform on.

As an extra added benefit, you'll find that this kind of attention to your 'instrument' — your voice, body and emotional self — will also help you improve every other aspect of your life, as well!

Motivation

Our subject here is motivation, and I'm choosing to read that as motivation in the way an actor would think of it. Your life's motivation might be to become a great magician, or to adopt better business methods, or to practice more... But that's for another time. In this article I'll discuss motivation as the moment to moment desire of the character you are playing when you perform.

When I was young, I studied to be an actor, and I've been fascinated by the actor's process for many years. I was fortunate while in NY to become friends with one of the world's great acting teachers, Bobby Lewis. Bobby was one of the founding members of The Group Theater back in the 1930's, and later served as head of the Yale Drama School. He was never patient with the American "Method" system as taught by Lee Strasberg at the Actor's Studio, and actually wrote a book called Method – or Madness? in which he methodically tore the logic of 'the method' apart, and suggested a more sensible and complete system for acting – one which, had Strasberg bothered to read more than the first book from Stanislavsky's trilogy for actors, he might have figured out, as well.

Bobby's acting places the dramatic action at the center of the actor's work. A dramatic story becomes interesting because of the interplay of different characters who have different goals. Each one is motivated to move towards their goals, and the setting of the play places them into situations in which their various motivations are in conflict. It is the working out of those conflicts that forms the core of the play, and of our interest in the dramatic action. Within that working out we learn more about characters,

characters change... and we come to many moments where we just have to know: "What will happen next?"

The popular crime drama genre may be one of the easiest places to see this. Will the lawyer be able to convince the jury of the defendant's innocence, or will the prosecutor convince them of his guilt? Two obviously conflicting goals, and motivations. The two attorneys proceed to do things that will advance their own goals and thwart the goals of the other. Along the way, witnesses — each with their own goals — will be motivated to tell the truth or to lie on the stand in order to protect their goals. Friends of the defendant or the victim will carry out actions in support of their goals... and the whole thing will work out into an interesting drama.

What does this mean to you as a performing magician? Well, in fact, at least on one level, you are an actor playing the part of a magician, even if that part is based largely on yourself. If you want to keep and build your audience's interest, you need to make sure your actions make sense to those audiences. A confused audience is not a happy audience.

The way to assure that your actions make sense is to make them fully motivated. "Why does my character pick up this prop? What does my character want from this moment? Why do I (as the character) ask someone to hold the deck of cards, or to choose one particular card? What is the overall story that this piece of magic is telling? Can I find a way to add more conflict to the story in order to make it more interesting? Who is my character interacting with, and what are their motivations? How will the working out of what I want and what they want take place? What sort of resolutions of our differences might be possible?

It is by answering questions like that – all arising from an understanding of your character's goals and moment to moment motivations – that you'll discover new and creative ways to make your magic more exciting, more meaningful...

and to make it more important both to yourself and your audiences.

As a solo performer, it's really worth thinking about who is the protagonist and antagonist in the story your magic is telling. Make no mistake, there is always a story happening. If there wasn't, what you are doing would be completely unintelligible. Your audience members will remember what you did as a story – and will remember it vividly if it is a good story, with lots of conflict and emotion. But if you don't carefully work out the story you want them to take away, you might not like the story they do remember.

Creating a great story is only half of what you need to provide though. Once created, you need to deliver — to act — that story to it's fullest in order to bring it alive for your audience. And for that, you need to fully understand your character's motivations at every step of the way!

Music

Music makes a fascinating addition to any magic act. We are affected by it on both a conscious and a subconscious level. Think of your favorite film for a moment, or your favorite TV show. I'll bet you can almost hear the sound track. When you first saw a particular film, the music of the soundtrack was probably almost a subliminal effect. You heard it, and perhaps noticed when it changed in some major way — shifting from soft and flowing to a sudden strong rhythm or fanfare, for example — but for most of the film you were affected on a subconscious level.

Music affects us by its rhythm, whether the key is major or minor, by using recognizable melodies, layers of harmony, and more. It has many, many ways of molding our experience.

One of my favorite exercises from the first volume of Beyond Deception is to try out several different kinds of music while performing a particular piece. Here is how it works: Make a playlist with 5 wildly different pieces of music on it. Each track should be about the length of a piece of magic you're working on, usually two or three minutes at most. Get out all the props you'll need for the piece, and run through it once with no music. This is just a straight rehearsal. Make it as good as you can. Then start the play list. Perform the same piece using each song from the playlist as a background. Go directly from one to the next, taking only the time you need to re-set the piece in between. I like to include a piece of hip hop, a piece of soft jazz, a TV cartoon theme, a bit of chamber music by Bach or Mozart, and one of my favorite Beatle's tunes. A good mix of fast and slow, ambient and dynamic, if possible. Each song should be as different from the one before it as possible. If possible, record the whole process on video.

You can choose to perform in rhythm to the pieces or just let the music inspire your style and character as you perform. Pay attention. If you're like most of my students, you'll find that you discover different 'new' things about your piece with each piece of music. You might find yourself simplifying moments with one piece, or adding interesting character moments and flourishes with another. You might discover an overall style or mood for the piece that you really like. Most likely no single one of the pieces will be perfect for your piece. That's not what this exercise is about. We're more interested here in letting the music affect you as performer, in inspiring your creativity.

For now, I hope you'll really try this on your own. It only takes a few minutes to create a playlist from your own music collection, and I think you'll be pleasantly surprised at what a quantum leap this simple practice can provide to your creativity as you rehearse pieces that might otherwise have reached an impasse.

On Becoming a Cloud

I've spoken before of the power real wizards gain by learning to view the world from different perspectives. This one might feel a bit 'off the wall' to you, but bear with me.

Let's imagine ourselves as a cloud. I've been watching a fantastic video of clouds forming, turning into thunderheads, then thunderstorms... and then dissipating again. This was a 'fast motion' video, and at the end of this article, I'll point you to where you can find it yourself if you like.

For now, though, let's imagine the cloud as a metaphor for what happens at a show. Performer and audience are like the tiny droplets arising from the sea. Each one alone is too small to be noticed. We don't see water vapor in the air until enough of it collects to become a mist... a cloud. Just as a crowd doesn't become a crowd until the people gather. Imagine, then, your audience members, each individual different from all the others, just as no two drops of water are quite identical, but enough alike that a sufficient number of them are drawn to see your show.

Before the show begins, some kind of publicity has been sent out in order to attract those audience members. Like droplets of water rising from the sea, they find their way to your performing venue. At some point, there are enough of those audience members gathered to form a group — your cloud. Let's put ourselves in the place of that cloud... no longer individuals, but a cloud with its own character, different from any of the individuals that make up that crowd, and different from any other cloud.

There are many kinds of clouds. Wispy Sirius clouds, flying high in the sky. Cumulus forming at lower altitudes, building ever higher until they grow so thick the sunlight can no longer make it's way through, at which point they become those ominous storm clouds we see before a thunderstorm. Sometimes low-lying fog climbs into low hanging mist, drizzling rain. Take a moment, and imagine yourself as that cloud that's about to become your audience. What is the special character of this cloud. What energies, colors, sounds, emotions... does it contain?

Can a cloud be controlled? Not completely -- but it can be affected by many things. How warm is the air surrounding the cloud? How fast does that air move? Does the cloud suddenly encounter a cold layer of air as it rises? Are the currents moving up, down, sideways or in circles? Like the cloud of moisture, your cloud of people can be affected by many things. How warm or cold is the area where they assemble, waiting to come into your theater? What kinds of pressure build up as you prepare to let them into the theater? Do they have expectations that doors will open at a particular point? Are they entertained as they wait, or left to their own devices? Once inside the space where you will perform, what kind of environment have you provided for that cloud? Again... warm, cold, stimulating or not, entertaining or not? Have you chosen music with which to massage the emotions of the crowd you've gathered before your show begins? What effect does that have? Have you thought of a way to build their anticipation towards the beginning of your show? Imagine yourself as that cloud. Stretch yourself and imagine you are the whole cloud, not just an individual within in it. You can do it.

And now the show begins. Perhaps the show is analogous to a storm, with you, the performer, as it's guiding principal. Can you sense all the energies within the cloud? How will you direct them? Perhaps you'll begin with a rumble of thunder, just to get them all to pay attention. A flash or two of lightning off in the distance... how does the cloud react? Now a blast of warm, damp wind to stir up the cloud a bit, and some big drops of warm rain. Then more thunder and lightning. A wall of water advances inexhoribly across the fields below. What must that feel like to the cloud? Imagine it. Can you orchestrate your own 'storm' in a way that will energize all the individuals that make up your cloud? What does it feel like to be at the center of that storm, barely in control, but guiding the tempest into a giant, spectacular crescendo, a climax of wind, thunder, electric discharge and tons of water pouring from the sky? Then that slow dissipation, the individuals in the crowd returning to their lives as individuals, each somehow transformed by your storm, filled with that delicious calm that comes after a storm, each one feeling cleansed and energized, ready to separate slowly and happily into the atmosphere around where your show took place.

What does the cloud feel like after your show? We've all gone out into that fresh, ionized, wonderful smelling air following a storm. The whole world feels clean and new... everything is possible.

As the force at the center of that cloud and then that storm, how do you feel? What did it feel like to be a part of the gathering cloud? To direct the energies of that cloud? To bring the whole thing to a giant, cathartic climax? What have you learned? What will you do differently next time?

I hope you've enjoyed this little journey of fantasy, and that it is somehow helpful to you as you plan your next show, or create your next experience. It is just one way of looking at your work from a different perspective. See what others you can come up with, and allow your imagination to run free with them.

The Role of Roles

The ability to transform ourselves by assuming different roles, taking on disguise, so that we appear to be other than what we are is one of the more magical things we can do.

In the Arthurian tales, we are told that Merlin would

sometimes disguise himself as an itinerant beggar or merchant and travel through the kingdom. In this guise, he could frequent inns and other locations, and go more or less unnoticed, whereas, as the king's wizard, he was always a focus of attention. He could do and hear things in this role which would not have been available to him had his "real" identity been known.

One of my favorite movies was "Moon over Parador," in which Richard Dreyfus plays a character who is a down on his luck, drunken actor who has been hired to impersonate, or act as the double for, the dictator who is ruler of a small Central American state. Something happens to the man he is impersonating, and Dreyfus' character finds himself in position as the new ultimate leader. He surprises everyone – not least himself — by being fully up to the position. Gone is the drunken, irresponsible actor, and in his place a new persona: The Great Leader, who wishes to rule his country justly and functions in a manner that, when he was the irresponsible drunkard, he could never have imagined.

Why do I bring these fictional characters up now? Because I want to talk for a few moments about the power of role playing. It is said "You are who you think you are," and to a surprising extent this is true. If you think you're a down and out loser – you are. On the other hand, if you believe yourself to be a brilliant and successful leader of men – that's likely to be who you really are! We all possess certain abilities, knowledge, emotions which are don't seem to us to be appropriate for "our position." This is true even for those of us who like to feel we're beyond being overly influenced by our surroundings or by what others think of us. It is something many actors discover. The mousy, timid little woman who keeps house for her family and serves them dependable but boring dinners each night, when cast in the role of the femme fatale in her local community theater show – is suddenly able to shake off the dust of her "normal" self, don the fishnets, develop the strut of a street walker – and take on the role. Who knew she had that inside her? But she does...and there are similar characters lurking inside each one of you.

So: who would you like to be that you are not? Try impersonating that person for a day. Imagine you're in one of those stories where you suddenly "change bodies" with your hero and have to live their life for a day. Get some clothes that make you feel like that person, and then go out and "be" them for a day or more. What does it feel like? What do you learn – about yourself, about your hero – and about how you get treated when you take on this new role?

As a performer, taking on a character vastly different from yourself can be a big step. I highly recommend trying it, though. Build one piece in your act where you become a character different than yourself. My friend Jeff McBride excels as this. In his famous "Mask Act" he transitions through a half dozen different characters in the first 2 minutes of the act. Those of you who might have watched Jeff's newest DVD: "Squeak Technique," have seen him perform "Bravo" his new routine with a metal bowl and ball...in the character of a slightly raunchy Italian Street magician. The character says and does things we would never expect of Jeff – taking on the character empowers him to perform a completely different kind of comedy than he would normally do. By assuming many different characters during the course of his full evening shows, Jeff is able present an hour and a half of entertainment that is far more richly varied and textured than most performers can do. There is something truly magical about seeing a single performer shift into so many different personas.

So: Your wizard assignment for the chapter is to either develop a new short piece of magic, or re-work one you already perform – as a character as different from yourself as you can imagine. Try doing linking rubber bands as Arnold Schwarzenegger's Terminator character, or cups and balls as Marilyn Monroe (doubly funny if you are male).

Can you do an impression of President Obama? Imagine him doing the 6 card repeat...and try it out. See what you come up with. Commit to the character (it doesn't matter if you're a great impressionist...just trying to be one of these people will take you far enough out of 'yourself' that it will have the desired effect) . . . and work the piece over and over for yourself, then try it out for your friends. I think you'll be amazed at the results.

Scripts

Written scripts are one of the things that separates the pros from the amateurs. For the pro, the piece isn't really ready to go until a complete script has been written, honed—and honed some more. Of course, everyone has his or her own way of getting to the point where the script can be written down. Some people start with the script. Perhaps they are playwrights at heart, and only performers as a means of getting their scripts heard. Others will get a piece of magic down roughly by working out a basic outline of how they'd like to present it, and then create the final script in collaboration with their first couple of hundred audiences. Some of those audiences get great, inspired shows, and others get crap. You have to take some risks, have to take a chance that something will be awful, in order to find those really fantastic moments that are going to seem like happy, spontaneous accidents—night after night.

Here's an example. I must have seen Jeff McBride perform his coin routine a thousand times. After every show, you can count on audience members coming up and telling Jeff, "Wow, you got a great kid for that tonight!" Jeff always agrees with them. But, in fact, the kid generally has no choice but to be great. The piece is so thoroughly scripted (even though no one speaks during most of the piece!) that 'the kid' picks up pretty much the same beats every night. Virtually every seemingly spontaneous moment has actually been worked out so that Jeff can cue the kid, and Jeff can then respond. It is all great acting, and the script writing is brilliant, but there is very little that is actually spontaneous. And that's why it is such a classic of magic!

So, what makes for a great script in magic? The same things that make for great scripts in theater, film and television. A great script has interesting, bigger than life characters that we can root for or against. It has a story with clear beginning, middle and end. Most great scripts have all the parts of a well-made play: Exposition, also know as 'the set up.' It has Rising Action, all those little moments of conflict and resolution that build the overall energy of the piece up to a moment of Crisis, followed immediately by a Climax, which resolves the conflicts, relieves the tensions the earlier action has built up...and then a Denoument, or wrap-up, which tells us what we've just seen and what we might want to make of it—"And the moral of the story is . . . ."

Remember: Every performance piece has a story. Your audience will tell it as a story after the fact. The only questions is how good a story, and how well is it told. Those are completely up to you as the creator and performer. It is a big job, but one that can be most rewarding.

I hope you'll all take time to look at the pieces you've been performing. Write down the script—even silent pieces can have scripts—and then begin the work of making your stories better. Check that they have all the parts that makes a great story. See if you can find ways to make what my acting teachers would have called "bigger choices" for each bit in the script—more colorful characters, stronger conflicts, more suprising reversals and resolutions—and a more satisfying climax and resolution.

The Five Senses

Today I want to talk about communicating beyond words. I'm sure you've heard that we each have 5 senses— and depending on how you look at it, there may be more. For example, touch actually includes the sensing of pressure, temperature, and physical pain and pleasure. Vision includes sensing color, shape, and movement, all of which seem to get into our brains through separate neuronal pathways.

Tony Buzan, the inventor of mind mapping, wrote a book called Brain Sell, in which he points out that different people tend to prefer communication through different senses. They tend to fall into three general types: Visual, Auditory and Kinesthetic. A visual person will tell you "I don't like the look of that." An auditory person is more likely to say, "It sounds wrong to me." And a Kinesthetic person will say, "It just doesn't feel right," or "It just doesn't move me."

Each of these types will tend to respond more strongly to communications directed at their own primary sensory type—and so when you're selling (and all communication can be seen as selling in one way or another) – it makes sense to present people with messages that speak to their personal sense preferences. Visual people might respond more strongly to words about color, beautiful design and pattern. Auditory people are more affected by sound metaphors – melody, harmony, noise. Kinesthetic people want to know how things feel. They will respond to metaphors that include physical sensations of movement, texture and feeling.

When communicating to a group of people, it's important that you address all the senses, because the group is likely to contain all three basic types, and a few of the less common ones as well. When writing a speech, a flyer, advertisement or press release—or when you are creating a performance piece—you'll find much greater success if you take the time to go through it and make sure you have included clear messages for all of the senses.

In the section on the business of magic, I talk about your elevator pitch – that 20 second speech you've written and rehearsed so you can use it to introduce yourself or your work to new people in a way that will really convey the essence of who you are and what makes you different from others. Here's your challenge for this week: Go back and look at your elevator pitch (or write one, if you haven't already done so). Go over it several times and see where you can include a visual metaphor. Make sure you have language that will appeal to the ear as well as the eye. And, finally, make sure you use language that will speak to that kinesthetic listener, and make them really feel what you're trying to get across. If you can also include language that will affect taste and smell, all the better!

Here's my elevator pitch for my new book and business, The Wizard's Way. It's still in early development, but I've just gone over it to make sure it hits all those sensual bases. See what you think.

Hi, I'm Tobias Beckwith, and I create wizards. Real wizards. That word probably conjures up an image of some old guy with a flowing white beard and a pointy hat. Dumbledore or Merlin. But real wizards come in all shapes and sizes – do the names Albert Einstein, Leonardo da Vinci, or Steve Jobs ring a bell for you? They're all wizards! You could be one, too.

Wizards are men and women who have developed their own special secret knowledge – their wisdom – by creating experiences for themselves and others that stretch boundaries, provide different perspectives–and ultimately give them the ability to do what others would say is impossible.

They are powerful movers and shakers who take on the responsibility to shake up the world around them, then put it back together in a way that is better than before. We live immersed in a world filled with the probabilities both of disaster and great excitement and joy – a world of rapid change. If you want to be a player in that world, and not just a pawn, the Wizard's Way is the way for you. Want to learn more? I can help–show you the way, so that you, too, can become a real wizard. Here's my card. Visit my web-site, read my book, and call me soon, and I'll make sure you get the help you need.

Well...that's my pitch. What do you think? Write me at tobias@beyonddeception.com and let me know what you like and don't like about it. I'm always open to improvements.

In any case...let this example inspire you to take another pass at your own elevator pitch, making sure it address as many of the senses as possible. Make us see, hear and feel your message. At first, you might feel your pitch really stinks. But as you work it, repeating it aloud again and again, making little improvements each time, before you know it your pitch will start sounding like music to your ears!

Silence

Have you every tried to create a performance piece completely without words? When I was younger, I studied dance and choreography, and discovered very quickly that telling stories without words was an entirely different proposition than putting dramas with dialogue and narration on the stage. In a very real sense, we create our sense of the world we inhabit through words. It is very difficult to see an object without naming it in your mind—and equally difficult to name an object and not see it in your mind's eye. Words can often create a kind of mask atop the experience of our other senses. Speaking magic often makes use of this mask of words to mislead an audience—but when that mask is removed, the magic itself must immediately be stronger. We no longer have words to misdirect, or to suggest what we are about to see. Audiences will be fixated on exactly what they can see, and their focus on that will be far more intense than for an act that is accompanied by speech.

I've worked with many magicians on many different kinds of acts, and I must tell you that where it might take a few days to create an effective two or three minute magical piece with speech—and then a few months to polish that piece to where it becomes really good, it often takes much, much longer to create a 2-3 minute piece with no speaking and get it just to a place where it is okay to show to an audience. Strip away the words, and it is suddenly necessary to make actions clearer and larger. Transitions linking different parts of the piece must be absolutely clear – and we must seriously consider things like pacing, visual composition and how they can assist us in telling the story that will appear as magic to our audiences. Once any part becomes unclear, your whole piece runs the risk of becoming confusing, and thus ineffective.

On the other hand: There was once a TV commercial with the line, "If you want to get someone's attention, just whisper." It was effective, but the silent mime or magician takes it ever further—"If you really want to get someone's attention, shut up altogether!"

I talk in my classes about creating a portal into your magical world at the beginning of a show or any individual piece of magic. This is something that's an integral part of any piece of performing art, from music to dance to circus, drama, opera—and most certainly for magic. Part of our job as magicians is to transport our audiences into a magical world—a world where they can have experiences not available to them in their everyday world at home and at work. There are thousands of ways we can achieve this, but one of the most powerful is to invite them into a world where your character can be super-expressive without the need for speech. It sets you off immediately as being "other"

– one with abilities that are special and worthy of note. It also forces your audience to pay attention in ways they are unused to, and thus draws them into your magical world.

In the words of the wizards, performing without words casts a certain spell over your audience. This moves you a giant step closer to being able to enchant them with a truly magical experience.

But it's not easy. You are communicating in a visual language where most of your audience has a limited vocabulary. Thus it may be difficult to provide the clarity necessary to adequately tell your story. It is much easier to confuse them about what you are doing if you're not speaking than it is when you are! Inadvertent movements will be interpreted as having meaning, and will cause confusion—so you must remove them! Actions which were perfectly clear when accompanied by speech—instructions, commentary, jokes, etc.—may be incomprehensible to your audience when you are not speaking.

And this leads to the need for a 'third eye,' a director or friend who can watch your act and let you know what they do and don't understand. If you are new to performing silent magic, some of the things they don't get will surprise you. After all, you know exactly what you're doing—how could they be so dense as to not get it? Even if you record the act on video, you may have difficulty finding these confusing points yourself. Again, you know what you'll be doing in advance, and you'll see yourself doing it and confirm to yourself that it is clear, even though it isn't clear to anyone outside your head.

As you can see, silent performing can be far more difficult than scripted performance. It is, however, very much worth the effort. Both as a final product and as a means of refining the magic you're already doing with speech. Try it. Take a piece you perform all the time, and work it out as a completely silent piece. Have a few friends watch it. Most often you'll find there are bits that are extraneous to the core story line, and you'll have to decide whether those bits are really a worthy addition or an unnecessary distraction. You'll find moves that are ambiguous when unaccompanied with words. You may even find that the overall story of the piece is now difficult to follow. Fix all those things in the silent version—then go back and perform this new version again using your script, and see how it has changed.

I love experimenting and playing with performance pieces like this. Not every piece improves with each new pass, but when you try several different new experiments with pieces you're already doing, you will invariably eventually come up with improvements—even to your masterpieces!

State of Wonder

I'm a big fan of defining one's purpose as a magician, and the answer I get most often when I ask magicians about their purpose is "to awaken wonder in my audiences." And I wonder just what they mean by that.

Those of us old enough will remember Doug Henning, who really took the whole idea of magic as wonder to heart. He wanted us all to live in a state of wonder all the time. And for Doug, "wonder" was truly something wonderful. I think it meant the ability to see everything and anything as being imbued with magic. As being truly worthy of awe.

On a more mundane level, 'wonder' is just what we do when we don't actually know something. I wonder what the weather will be like tomorrow. I wonder why there only seem to be 4 or 5 colors of cars on the road. I wonder if wondering about so many things means I have a sense of wonder?

Einstein was known to have said, 'the man who has lost his sense of wonder is dead.'

So, what is this 'sense of wonder' that we're all so intent

on creating? I'm not sure I can define it really clearly. There are some things I think I do know about it, though.

One is that it is more likely to happen if it is given a bit of time. The performer who comes on and assaults his audience with one effect, then another, then another, all in lightning succession, often kills the sense of wonder we might feel at any one of those effects. He is able to surprise us, to dazzle us, certainly...but to create a sense of wonder? I think not.

Another thing I know is that the performer who challenges me with an attitude of "Betcha can't catch me" is unlikely to achieve a sensation of wonder. Wondering how he did it is not the same thing as feeling a sense of wonder.

Still another thing about wonder is that, at least for me, it seems to have something to do with beauty. I feel wonder when I watch a time lapse sequence of a flower blossom opening. I experience when I witness amazing cloud structures as I fly over them. I guess this has something to do with suddenly awakening to aspects of the natural world, to suddenly seeing them in new ways. They were always worthy of my wonder, but I don't notice how wondrous they are until I experience them from a different perspective.

This is actually one of the functions of art – to hold nature "up to the mirror" in such a way that we will notice and appreciate it in new ways. Following on with this thought:

I experience wonder when I encounter something new. Wonder comes with discovery...and the same item that inspires wonder today is unlikely to do so after I have encountered it a hundred times.

I'm not sure how useful this chapter might be to you. I certainly enjoyed thinking about the subject. If you think of your purpose as being to reawaken a real sense of wonder in your audiences, you might want to take on the challenge of writing out an article like this one about just what that really means to you. It will help you clarify your thinking, and might even inspire you to create some new magic.

Story Telling Revisited

I know—I know. Many of you classify yourselves as 'not story tellers.' But, I'm sorry—you're wrong about that. Stories are how humans make sense of the world. They are the basis of how we both understand and remember the events of our lives. Without story, pretty much all performance pieces would become unintelligible.

Even something as abstract as gazing through a kaleidoscope gradually becomes a story in our minds. "Oh...what a cool pattern...all jaggy and mostly blue and violet...oh, and look, there it shifted suddenly, and now it's all yellow, with bigger bits and bright like sunshine. And there—look how it just kind of floats into the next pattern . . ." Whenever we describe events, we are telling stories.

So, the question really is, what makes a story a good story. I know you've heard me talk about the importance of stories before—how characters with motivations and goals come into conflict and that the resolution of those conflicts is how we create drama. All good information, but I'd like to take things a bit further.

Think for a moment of your favorite movies and books. Most of us have a preferred kind of stories we like to read and watch. Do you love mysteries? Romances? Action and adventure? Spy Stories? Ghost Stories? Each of these KINDS of stories has a slightly different kind of structure. And for those of us experiencing the story, there are certain expectations we have for each kind of story.

In a detective story, for example, we'll almost always start off with a crime. And not just any crime—it has to be a crime that presents a mystery. We'll be presented with the likely culprits, and be introduced to a detective character. The story will be made up of the detective interacting with all the likely culprits until he or she figures out who the perpetrator is. Then we'll have a climax where the perpetrator is identified and captured. That's the basic structure of the detective story. There will, of course, be false leads, sudden reversals and a bit of thrilling danger on the way to figuring it all out. That's the joy of the detective story.

A romance will have quite a different structure. A comedy or tragedy will be different, too.

So, what kind of stories do you like most? What sort of television shows do you enjoy? What are their distinguishing characteristics? Can you find ways to tell that kind of story with your magic? Once you identify the kind of story each of your magical performance pieces is, then you can go through and find out if all of the parts you would expect from that kind of story are present. If not, you can add them in.

Have you adequately introduced all the primary characters in your story—the hero or heroine, the antagonist, the other significant parties? Have you let us know what each one's goals are? What their plans for achieving those goals might be?

Have you defined what your story is about? Have you built appropriate rising action, reversals and the like into the story? Do you know what the crises and climax points are? Have you constructed an appropriate denouement— that is, a good tag line that lets your audience know the story has come to a satisfactory conclusion and it's time to applaud? Have you wrapped up all the loose ends for each of the story's characters?

If you have done all that, you may still be able to find ways to make each aspect more interesting and exciting. I had a great acting teacher who, once we had worked through our scenes several times and made them as true to life as possible, would challenge us to go back and "Make bigger choices." This was the key to moving the story we were telling with our acting from the merely interesting and "good," to becoming really special—to achieving real creativity and excellence. It's a great challenge to give yourself, again and again!

Who Am I - Self Awareness

In this fast-paced world, we often find ourselves spending most of our time reacting to other people and to situations around us. Sometimes this is fun – life can be like a game of ping pong where we take delight in our ability to 'get' everything our opponent throws at us. Other times, we can feel like we're trying to carry the weight of the whole world, and that torrent of things coming at us becomes overwhelming. You might just find yourself wishing not to deal with it all.

One of the problems we encounter living in this kind of world is that we can lose track of ourselves and who we really are, and who we want to be.

Every so often I find myself in a situation–maybe someone has cut me off in traffic—where I hear something come out of my mouth that makes me think, "Wow...where did that come from? I would never say that to anyone!" And yet, there it was, popping out of my mouth without my brain having been consciously engaged at all. Who is the person who said that?

On a larger scale, how many people do you know who find themselves stuck in a career they never intended? In fact, who do you know who has really followed the dream they had for themselves when they were young? How many truly creative young people wind up in jobs they hate, doing uncreative things and somehow managing to convince themselves they've created good lives for themselves?

What I'm getting at here is the importance of knowing–being in touch with–yourself. You would think this would be easy. Who can know you better than yourself, and what could you possibly know better than what it's like to be you, and who you are? And yet—we don't.

During the first years of the Mystery School, we met at the Ananda Ashram in upstate New York. Their favorite meditation there was just the question "Who Am I?" I believe this is common in many different spiritual traditions. I have found it useful, myself. I like to take a few moments when I wake up, or before I go to sleep at night, to ask myself just that, and to let my quiet mind answer.

One of the surprising answers that comes is that I am actually many different people. At one moment I might be someone who embraces a particular principle wholeheartedly—and half an hour later I find myself tearing apart arguments for the belief I had been espousing earlier. Sometimes I love every individual I meet, and humanity in general—and at others I can't fathom how unbelievably stupid or cruel my fellow humans can be. Yet, somehow, beneath it all there is a persona—a basic sense that I am me—and that I do have certain strong values, certain dreams and desires, certain talents—that define who I am to myself. And when I manage to stay in touch with that basic sense of who I am and what I want, I think I'm a better, stronger person. When I manage to integrate all those different personas and start to understand how they all fit together, I become a person with infinitely more power and creativity, because I become able to focus on the things that will move me toward my dreams, that will help me change the world in ways that are meaningful and important to me, and that will help me sort out the distractions coming at me from the things that are truly important.

It is one of the defining characteristics of wizards that

they are able to do this—to separate out the truly important from the merely urgent, and to focus their attention and energies on the things most important to them.

So, I would urge you, for the next week, to take a few minutes–it needn't be a long time, and you can even do it, as I often do, before you get out of bed in the morning—to ask yourself each day, "who am I? How am I inhabiting this body? What are my strongest values? What is my biggest dream? What is the one big thing I want to accomplish today? This week? In my life?"

Try it just for a week. See how that works out for you. If you're not used to doing this, and you try it just a couple of times a day for a week or so, I think you'll begin to see a difference in your life even within that short amount of time.

As a stronger, more fully integrated person, you'll also find that you are a more creative artist and a more effective performer.

What is Impossible?

For many of us, doing the 'impossible' pretty much encompasses what we mean by doing magic. And there is great delight to be had by witnessing, by actually experiencing, something you had believed to be impossible. I take great delight in various optical illusions, for example, because they allow me to have an experience of something I somehow know cannot be. And yet through the operation of that illusion, my mind allows itself to experience something outside of its own belief system. Back in the 60's we called that "mind expanding," and we had some interesting ways of attempting it. If you were to believe Timothy Leary and others of the time, LSD and other drugs were the key. I've always wondered where all those "expanded minds" and enlightened characters went to. Perhaps the expansion they accomplished was only a temporary, easily forgotten phenomenon. Perhaps they simply didn't discover things in that expanded mental state that were then applicable to our every day lives. But I'd like to think that there could be a more lasting effect for those of us who enjoy expanding our views of the world through the conscious experience of illusion.

It's interesting that I can actually know how some of my favorite illusions work, but still have the experience of that illusion! This is, I think, also true of the best magical performances.

For me, this is not an experience I get from most big box illusions. I do get it from seeing some of Paul Harris' pieces performed well, though—even after I've read them and learned to perform them myself. Knowing the modus operandi doesn't detract from the experience of the illusion one bit. My conclusion, at least for myself, is that it's possible to be 'fooled' on several different levels. On some of those levels, it is, indeed, "Fun to be fooled." On others, not so much.

There is the level of being fooled because the magician is tricking me. I think of that as 'gotcha' magic. Not my favorite, as it leaves you with the predominant feeling that you're not quite as clever as the performer. It makes the viewer the victim of a practical joke.

Then there's a level of being so involved in the magical story that the performer gives us, with the magic trick as a metaphor, that we really don't even stop to think of how it may have been accomplished. We simply accept it as an amusing illustration that deepens the impact of the story being told.

But, finally, there is the performer whose magic itself just completely destroys your sense of reality for a few minutes. The world stops in its tracks as your mind tries to grasp what it has just experienced. At that moment, the magic opens up your whole idea of what is and isn't possible in the world. Physical laws become mere suggestions – and my mind is suddenly open to all kinds of new possibilities.

That's the moment of astonishment, and I think it's a kind of moment that is unique to performing magic. It's on a par with the moment a new baby comes into the world, that the Olympic athlete shatters both her own personal best and sets a new world record, or a young couple falls in love and experiences their first kiss. It is a moment devoutly to be wished for, worked for—and one that we actually experience too seldom. To get to that kind of moment of pure astonishment requires more than just a good method of performing an effect. It requires the proper set-up, building of rapport, timing and much more. But when it all happens in just the right way, well, that's why we call it magic!

Entering Magical Space

When does the magical experience you provide as a magician actually begin? Is it when the curtain goes up on your show? When the audience enters the theater? Maybe when they buy their tickets, or even before that, when they first encounter your advertising.

All performances, all stories, films and the like, start out by bringing the audience, readers or whoever is to experience the performance, into the space. In fairy tales, for example, we know we are entering that magical world when we hear the words, "Once upon a time." After those words, we are no longer in our everyday world, but have stepped into the world of the story. It's the same with performances.

If you perform in a theater, you may not have a lot of control over the configuration of the space – seats tend to be bolted to the floor, the stage is a certain height, and so on. However, you do have some things you can control even in the most rigid of situations.

What sort of lighting will greet your audience as they enter your space? Will they be coming from bright lighting outside to a different kind of lighting in the performance space? Or perhaps it will be the other way around. I'm a big fan of the idea of entering a magical space through a 'portal,' and most theaters provide this experience through their architecture. You leave a street scene outside and come through doors into a lobby, where it's likely to be crowded and noisy, everyone excited about what they are about to experience. Then you enter through doors where your ticket is taken and you are directed to your seats. Inside it is likely to be quieter and the lighting more subdued. There may or may not be something for you to see on the stage. The lighting in the house and on the stage will set up some expectations for you. If you're going to a Cirque du Soleil show, there are probably costumed characters working in the audience–helping set the tone for what is to come. In Jeff McBride's shows for the past few years, Jeff and his assistants are likely to be there greeting you and making you feel at home. Some performers prefer not to be seen before their first appearance on stage – it's a choice we must each make for ourselves, but you must be aware that whatever the choice, it will have an effect ton what is to come.

What sort of music might be playing as audiences enter? When we designed shows at Caesars Magical Empire, I liked to have patterned lights moving slowly over the audience, to slightly disorient them and give the feeling they had entered a particularly magical place, even before the show was to begin. Depending on the theater, we played either vaguely Arabic or Chinese music to fit with the architecture of the space. Many of the large corporate meetings and shows I work on use a similar technique, but with the lights moving more rapidly, and rock music playing to help generate energy and excitement before the show begins.

Back when I was managing theaters on Broadway, we would pay a lot of attention to how we trained our box office staff, ticket takers and ushers. Always remember that, although there is almost always a 'curtain' moment when a show appears to begin, the experience of the show begins much earlier, with the buying of tickets, entry to the theater and so on—and you can use each of these encounters in a way that will enhance the overall experience of your audiences. If you don't pay attention to them there's a chance they will detract instead of enhancing.

Even if you're table hopping or working behind a bar, even if you're working hospitality suites—there are things you can do that will help 'set up' your performance. How will you approach groups for whom you intend to perform? What part of the room will you choose to work in? Are there bright spots and dimmer ones? What will your dress convey to those you intend to perform for, even before you reach them? All of these things help, or detract from, the overall experience you wish your performances to provide, so please, take a few moments—or preferably considerably more than that—and consider the overall experience you want audiences to have with your show. Every detail is a choice that will get made for them—with or without your conscious consideration—and I can tell you, it can make a huge difference to the success of your performances if you make sure that you have considered and had input into all those details.

Gigging

I've included pieces in this section that apply particularly to the magician who performs regularly in different locations. Some of us do keynote talks at conventions and corporate meetings. Others perform at parties, tradeshows, or various other 'gigs,' moving from location to location, job to job. Both of the clients I've managed for the past twenty years do that, so I've have had quite a lot of experience in dealing with travel, with different venues, technical crews, etc. I hope you'll find my experience useful.

Dealing with Challenging Circumstances

The more you work, the more things will go wrong. Over the years, I've collected a fair number of memorable 'war stories' about just such occurences.

For example, there was the night I went with Jeff to Thailand, where he was performing out doors in 100% humidity. The cards he was going to use for manipulation at the end of his performance were soggy with dew by the time he got to them, just from being on stage with him for 20 minutes. Somehow he managed to power through his already difficult card manipulation routine.

There have been many nights at major gigs—International Arts Festivals, and even some casino gigs—when the tech rehearsal we had scheduled (liberally, we thought) for 6 hours, was barely getting started by the time they were supposed to be over. Equipment hadn't been installed on time, or wasn't available in that locale, or the local crew decided if they dragged their feet they could get themselves into an overtime situation and blame it on us. Whatever. There have times I've actually run Jeff's lights as the lightboard operator, simply because the local guy supplying the equipment had more than he was really capable of handling just to get it up and operational, leaving no time to actually write cues and rehearse.

One of the skills I've developed that has served me best over the years is the ability to remain calm and deal with this kind of situation. The longer you are in show business, the higher the likelihood you'll have to deal with them, as well. Even on the uppermost levels of our business, artists are faced with extremely challenging situations, on a more or less regular basis. There's a story about David Copperfield having his show props (all 9 truck loads) held up at gunpoint 'for ransom' in Russia. Another about Siegfried and Roy being confronted with seemingly insurmountable problems in connection with getting their animals – upon which their show depended – in and out of Japan.

So one of the more important skills you can develop as a professional is the ability to stay calm and persevere when you have to deal with these things. You won't always be successful, but you can be sure that, at some point, the ordeal will end. And more often than not, you will be successful, if you just take a few deep breaths and think clearly about the situation you find yourself in. Often, the solution is simply to let yourself think creatively. "Oh, my God, we're never going to get all these cues into the light board in time!" can be resolved with, "OK, I know I can run this show with just 8 different lighting "looks." If I can just get those programmed, and into sub-masters, then I can run the show myself, and it will still look reasonably good." Or: "Well, I guess tonight we run the show with just one look, and fade it in and out as needed." Not your original intent, or what you would choose for the artistic integrity of the show you've brought with you – but there is always some way through. Often compromises like this will 'save the show' and make you a hero with those who have hired you.

I remember sitting in a show at Caesars one night when the Pendragons were performing—and there was a blackout. Not just in the room, but all up and down the Las Vegas Strip. Casinos, always a bit strange, can be really weird with no electricity. We could have had major panic and a dangerous situation. Instead, we heard Jonathan Pendragon, from the stage, say, "Wow...that's cool. Could someone find me a candle backstage?" A few minutes later, stage hands with flashlights did just that. Jonathan set the candle beside him onstage, did some "in the hands" magic and talked to the audience, telling stories by candle light. Everyone had a great time, and a very special story they could tell their friends afterwards. When the lights came back on and it was time to leave, I think everyone wished it had gone on longer. Because Jonathan kept his cool and rolled with the situation, just assuming it would all work out alright—it did!

In situations like those above, your expectations can be your enemy. If you expect things to go in a certain way, you may be thrown for a loop when they go another. A looser grip on those expectations—what the Buddhists call 'non-attachment'—can serve you admirably. An attitude of "Wow—this isn't what I expected—but it's cool. What shall we all do now?" can go a long, long ways towards helping you cope. In the case of my story about our tech support and lighting not going as expected, a retreat to, "There's a great show about to take place. What can I do with the limited resources here to enhance it, and make it the best I can?" was what saved the day. In the case of Jonathan Pendragon on the night the lights went out, the retreat was to, "Wow, here's a theater full of people sitting in the dark, who came to be entertained—and I'm here to entertain them. What can I come up with?" led to a very special evening for all involved. I know I'm glad I was there to experience it!

So, when you find yourself stressing out because something you had expected at a gig hasn't come out the way you expected, take a deep breath and relax. Let go. Retreat to the basics, and do your best with what is at hand. You may surprise yourself at how much fun it can be to deal with those 'difficult' situations—and just how creative you can be under pressure. Sometimes what you come up with on the spot will be so good, you'll want to find a way to 'keep it in' for future shows!

Pre-show & Post-show Routines

There is a time between when a performer arrives at a venue and when the show begins, and then between the time the show ends and when the performer leaves the venue. Even more broadly, there is a time that begins when your potential audience or buyer first learns about you. That might be through an article the press, a video online, a poster, your website, or through a friend telling them about you. Their experience of you as a magician starts right then, don't you think?

When I lecture, one of my favorite themes is how our entire business as a magician needs to have integrity, by which I mean that all the different parts need to fit together and support one another. Any time anyone has contact with you or your business, they should have an experience that you have designed so that it fits in with all of their other experiences with you. That is one of the things that branding is all about. And that only happens when you're able to define your business with a clear purpose. If you don't know why you're doing what you're doing, it's hard to design all those experiences in a way so that they will all go together. But when you do know—that difficult task becomes a bit easier.

Let's imagine for a moment that you like presenting really creepy magic. Horror show magic. Your goal might be to help your audiences confront their own mortality, to accept the gruesome truth that we will all die and our bodies rot away one day—all the while giving them that little extra dose of adrenaline and excitement that makes them feel all the more alive in the present moment. By facing our mortality, each of us may be encouraged to live our lives more fully. So you want to help us do that, through the experience of your "Master of Gore" performances.

So: How does the "Master of Gore" answer the phone? What sort of graphic images appear on his web-site? What kind of language? What are the messages conveyed? Some of your props will undoubtedly have a frightening aspect to them...but what about the cases they are packed in? How far do you need to expand your image?

The onstage "Master of Gore" might be too strong a character for basic business dealings offstage, so what will your 'business character' be? What sort of manager would we expect for the Master of Gore? Will your contracts be printed on parchment, bearing a wax seal?

Of course, there are certain elements of basic practical business etiquette you'll want to observe, no matter what the purpose and nature of your business might be. I imagine that the "Master of Gore" might want to look quite businesslike and normal and friendly as he enters a theater for the first time and begins unpacking his props. He might be wearing a T-Shirt or other clothing that bears a logo or image of him in performance, though. He will, as we all should, be unerringly polite to the whole staff and crew of the theater—but perhaps he will have a little something special—a scary but funny bit of magic or spectacle that has been prepared just for the crew, so everyone will feel they are in on the act, that they are contributing to what it's all about. He might even have special Master of Gore T-shirts he can give as gifts to the staff.

And how will the box office answer their phone when patrons call to buy tickets? Will there be screams in the background? Spooky pipe organ music? The more you consider ALL of these details, the more your show is likely to achieve that purpose you've set for it. And the more likely you are to build a successful business around your performances.

Oh...and one more thing: Don't forget that the experience isn't over when the curtain falls at the end of the show. That audience must still leave the theatre, and you have a chance to decide what the experience of leaving the show will be like for them? What sounds will they here, what sites will they see? Will they meet you in the lobby and be able to get a photo or autograph? How will they be treated?

What about those who have hired you? Remember, the experience isn't over for them until you are gone from the theater. How long will they have to wait for you? Will they want to invite you back? If you're really smart, their experience with you won't end at all, because you will follow up with a thank you note–in the case of the Master of Gore it may be on wrinkled parchment and appear to be written in blood—but it will arrive. And then, for years after, they will occasionally hear from you. Again and again—until they invite you back, because the experience of having you with them the first time was so memorable and such a success!

Storage-Display-Organization

In spite of the fact that I've really only recently begun to actually perform magic for the public again, I seem to have collected more than my fair share of special decks of cards, coins and the like. And until recently, it would have taken me some time to lay my hands on any specific magic object in my collection. Not long ago, though, I started an "organizing magic" project. For years, I've stored most of my small items in those little sets of plastic drawers they sell in hardware stores, designed to store different size nails, screws, washers and other small hardware bits. And larger plastic drawer units for the few larger props I've collected. My recent "innovation" such as it was, was to get one of these (label-maker), and start sorting and labeling the contents of all the drawers. I found there was about 1/3rd of the stuff I could just get rid of, and that the rest began to fall into logical sections: A coin magic section, a silk & rope magic section, gaffed and ungaffed cards, and so on. Now I can find things I know that I have much more quickly than I used to.

That was my system before I began really developing fully fleshed out pieces for performance, which I only started doing about 4 months ago. For those of you who do perform regularly, either for money or not, I have one *most* important thought to help you improve your life: ***Organize!***

For myself, I got a couple of dozen little cloth-mesh zipper bags, and I pack everything I need for each piece I perform into one of those bags. I insert an index card with the name of the piece in large letters inside each bag, and make sure they don't get stored back into the plastic drawer sets where I keep them unless they are fully "ready to go" for the next performance. When I go to do a show, I pull the bags for all of the pieces I intend to perform, toss them in a briefcase, and I'm ready to go. Since I never file them away without making sure they're fully supplied, I don't have to worry about whether or not I'll be missing something when it comes time to perform.

The more thoroughly organized you can be with your magic props, the easier your life as a performer will be. I remember when I first started working with Marco Tempest, being amazed at how organized he was. Every act he performed had it's own hard sided camera-equipment style small suitcase, each one lined in foam, with cut-out spaces to hold each prop. There were separate spaces to hold the disposable supplies that went with the piece – the snowstorms, streamers, etc. Separate spots for the chargers to charge his various gadget props. Even a space for a power strip he could use to plug into a single outlet and charge all his stuff.

The result of this "super-organization?" Marco's many

delicate props seldom got damaged. He never forgot a prop, or failed to arrive without all the right disposable supplies. All he had to do was open a case and glance at it to see if there were empty slots, and to know exactly what needed to go into each of those slots. Having thought exhaustively— once—about how he wanted the act organized for travel, he never had to waste his time thinking about it again.

Today, I would even go a step further. I would create a database, stored on my computer and in the cloud, listing every prop that is stored in each case. I would name the prop, list where it was originally made, when I bought it, its cost then, and it's approximate weight. I might even include a field or two where I could record when the prop was refurbished, and other similar information. This probably seems like a lot of useless work, just to organize your storage, doesn't it? But if you're going to be traveling with large pieces, this long tedious set-up of your system will actually save you a lot of time and inconvenience. Why? Because you'll be able to quickly organize and pack just the cases you really need when you're putting together a new version of your show, for one thing. For another, you will be able to easily give your shippers, insurance companies, and customs brokers the information they need to serve you best.

We ship Jeff McBride's illusion show overseas a couple of times each year, and each time we have to file detailed information with our shippers and with customs brokers and others. If we had to go through each one of his cases and catalog everything each time we shipped them, it would add a full day to our preparation time each time we have to ship the show. As it is, we can usually take care of the necessary paperwork in an hour or less.

I remember the first time we shipped Jeff's illusion show overseas: It took two of his assistants two full days to get the information together that we needed so that our shipper could file a carnet with customs. A carnet is a certified document you can file when sending things out of the country that are going to return after your gig has ended, and thus avoid paying the customs fees you would normally have to pay if you were actually importing and exporting the items. If we had then had a database with all of the information on each prop and where it was stored, I probably could have prepared the full statement for the carnet in an hour or less—as I do now—without having had to pay the assistants for those two additional days cataloging at the last minute.

So, remember that word "Organization." Learn about ways to get and stay organized—not only with your magical props, but with your contracts, marketing materials, and as many parts of your life as you can think to organize— Just do it! Every minute you spend keeping organized will save you many, many minutes in the future.

When I started running my own business, I used to waste as much as an hour almost every day just trying to find things. I was fairly organized then, but over the years, I've managed to become much better organized. It's not an easy habit to form, but believe me, it is worth every bit of time and effort you put into it.

Smart Travel

Travel can be a great joy…or a big pain in the butt. Which it will be depends mostly on you and your preparations – though not always. As a manager, travel is one of the areas where I often find I am most useful to my clients. Our buyers understandably often want to save money on travel, and my clients want the most convenient and safest means of getting them to and from their engagements. These two interests, coupled with the vagaries of airline schedules and pricing, often make the situation more complicated than it needs to be. Here are a couple of ways I've found to make that aspect of things go more smoothly:

First: Make sure your travel needs are clearly conveyed, in detail, right when you name your price to a client. "My fee is $2,500 plus round trip airfare on the most direct routes available. Economy fare is fine, but it must be full fare so I'm not penalized if I have to shift flights at the last moment. I also need you to provide professional local ground transportation, and lodgings in a 3 star hotel or better, as close to the performance venue as possible."

Not that your buyers will always be able to provide exactly what you ask for—but if you ask for it up front and spell it out in your contract, it doesn't come as a sudden surprise to them that they have what many will consider this "extra" cost.

Once we have an agreement, someone has to buy the airline tickets – either us or the buyer. Whichever way it is, I always try and have the other party look at the reservations and confirm them before finalizing the tickets. Will we have time to make it to the airport after the performance in time for this flight? I'll ask. Are you sure you don't want him to arrive the evening before – just in case there are weather delays, or other travel problems? These discussions often save grief on both ends about arrivals and departures.

Then there are the airport pickups. I always try to confirm who will be meeting my clients at the other end of a flight, the fact that they'll have a vehicle large enough for my client and his luggage—and I always try and get the person's mobile phone number. All too often these people will show up and the wrong terminal, or baggage claim, and the performer is in trouble if he can't call them and get them to him.

Another point: I always try and get full hotel information: Name, address, reservation number and who made that reservation–including their phone number. When possible, if my client is arriving in the middle of the night or early morning—or some other time which is odd by hotel standards, I get my client to confirm their room will be ready when they arrive. It's never fun to sit on a plane for 12 hours, then have to wait in the hotel lobby for 2 hours more before your room will be ready!

The same comes for dealing with shipping and luggage. You need to work out all of the details as far in advance as possible. We sometimes send props by FEDEX – in which case, I have to find out where they will be delivered at the venue. Many big convention hotels now have FEDEX offices within their conference centers, and that is where we—or our clients—have to arrange to pick up the things we've sent. There are often pick up and drop off fees that must be paid—not a problem if you're expecting them, but it's always good to know about them in advance. So be sure you ask. Also, check to see where the props will actually be delivered. If it's to an internal FEDEX office, how do we find it? If not, who is the individual responsible to receive it? How do we contact them? Will it go to the backstage of the venue, or get held in a receiving area? You get the idea.

However your props will travel—make sure you know as much as possible about all the details of how, when and where they will be picked up and delivered to. If you're going out of the country, make sure all of the details you need to deal with for customs at either end have been taken care of well in advance—and always plan for customs to cost you a few extra days before your props will actually be available to you!

As you may as you may have gathered, the real key to being able to enjoy your travels is to be sure and nail down as many of the details as possible long before you actually set foot aboard a plane! And then be prepared to be flexible, because travel is never a sure thing. Make sure you have a good book, and that you have enough items in your carry-on that you could deliver a show even if your luggage doesn't arrive.

When you do all that, travel real is one of the great experiences that life as a performer can provide you. There's no better education than being able to immerse yourself in cultures not your own, in seeing new places and experiencing new ways of being. When you travel as a performer, you get to work with locals, and if you're the kind of person who makes friends easily, they'll often be eager to show you a good time. You'll get to experience those other locales not as a tourist, but a special guest. Have fun!

To Reset or Not to Reset

To re-set or not to re-set – that is the question!

Well, I should think it would be obvious, but I'll state it anyway:

This is a question with different answers for every different show and every different performer. If you're a performer working a cocktail party, you had better be set up for at least several groups in a row. If you're doing material that automatically resets itself at the end of the piece, grand. If not, perhaps then you need to find a way to have several set-ups prepared in advance, and carried with you so that you can work several groups without taking time out to re-set.

One consideration here is that you do not want to interrupt the flow of your show in order to re-set a piece for the next one. If your re-set process doesn't look like the natural putting away of the prop once you're done with it, you need to find a way to either wait until later, or re-choreograph the re-set so it does look like part of the show. Awkward transitions between pieces, is the mark of the amateur.

For a platform show or small stage show, it's great if you can reset the show and leave it, but often you'll need to completely pack up and clear the stage, then come back and set up again the next day or a few hours later, before your next show.

With large theatrical or casino shows, you'll set up specific routines for both before and after the show. Props and illusions will be stored in a certain way, then got out and be set in a certain way before a performance. Specific rules are set for who can and cannot handle props backstage. Someone will have the task of checking each and every prop just before a performance, to make sure they are set correctly, not broken, etc.

If you're working in lots of different kinds of venues, you'll find you need to find ways of enforcing who can and cannot touch what. While it might be obvious to experienced stagehands working with magicians, it is not so obvious to executives and others walking backstage during corporate events that they cannot pick up and move something they might think is in their way. At cocktail parties or other hospitality events it may not be obvious to the waiters working the venue that one of the apparent 'wait stations' is actually the magician's pre-set area. So you have to go out of your way to make it obvious to these people, if you don't want them picking your stuff up and playing with it!

I've recently started doing my Wizard talks, which use magic to reinforce some of the points I make. I have been able to design the talks in a way that, by and large, when I finish a piece and put the prop away, it is automatically re-set and ready to go for the next time I do the talk. There are one or two things for which this isn't the case, but for the most part, the show re-sets itself. Of course, that doesn't mean that I don't go through and check it all before going out to deliver a talk, and again right before I go on stage. There's plenty that can go wrong without my setting myself up for it to go wrong by not being properly prepared!

Whatever works for you and your show, whatever you decide with regard to setting and re-setting your performance, please don't forget to make yourself a checklist and get in the habit of using it. Don't add this one extra task to your already overtaxed memory. Put it on paper or in a file on your smartphone. You need to be putting your attention on the performance itself—and not worrying if all of your props have been properly set!

Theater Tech

The phrase, "Whoever can do the most with the least, wins," really applies when it comes to ways to technical support your show. I've seen way too many performers who think that because they have invested in, and are willing to schlepp around, backdrops, lighting equipment, sound systems and the like, they are more professional. Well—maybe, but probably not.

Too often, collecting tech support equipment is like buying more tricks at magic conventions. It's an excuse for not doing the real work of practice, rehearsal and improving your scripts.

You wind up with a lot of stuff, none of which really makes you a better magician, and none of which actually enhances the experience audiences have with you. So, before you go shopping for lighting equipment, study lighting design. Take a course at your local college, or read books on the subject. Find a way to try out different lighting set-ups to see what kind of lighting will do the most to enhance your show. Be realistic about the kind of space and audiences you are likely to perform for, and let that determine your technical requirements. Remember, if you work mostly in theaters or at large corporate events, you are actually better off letting the event planners who hire you provide the technical support. Invest your time and energy in creating a great technical rider and simple cue sheets, not in shopping for equipment you don't need.

Neither Jeff McBride or Marco Tempest supply sound

and lighting equipment. They both perform in such a wide variety of venues that we would have to stock a warehouse full of equipment in order to be able to support all of those situations, and today the equipment in those areas is out of date six months after you buy it. Much better to really understand how best to ask for what you need, and what will be the minimum necessary to best support your show in each of those venues.

That said, there are times when it pays to be able to supply your own tech equipment. I know performers who work the county fair circuit, and sometimes they are actually hired because they can supply a stage and lights. Their stages get used for their own show and a half dozen others each day. They become more than just a performer to the fair owners, and they definitely increase the number of their bookings and their income from each booking that way—but the price is that they are then tied to the stage as the tech support all the time the fair is open. They're also tied to the loans they have to take out to pay for all that equipment. It can be a good business, if it is one you enjoy doing.

There is a similar situation for a certain level on the party circuit. If you are providing sound and lights that will serve not only for your show but for a DJ, party announcements and the like, you are adding an aspect that will be attractive in certain instances, and you can build business around that. However, do be aware before you consider going this route that it really is another business, and you need to as be fully competent to provide and maintain that equipment as a tech company who makes that their primary business would be. If your system goes down at the height of an event, you will have very unhappy clients, and word will get around quickly.

Falling in love with technology can be great fun, and it can certainly add to the business you will get if you're willing to take on that business and keep up with it in the same way you would your performing business. If you are going to be happy maintaining not only the sound and light equipment that you'll be bringing with you, but also backups for all that equipment, if you'll enjoy dealing with the problems of having proper power set-ups, putting in the extra time to pack, transport, set up and take down the equipment, and to deal with the other performers you'll be providing tech support for—then by all means, go for it.

If not: Do what you do best, and avoid becoming a 'chief technical officer' on top of your job as a performer. Learn all you can about creating effective lights and sound. Learn how to communicate with the technicians who will be supporting you in ways that make them feel empowered and excited about helping you create your magic—and save yourself the added aggravation of shopping for, maintaining, storing and setting up and taking down the technical equipment needed to support your performances.

The Business of Magic

When I was studying to become a young theater artist—actor, director, designer—I never imagined I'd become truly interested in the business end of things. I thought of myself as an artist, and above all that. The creative genius who could create the great works and then the money would just roll in. How wrong I was!

Only after falling into the job of managing New York shows on and off Broadway (kind of a trial by fire, since I had never studied management), did I begin to really appreciate the roles of producer and manager. While it's easy for the artist to think they are somehow above the exigencies of running their careers as a business—in fact it is the business people in show business that make it possible for the 'pure artists' to make a living.

For most of us in the world of magic, we have to be both artist and producer, both creator and business manager. We run one-person businesses, and the more we know about business, the more likely we are to have enjoyable and rewarding careers. As your own producer and manager, you will soon realize the necessity of taking not only the purely artistic concerns of how you create and perform your magic, but also the necessity of creating for a particular market, of balancing your artistic desires against the revenues you might be able to earn when you perform. Over the years, I've found that I actually enjoy the limitations placed on the artistic works I'm involved in by things like the budget available, the kind of venue and audiences for whom we perform, and the like. Limitations can be truly inspiring!

This section, then, is for those of you who want to have a career, to run a business, performing magic. It can be a most rewarding career, and I wish you the best of luck in pursuing it!

Selling Magic

I'd like to talk for a couple of minutes about the power of stories. Many people coming into business for the first time think they need to really study the art of the pitch—how to hype themselves to clients. They usually learn to list all the features and benefits of their work to their target audiences, and overwhelm them with testimonials. And it is good to understand how that kind of selling works, and how it doesn't. However, it is still true that the most powerful way of selling anything is through the telling of a story.

I distinctly remember a time when I started working with Jeff McBride, and was learning how to talk about his work in a way that would excite potential clients. I could tell them about all the awards he had won, about his work as the "opening act of choice" for Diana Ross, Tom Jones and others—and they would generally politely express that, yes, that was impressive—and then go back to their cocktail chit chat with their friends.

When I chose to tell a story, though, things were different. "He's an interesting kind of performance artist who combines pantomime and magic to tell these amazing magical tales. He performs in masks and whiteface. He appears onstage at the end of his show and wipes the whiteface make-up off his face as this strange, kind of ghostly music is playing. Almost as though he is trying to wipe away that persona. Just as he finishes wiping his face clean, a white mask appears back on his face. He tries to pry it away, but in snaps back on his face. He drags it off his face with both hands, down to his knees—but when he lets go, it snaps back on his face. No matter what he does, the mask won't go away. Finally he manages to break it in half, and there's another, stranger one underneath! He breaks that away, and there's a skull—and then a robot. He struggles with one mask after another, until he picks up the mirror he was using to help remove the make-up, and looks into it. At that point both the mirror and the mask explode, and he is left, bare-faced and free, in a pool of fading light."

At this point, I would usually find I had drawn a small crowd, all of whom wanted to know where they could see this performance take place. The story of the performance sold it far more strongly than any 'advertising copy' could have done.

Roy Williams is the author of a series "Wizard of Ads" books. If you want a fast, graduate level course in writing copy that sells, I highly recommend that you pick these books up and read them. They aren't expensive, and they'll teach you not only about marketing, but about how our minds work. They might even give you some ideas for new performance pieces.

Learning about what it takes to market and sell your show can take a lifetime. Learn the principles first, then how to go about it using the tools and channels currently available to you. When I started in the business, those tools included print advertising, direct mail, and phone calls. Today, marketers reach their audiences through different channels. Web-sites, social media, mass media, e-mail, and other mediums can get you a much bigger overall effect for the effort put in, if you use them well. They can also provide major distractions and you can spend lots and lots of time trying to learn to use them effectively. So try and team up with experts who do know the current market, and who know how to help you get the very most from your advertising time and money using all these new tools. And keep learning. The world is changing so fast that what you learn today may be completely outdated and wrong within a year.

Exciting times to be alive and in business!

Career Development

Let's talk for a few minutes about what you can do to help build your career. I want to offer you some thoughts that should help you, whether you're building a career in magic, or some other kind of career.

First, you need to recognize that while building a successful career as a performer, or any other kind of artist, does require—at a minimum—that you become excellent at delivering that performance—or whatever your art is, it also requires a lot more than that. To build a successful career in any business, you must have a basic understanding of that business. What is the end product? Who are the buyers for that product, and what benefits do they expect from having made their purchases? How does that business actually generate revenues, and what portion of those revenues will actually become profits? Those are just the most basic questions you need to answer.

So, if you're not excited about the prospect of learning all that, you're probably better off not pursuing magic professionally. The odds aren't good for your success. Last I checked, there were about 14,000 IBM members. Probably about 20 of those make a really good living, another 400 or so make an OK living, and the rest either live in their parents basements or have day jobs in order to pay the bills. If you want to maintain your love of magic, it might be better to pursue it as an amateur. You can become just as good, and perform as much as you want, without becoming dependent on those performances for your living.

Remember: Successful careers are, by and large, not something that happens to you 'by luck.' They are something you create through your own vision (or lack of it), by planning, by taking action, and through lots and lots of hard work — not only on your magic, but on your business as a magician.

Networking

Learning how to build a network is one of the keys to having a great business and a great career - no matter what that business or career might be.

I can still remember the day Jeff McBride asked me if I would take over as his manager – and I said no. In my mind, managers were glorified agents, and my image of agents was right down there with the stereotypical used car dealers. Hard-sell artists. Do anything to get the sale now kind of guys. Definitely not who I aspired to be.

After some time, Jeff managed to convince me that he wasn't asking me to become one of those hard-sell guys, and that my 'softer' way of doing business was, in fact, exactly what he needed. He explained that he wanted me to work with him precisely because, "people trust you." That's when I got it that we might be on the same page about how to build a long-term business.

So, what is this softer way of selling? In today's terms it is the difference between 'relationship' marketing instead of 'transactional' marketing. That means that building a strong business is much more about building lots of strong relationships. It's about really serving those potential clients even when they aren't immediately buying what you're selling, and less about making the immediate sale in the moment.

As an example: Many magicians feel that if they get a call from a corporate producer asking if they can do something, they should answer "yes!" whether or not that particular thing is currently a part of their repertoire— and even if they have no idea how to do that thing. They'll hang up the phone and begin figuring out some way to do that thing, even though they know several other people who already do that thing very well. The result? They deliver a mediocre product, when they might have better served the client just by putting them into contact with another performer who already does exactly what is required and does it well. They get the job, but burn the bridge. That client won't hire them again, and won't recommend them. It's almost always better to build bridges than to burn them. And that's the first level of networking - those contacts who are your direct contacts—the ones who hire you and who you work with to put on shows. The more you work, the more of this kind of contact you'll have.

The tougher part is in extending your network. You want a network of people at least 2 or 3 deep—and you get that by inspiring your first ring. Tell them interesting stories, share exciting news – the object is to develop them as your fan base, to help spread your news and information to their friends and colleagues.

As magicians, we are uniquely skilled to do just that. Your business is the doing of things that people will remember and talk about. I know some of you feel "I should get paid whenever I do magic," and I can see your logic. Sometimes it might pay you to look at it differently, though. Your job is to spread wonder, or to excite people about doing the seemingly impossible—or however you define your purpose—and if that's your mission—well, whether you get paid or not for each performance is kind of beside the point, so long as you do get paid for enough of them to make the sum total you need.

Here's an example: My friend and client Marco Tempest set out a few years ago to produce a series of magic tricks for YouTube. Free—given away, even though it cost him significant time and money to produce some of the segments. He wanted to build an audience, and so he challenged people to figure out how he did it. People submitted their own Rube Goldberg solutions in response to his postings, and he often went on to post his 'backstage' view of how things actually worked. These were his own creations, so he wasn't giving away anyone else's secrets. Marco spent days creating some of the pieces, just to give them away. What did he get out of it? Besides having a lot of fun, he built an audience—a network of people who had seen and remembered—and sent others to see those videos. And that network has changed the course of his career. Things have happened directly as a result of having that audience. He got an invitation to speak at TEDx events, then at the World Economic Forum in Davos, and then, as a result of being seen at those events, at the main TED event in Long Beach. He appeared on The Tonight Show, and had featured pieces in Wired Magazine, on CNN— and much, much more. And every appearance is designed to reach out, invite more connections, and to build on his global presence. As a nice side-effect, the requests for him to come and do the work he does get paid for have increased exponentially.

Now, that's building a useful network.

That was Marco's way. It suited his persona and talents perfectly. What will your way be? Go and start now. Remember, once you hit a certain point, your network will take off and build almost exponentially, with very little additional help from you. Then you, too, can wield the magic power of the network.

21st Century Promotion

If you're going to be in business, you need to figure out how to promote that business. How to get it in front of the people who might buy your product, and how to make them want to buy that product. How you go about this will be slightly different for each one of you, since you are all in different markets. The details of how one promotes oneself in the private party market are quite different from the way you would promote yourself in the theatrical touring or corporate markets.

So, perhaps the first thing you need to know about promotion is: Who am I promoting my work to? And what sort of promotion will they respond to? Who are the individuals who have the power to hire me, or to buy what I have to sell? How are they likely to find out about what I have to offer? What are their concerns about hiring me?

Note that the person and their concerns will be very different for different kinds of performers, and that sometimes you have to do multiple promotions for a single job. Selling yourself to the agent who can book your shows for you will mean dealing with a whole different set of concerns than the ones that the actual buyers of your services will have—and that you'll encounter yet another set of concerns from those who will actually be buying tickets or attending the show. The agent and promoter want to know "can I make money?" The theater wants to know you'll behave professionally and respectfully in their space. The audience wants to know you'll be entertaining, and appropriate.

All of the above is, of course, a big generalization—and we want to talk particularly about promoting your particular self right now. We live in a very different world from the one we did just a few years ago. Agents and buyers no longer expect or want to receive printed press kits and video tapes or DVD's from performers. Audiences find out about shows as much from online sources as from traditional news media. People still watch TV and listen to radio, but these are no longer the primary or most economical ways of reaching potential buyers and audiences.

Marco Tempest recently suggested to me that "today, you are who you are online." And being online means being on social media, reaching out via blogs, posting on newsgroups, YouTube, and more. You can have a presence online without a major financial investment – you can, for example, fund a web-site for around a hundred dollars a year. Facebook, YouTube and the like cost nothing to post on.

However...the competition for attention is severe. With more than 72 hours of video being uploaded to YouTube every minute, how do you get anyone's attention long enough to watch what you have posted there?

The answer is that if you want to succeed online, you need to show the same qualities that will make you stand out as a performer. You need to consider what you can post that will make those who view it want to share it with their friends. What can you put online—as a video, a graphic or verbal post—that will make those who see it want to re-tweet, like, plus one, share, pin, or otherwise help you propagate it?

More and more, we live in a world of one minute video and sound bites. Because we are all inundated with 'marketing' messages, we have learned to filter most of them out, and to give only enough attention to any potential source of marketing to see if it interests us. That means you have a few seconds at most to really capture someone's interest. And you'll be competing with professional marketers working in graphics, video, copyrighting, etc. How are you to get through the noise?

It's not easy. You must be at least as creative promoting yourself as you are in creating your show. The good news here is that the process you must go through to find your market is very similar to the one you will go through to satisfy that market – you need to learn to deliver the same kind of interest grabbing magical experience online as you will need to deliver live in your shows. If you can't do it online, there's a good chance you won't be able to do it in your shows, either.

So...before you go out and start promoting yourself— figure out who it is that you need to promote yourself to. Then figure out where that person is likely to find you. Are they a part of event planner newsgroups on LinkedIn? Or are they young mothers who like to post and browse Pinterest? Can you find them on Facebook and get them to accept your friend requests? Can you post things on Facebook and YouTube that they will want to forward to their friends? Perhaps they read a certain kind of trade publication or journal, and you can either buy advertising there, or try and get an article published that they will find useful and, at the same time, make them aware of your abilities to help them out.

Once you've figured out who these people are, where you need to be so they will discover you, and what will catch their attention and imaginations, then you just need to create the material that will do that, and get it placed where they will find it. You'll find yourself becoming 'known.' Then you can take them to the next step, where they begin actually buying your product.

Promotion, in all its aspects is a HUGE subject. You can go to business school for 4-6 years and major in marketing and communications, and still not know all there is to know. So I hope what I've said piques your interest—and sets you on a path to learn more.

Relationship Beginnings

The other day my phone rang, I picked it up—and thought I'd made a mistake. It was as though I had picked up in the middle of someone else's conversation. I always pick up the phone and say, "Hello, this is Tobias."

This time there was along silence, and then, finally, "That magic school." said the voice at the other end.

"Ah...Hello?" I said. Another pause.

"I want to learn magic."

"I'm sorry, who am I talking to?"

"Mike."

"Okay, Mike—I gather you're interested in our Magic and Mystery School."

"I want to learn magic."

"Great..."

and so on.

Why am I telling you this? Well, because I want to talk about the importance of relationships, and how we establish and maintain them. My friend "Mike" could use this lesson, but I'm pretty sure he's not reading this. Mike just doesn't 'get' the relationship thing.

In business, during the course of a show, and in life, few things are more important than our relationships with others. There's a common phrase, "People do business with people they like." It's very true. You've probably encountered someone in your life who is brilliant at whatever they do—but who you can't stand to be around. Let's imagine they're a brilliant graphic artist, for a moment. Would you hire this person to create your new business card or an advertisement for your business? Or would you be more likely to want to work with your friend, or friend of a friend, who may not be quite so brilliant, but is fun to work with, and who treats you like an intelligent human being? There's no right answer to that, but many top, experienced corporate executives will tell you, again and again, "always take the competent team player over the brilliant loner." The end results are always much better.

Since most of you reading this are performers of one sort or another, let me give you an example of how this works in the context of a performance. In the course of my work, I've seen many, many performances. A very few of them were really fantastic, many were good, and there was something to be learned from every one. But I've actually seen many performers who, in terms of technical ability and the polish on their performances really weren't that wonderful—but whose performances everyone thoroughly enjoyed. In those instances, it was invariably because the performer understood how to relate to and connect with their audiences.

Relationships begin the moment you are introduced. Have you planned your introduction? An introduction sets up the audience for your performance. Does yours set up expectations that you'll be fun, funny, serious, impressive, scary—or what? Introductions are one of the things we work on at sessions of the Magic & Mystery School—because they are so important, and because they are one of those areas that many magicians fail to consider adequately.

After the introduction, the performer comes on stage and begins his or her performance. Remember Mike, and our phone call? Too many times beginning performers, in their nervousness about their performance, are just like Mike. They forget to make the connection – to reintroduce themselves and set the tone, the expectations, for the experience they want the audience to have, before they launch into their first trick. There's no one right way to do this – each of you will want to create a different experience with each of your performance pieces—but there are many, many ineffective 'wrong' ways to do it.

I've seen performers walk out, go directly to someone in the front row and fan a deck of cards, and, "take a card." While this might be okay at a magic club, where everyone already knows one another and knows the drill—it's not really a good approach even in that situation. When you come onstage after your introduction, the first thing you need to do is connect with your audience and establish a relationship. Walk on with the kind of energy you want to convey. Stop. Make eye contact with at least a few audience members. Take a breath or two, smile, if your character would smile. Scowl if that's the character—but let us see it. Silence is actually your friend at this point—there's no need to rush into that first trick before we get to know you.

One of my favorite moments in magic is the opening of Max Maven's shows. Max is introduced and the curtains open on a shadowy, back lit stage. Max is standing far upstage in shadows. He walks slowly and purposely downstage into the light, looks from one side of the audience to the other, then straight ahead, and aggressively says, "Boo!" with his tongue firmly planted in cheek. We know immediately that Max is master of the situation, that we might be in for some slightly bizarre experiences, but that we are not to take any of it too seriously. In just a few seconds and a single word, Max has set up the experience he is about to provide us. He has established a relationship with us—and, I think, most audiences are immediately drawn into the fun of that relationship.

Oh, Mike, if you're reading: When you call someone on the phone, if you want to be more effective, take the time to say "Hello," and to introduce yourself before launching into your reason for calling. You needn't waste a lot of time— just enough to let the person on the other end know that you know you're talking to another human being. You'll get much better results, and might even begin to develop some interesting and fun relationships in the process!

For the rest of you: Take some time this week to think about the beginnings of your performances, and the way you enter into new relationships in business and personal life. How do you introduce yourself? How do you acknowledge others? How do you make your connections? What kind of expectations do you create for those meeting you? Just as our mothers all told us: First impressions are important!

In the next chapter I'll talk more about building relationships—things you can do to assure that your circle of friends and colleagues continues to expand, and that you are never without a number of people who want to do business and spend time with you.

Maintaining Business Relationships

In the last article, I spoke about the importance of

establishing good relationships. We talked briefly about such simple things as how we answer the phone, and how to spend a few moments at the beginning of a performance to establish the relationship you want to have with your audiences.

While first impressions are, indeed, important, even more important in your life are the relationships you build and maintain over the years. While some people enjoy being 'loners,' socially, and having only a few really good friends, instead of diving in and enjoying the benefits of being a part of a larger community—in business we really don't have that option. In business, your success will be directly proportional to the number of good relationships you create and maintain.

You have, no doubt, heard the phrase, "It's not what you know, but who you know." While this has a clever ring to it, it really misses the point. It's not who you know, as much as it is who knows you—and thinks well of you. If you 'know' the president of the US, but he doesn't know you, well, 'knowing him' doesn't really give you any advantage over any of the other 300 million Americans. However, if the president knows you and likes you—perhaps because you've helped him out in some way, or are known to have said kind things about him (that he knows about) in places that it matters—well, that's a relationship that might be valuable to you.

We all swim in a sea of social relationships—friends, co-workers or fellow students, people we encounter in stores, at the coffee shop—wherever. Some relationships are casual, others far closer. There are those you have contact with every day, and those you might only see once every few years. We all have both friendly relationships and not so friendly relationships. There are people we spend time with because we must—co-workers for instance—and others who we continue to see out of habit, and still others we go out of our way to have a relationship with. All together, they create a huge web – your personal network.

The people you choose to associate with you will affect your life more than you can imagine. T. Harv Ecker is the author of Secrets of the Millionaire Mind, and he'll tell you he can predict your personal annual income accurately based on knowing the 10 people who you spend the most of your time with, and their annual earnings. His method? He simply averages the incomes and net worth of those ten people, and predicts that as your annual income. He says he has an accuracy rate of over 90 per cent. The same goes for general attitude towards life, happiness level, social status, and other major success indicators. So, take a few minutes and think about all your relationships. Are you putting effort into the ones who are leading life according to the standards you want for yourself?

How do we nurture relationships? It's really not that difficult. One simple way is just to stay in touch. Send personal notes or e-mails. Always send thank you notes after you've worked with someone, whether they actually hired you or not, and whether or not they were actually helpful while working with them or not. You need not lie. Just send a note saying, "Thanks for everything. I look forward to doing this with you again soon!"

Along these lines, I do a number of different things to stay in touch and nurture relationships with business colleagues. I do send thank you notes, ideally via snail mail, and hand-written. I send irregularly timed, personalized, e-mail blasts with news about myself and my clients, always with a personal tone. Occasionally, I send out postcards. I post and respond to posts by friends and acquaintances on the various social media sites. Since a lot of my business is with magicians, I make a point of getting to a magic convention or two each year, and attending events related to the magic community. When I see an article that's about something I share in common with someone, I send them the link to that article with a short note: "I remembered chatting about this with you when we were in (wherever we were), and thought you would enjoy seeing this new article on the subject." Get the idea?

Maintaining as many good relationships as possible with people in my business is the greatest key to my success in my work as a manager. My clients do the same—between us, we cover quite a large swath in the world of live entertainment. And those relationships are what have generated well over a half million dollars in bookings each year for the past 10 or 15 years. Yes, I am blessed to work with clients who are unique, and who are at the very top of the magic world in terms of the performances they give—but it is the work of maintaining relationships, of making sure we are 'top of mind' with as many people who can hire us as possible, and making sure that those people think of us as 'someone I'd like to work with again,' that keeps us in business, working even when many of our colleagues are not.

So, spend some time thinking about the relationships you have created for yourself and your business. Think about the ones you really want to cultivate, and the ones you just need to maintain on a friendly basis. Spend no time at all worrying about enemies. For the most part, it's best not even to acknowledge them, unless by doing so you can generate press for yourself. Instead, spend that energy building more good relationships. Make lists. Set up your contact managers. Make notes on each contact.

Then plot your own strategy for maintaining those relationships. How can you make sure these people really know you, and that when they think of you, they think good things? This is the true art of marketing and building a business. The more great contacts you have, the richer your life will be, both financially and emotionally.

SupportTeam

When I teach magicians about the nuts and bolts of running a business, I like to talk about a model that looks like a pyramid. At the base of the pyramid there is a large, thick slab – the purpose or mission that will drive the business. Like a building, a business without such a foundation is unlikely to survive.

Three additional slabs make up the sides of the pyramid: Strategy, leadership, and team. All of these work together to help you with building and leading a strong team in order to bring about the dream you have stated as your mission. If you were to have a discussion with great entrepreneurs—people like Larry Page and Sergey Brinn, or Steve Jobs when he was re-building Apple—they would tell you that their primary job as leaders of their companies was to "get the best people" and then "inspire them."

It's really quite simple: the company, or the performer, with the best team, wins. But few performers really give a lot of thought, or put in the effort, to attract and inspire the best possible teams. Speaking for myself, I'm deeply honored to be on the team of two of the greatest magicians I know: Jeff McBride and Marco Tempest. Each of them has built incredibly strong teams around them—in Jeff's case, Eugene Burger as a wise advisor, Larry Hass as Associate Dean for the magic school and publisher, Jordan Wright as lead assistant and videographer, and so on. Marco has enlisted the aid of David Britland as writer, and top experts in the fields of augmented reality, 3-D graphics animations, and so on. Through his recent appointment as a Director's Fellow at the MIT Media Lab, he has been able to add the resources of many of the faculty, staff and students working there, as well. Neither Jeff or Marco, on their own, could have taken their careers and their magic to where it is today without those teams.

Each business, each artist, will have different requirements when building a support team. We need our teams to extend our own abilities, and to leverage our own time and effort. One of the biggest mistakes people make when building their own support teams is to want to hire people who are less intelligent or less powerful than themselves. They are afraid that such team members might overshadow the leader. As a result they create companies not quite as good as they might have been otherwise. The wise leader and artist builds teams of people both smarter and more powerful than they are. They are willing to pay a bit more, to risk a bit more, in order to surround themselves with people who will challenge them to up their own game—to create on a level beyond what they have imagined and achieved on their own. That is the path to excellence, and in today's world, you can't really expect to succeed with anything less.

One of our goals at the Magic & Mystery School is to provide you with the tools you'll need to build your own lives in magic. Careers, if you chose to work as a professional, or just ways to improve your magic if you are a hobbyist. Part of our job is to help you build your own teams, and to offer our own services as a part of your own teams. Speaking for myself, and I know for Jeff McBride, as well, not a day goes by when I don't field several e-mails or calls from former students who have questions we can answer that will help them with their magic. While we both also consult for fees, for students who have attended our classes, short responses are never charged. They are our alumni, and it is in our interest to see them succeed. In a like manner, many of our former students have joined our team. Jeff tours doing his McBride Magic Experience, where he performs a show, lecture and workshop in towns around the world—and they are most often sponsored by one of our former students, or the magic clubs they are a part of. It helps us fill in the gaps when major touring or corporate engagements aren't in place, and lets us pursue our mission for Jeff's career and for the school, of getting the word out and doing what we can to raise the level of this art we all love so much.

Marketing Magic

Here's one of the subjects I get asked about most—how to market magic. I find myself drawn, again and again, year after year, to books and classes on marketing. I suppose I'm fascinated because I know that a deep understanding of marketing can provide such a useful point of view into achieving real success in so many parts of your life.

That's partly because marketing is so much more than people often think. We tend to think 'marketing" is a synonym for 'selling.' That immediately makes us think of annoying late night television commercials, sleazy salesmen trying to push us into upgrades we don't really need, and things like that. Fortunately, that's not what it's really about at all.

Truly successful marketing is about creating value for the members of a group—your market. I'm talking about real value—something that will improve their lives. Then you connect that value with the group—that's the advertising/PR and selling part. But that part doesn't come until after you've gotten to know the group, imagined ways of improving their lives, and then created the things that will do just that—in a form and at a price so that their acquiring those things will truly improve their lives. That kind of marketing adds to the overall quality of the society we live in.

The kind of salesmanship that pushes junk on a public that doesn't need it, and for whom that junk might actually be detrimental, though — that idea of marketing is missing half the equation.

Let's look at the example taking this approach to how you might want to market your work as a magician.

First: What sort of market do you imagine would be best served by the magic that interests you? Is it made up of mothers looking for ways to give their children a memorable birthday? Perhaps your ideal audience will be corporate marketing people looking for ways to increase their return on the investment of taking their product to a trade show? Are they couples out looking for a romantic evenings' light entertainment? Perhaps they are entrepreneurs looking for new ways to inspire their employees. Or church pastors looking for new ways to make the church message relevant to young people. There are many different ways different kinds of magic can serve different markets.

The product you will need to create to serve each of these different potential markets will be different from what will serve all the others. And these are just a very few of the markets that magicians regularly work in. With a bit of creativity, it's easy to come up with hundreds more. Each one will require a unique kind of magical presentation to serve it best. Each market is made up of different kinds of people. Different levels of experience, economic levels, ethnic backgrounds, different ways of looking at the world. Each group will have different concerns, different ways of measuring the value of your offering to them.

If you create the magical product that will best serve the particular needs of any of these markets, you'll stand a much better chance of being able to connect your product with that market when the time comes to get out there and sell it. If you are fully meeting the needs of a particular market, you will rapidly become well known. Word of mouth about what a success your show is for your clients will travel quickly.

If, on the other hand, you have one show—the show you insist you want to do—you will probably only satisfy a market of one, and that one will be yourself. For some of you, that's just fine, but don't count on building a big career based on that show.

If you're more like the rest of us and really want to build a career in magic that will connect you with audiences you enjoy working with over many years—I recommend the deeper marketing approach. Continue learning about that audience, that market, as long as you want to continue in magic, and continue to upgrade your performances in ways that will better serve that audience and their needs.

Oh—and remember, markets don't always know what they most want and need themselves. Sometimes you can see ways of improving the lives of people making up a particular market in ways they never imagined until you showed it to them. This was one of the great secrets to the success of Apple under Steve Jobs. No one knew they needed an iPod, or an iPhone, or an iPad—until Apple created them. But Jobs saw the need. He understood the market and his audience, and continued to offer them miraculous products that served those wants and needs in ways that always delighted.

Can you do the same with your product as a magician? Think about it. Be creative, and have fun.

Power of Team Building

I've written elsewhere about the importance of having a purpose for your work as a magician? How each show can be improved by having a clearly defined purpose? Working as Cyril the Wizard, our friend CJ May uses his magic to help educate children and adults about the importance of re-cycling. As a result, he has a show that knows it's audience, what kind of magic he'll include, and is provided with a whole set of stories he can use to create new performance pieces. Audiences know exactly how to respond to him – everyone knows what a wizard looks and sounds like, and CJ looks and sounds just like that when he performs!

What's more, his clear purpose gives the press an angle – a 'hook' if you will, to know how to write about "Cyril the Wizard," and he is getting more and more press (that is, free advertising!) all the time.

But having a purpose isn't the only reason I've brought up CJ May. As I mentioned at the beginning, he was the active force behind sponsoring Jeff McBride in his "Jeff McBride Experience" at Yale in New Haven. We talked last week about the importance of building your team and keeping your relationships fresh, and my relationship with CJ is a great example of that. He first contacted me quite a few years ago, interested in finding a way for his local magic club to bring Jeff to New Haven. At the time, we hadn't developed the whole idea of "The Jeff McBride Experience," with his show + lecture + workshop format, and Jeff was mostly only lecturing when he was in an area for a show sponsored by someone else. So we didn't manage to arrange the lecture back when we first started talking.

But CJ and I stayed in touch, trading e-mails and occasional phone calls over the years. Then just a couple of years ago, CJ decided to come to one of our Master Classes in Las Vegas. We finally got to meet face to face, and I think I can safely say, he left more or less overwhelmed by the experience of the Master Class. Students there get so much information, and have such an intense time learning and experiencing magic from Jeff and all our staff, and from each other, discovering new ways of thinking about their magic, that it's not uncommon for them to tell us, "It's going to take me months to process all of what I came away with." The next year (I think), CJ made it out to Las Vegas again, this time for the Magic & Meaning Conference. Since then, he and I have been in touch regularly by e-mail, as he has been looking for ways to build up his career and get his message out as a performing wizard. I'm always happy to help anyone who is a former student of ours in any way that I can, and especially one with whom I've developed a friendship over the years.

So, just a couple of months ago, we had a call from the "It's Magic" people – Milt Larsen and Terry Hill – inviting

Jeff to appear in a couple of shows they were sponsoring at the Mohegan Sun Casino...just an hour or two's drive away from New Haven. Almost as soon as I got off the phone with them, saying yes to that engagement, I picked it up again and called CJ. "Remember how you wanted to get Jeff to Yale?" I asked him. "We might have the perfect opportunity!" And so we began our talks, and he got busy finding space, sponsors, etc. As a result, the Wednesday after his Sunday show with It's Magic, Jeff performed and lectured at Yale! And it's all because CJ and I spent years and years keeping our relationship alive. Jeff and I both have a number of friends in the Connecticut / Massachusetts area – but CJ was the one I thought of most immediately, because he's the one who has been most active staying in touch. We feel very lucky that we were able to just pick up the phone, make a call, and set this whole event up, adding significantly to the value of Jeff's trip back to the East Coast. Not only did he pick up some extra income, but we've discovered that The Jeff McBride Experience almost invariably recruits one or two new students to come to our classes in Las Vegas.

This is a perfect example of the kind of business package anyone can design, if they are willing to move out of their own mind-set and adopt that of their potential clients. You may remember me talking about how important it is for you to be able to adopt the mindset of your potential clients. We designed the experience initially to make it possible for local groups to bring Jeff in to lecture. Since a lecture doesn't really pay what we like to have him make when he goes out, we wanted to come up with a package that would both provide Jeff (and the hosting organization) with the opportunity to make a bit more, and at the same time to give them a way to sponsor a larger event and give their local communities a chance to see some world class magic while he was there. All that, wrapped up in a package that we could make available for even less financial risk than the club would have if they booked him just to lecture. Not long ago, we discovered that hosting a McBride Experience was a great way for local magicians and organizations to get press for themselves.

The Jeff McBride Experience Package, like everything we do – is still a work in progress – we know we can always find ways to improve it. But by listening to those who have already hosted the packages, we learn a little bit more each time it goes out, and continue to improve it. It's a perfect example of an innovation that can generate hundreds of thousands of dollars in income over the course of a few years– created by listening to and adopting the mind-set of our potential sponsors.

So I hope you'll follow our example, and see what can happen if you spend some time getting yourself into the mindsets of your potential clients. What are their needs, their concerns, their dreams? How do they feel when they encounter you or a piece of your marketing? How do they feel and what do they think when they attend your shows? See how deeply you can go into your client's point of view, and then think of what you can do to help that client reach their goals, and make their dreams come true. In my experience, when you can do that, you won't have to worry too much about how to market yourself. Your clients will take care of that for you.

Final Words

Well...that's it for this volume. I hope I've provided you with food for thought and some enjoyable reading. Please visit the web-site for this book and Beyond Deception, Volume 1 at: http://www.beyonddeception.com. You'll find some essays not included in the books, and there's a place there for you to leave comments and corrections for future printings. Thanks for reading!

* * *

Printed in Great Britain
by Amazon.co.uk, Ltd.,
Marston Gate.